PANDEMEDIA

PANDEMEDIA

HOW COVID CHANGED JOURNALISM

Edited by **TRACEY KIRKLAND & GAVIN FANG**

This book was conceived as the storytellers' story of the pandemic, written on many lands of the Aboriginal and Torres Strait Islander peoples. We acknowledge the original storytellers of these lands and pay our respect to Indigenous elders past and present, including our many brilliant colleagues who keep this tradition alive.

Pandemedia: How COVID Changed Journalism
© Copyright 2023
Copyright of this collection in its entirety is held by the editors, Tracey Kirkland and Gavin Fang. Copyright of the individual essays is held by the respective author/s.

All rights reserved. Apart from any uses permitted by Australia's *Copyright Act 1968*, no part of this book may be reproduced by any process without prior written permission from the copyright owners. Inquiries should be directed to the publisher.

Monash University Publishing
Matheson Library Annexe
40 Exhibition Walk
Monash University
Clayton, Victoria 3800, Australia
publishing.monash.edu

ISBN: 9781922633811 (paperback)
ISBN: 9781922633828 (PDF)
ISBN: 9781922633835 (epub)

Editor: Paul Smitz
Design: Phil Campbell Design
Typesetter: Cannon Typesetting
Proofreader: John Mahony
Printed in Australia by Griffin Press

A catalogue record for this book is available from the National Library of Australia.

Contents

Cartoons by Warren Brown	xii
Introduction	xiii
COVID Timeline	xvi

PART I MORE THAN THE HEADLINES

The Storytellers' Story — 3
Tracey Kirkland, Continuous News Editor, *ABC News*, Sydney

An Honest Conversation — 15
Michelle Grattan, Chief Political Correspondent, *The Conversation*, Canberra

The Daily Presser — 23
Andrew Lund, Head of Communications, Melbourne Airport; former state political reporter, Nine Network, Melbourne

Breakfast Television — 30
Lisa Millar, Presenter, *ABC News Breakfast*, Melbourne

The Economic Pandemic — 36
Patrick Durkin, Melbourne Bureau Chief, *The Australian Financial Review*, Melbourne

Pandemedia is dedicated to storytellers everywhere.

CONTENTS

PART II THE CHANGING NEWSROOM

Fit to Print — 49
Tory Maguire, Executive Editor, Nine Publishing, Sydney

Power Switch — 56
Grant Sherlock, Managing Editor, ABC News Digital, Brisbane

Nightly News — 67
Max Futcher, Presenter, *Seven News*, Brisbane

A Media Newcomer Bringing Hope — 76
Anita Savage, News Director, 103.2fm, Sydney

Kohler's Book Stack — 81
Alan Kohler, Finance Presenter, *ABC News*, Melbourne

PART III THE TRUST EQUATION

A Question of Balance — 87
David Speers, Presenter, *Insiders*, ABC, Melbourne

Public Backlash — 96
Rachel Baxendale, Victorian Political Reporter, *The Australian*, Melbourne

The Role of the Expert — 100
Prof. Raina MacIntyre, Professor of Global Biosecurity, University of NSW, Sydney

Behind the Hard Border — 107
Peter Law, former political reporter, and Josh Zimmerman, Political Reporter, *The West Australian*, Perth

The Slippery Truth — 113
A Q&A with Rick Morton, Senior Journalist, *The Saturday Paper*

Febrile Nation — 118
Prof. Mark Kenny, Australian Studies Institute, Australian National University, Canberra

CONTENTS

PART IV THE JOURNALIST EXPERIENCE

The Power of Purpose — 133
Gavin Fang, Deputy Director, *ABC News*, Sydney

From Moral Injury to Trauma Resilience — 143
Dr Kimina Lyall, Deputy CEO, and Dr Erin Smith, CEO, Dart Centre Asia Pacific, Sydney

The Great Resignation — 149
Emily Arnold, former reporter and producer, *7NEWS*, Brisbane

Making Your Way — 153
Jess Malcolm, Political Reporter, *The Australian*, Canberra

Investigative Challenges — 158
Anne Connolly, Investigative Reporter, *ABC News*, Sydney

PART V INNOVATION AND NEW MEDIA

The Use of Data for Storytelling — 167
Casey Briggs, Data Journalist, *ABC News*, Sydney

The Rise and Rise of TikTok — 177
Lee Hunter, General Manager, TikTok, Sydney

Staying the Course — 184
Claire Kimball, Founder, Squiz Media, Sydney

The Success of Podcasting, Corona Style — 189
Dr Norman Swan, Health Expert and ABC Broadcaster, Sydney

***The Virus*: Live, Daily Programming** — 194
Jeremy Fernandez, Presenter, *ABC News*, Sydney

The News Media Bargaining Code — 199
Bill Grueskin, Columbia Journalism School, New York

PART VI A PLACE IN THE COMMUNITY

Digital Transformation: ABC — 211
Gaven Morris, Managing Director, Bastion Transform, Sydney

CONTENTS

Multicultural Messaging: SBS — 222
Mandi Wicks, Director of News and Current Affairs, *SBS News*, Sydney

Community Connections: NITV — 227
A Q&A with Tanya Denning-Orman, Director of Indigenous Content, SBS, Sydney

Rural and Regional Media — 230
A Q&A with Gabrielle Chan, Rural and Regional Editor, *The Guardian*, Harden, New South Wales

A Tale of Two Cities: A Divided Sydney — 234
Tu Le, Lawyer and Community Advocate, Marrickville Legal Centre, Sydney

Generation COVID: Storytelling for Gen Z — 239
Sarah Curnow, Senior Reporter, and Ben Knight, Senior Reporter, *ABC News*, Melbourne

PART VII GOING GLOBAL

Tom Hanks, Trump's America and COVID Journalism — 247
Damien Cave, Australian Bureau Chief, *The New York Times*, Sydney

Chasing Truth and Facing Jail — 252
Drew Ambrose, International Correspondent and Investigative Journalist, Al Jazeera, Kuala Lumpur

Dome of Despair — 257
James Oaten, North Asia Correspondent, *ABC News*, Tokyo

Hong Kong's Citizen Journalist — 262
Aaron Busch, the brains behind @tripperhead, Hong Kong

China and the Virus of Tyranny — 266
Stan Grant, International Affairs Analyst and Presenter, *ABC News*, Sydney

Acknowledgements — 277
***The Betoota Advocate*: Light Relief in Dark Times** — 280
Contributor Bios — 282
Notes — 294

Cartoons by Warren Brown

THE FIRST DRAUGHT OF HISTORY...

Introduction

In January 2020, devastating bushfires were burning out of control across Australia's east coast, the nation gripped by an emergency that dominated the headlines. So, when the World Health Organization announced concerns about a mysterious virus in China, few in the Australian media initially took much notice. Little did we know that for the next three years, the story of COVID-19—a global pandemic the likes of which hadn't been experienced for over a century—would come to not only dominate journalists' lives but also reshape the industry we work in.

At the time, the editors of this book were in key roles leading the ABC's news coverage, including running agenda-shaping daily editorial meetings. Like journalists around the world, we would undergo a crash course in viral transmission, reproductive or 'R' rates, social distancing, mask-wearing, mRNA vaccines, lockdowns and 'the curve', to satisfy the audience's seemingly unquenchable thirst for COVID information. Soon, 'What is today's COVID angle?' were among the first words uttered in every editorial planning discussion, stretching our capacity to fully understand and explain this one intense, huge and ongoing story.

Behind the scenes, we were grappling with a workplace turned upside down by unprecedented issues, forcing us into decisions that would change how we worked. How do you tell a story when you can't get in a room with the people impacted? How do you protect your reporters and camera operators when the public's right to know means putting their health and safety at risk? Technology would come to the rescue there, opening up new ways of communicating and, in the process, creating new media stars—often scientists and data analysts—and a more egalitarian media environment where talent beyond our cities was given a greater voice.

There were opportunities for the disruptors too, some good and some not. The pandemic supercharged all news consumption, including on social media, opening up space for innovators to tell stories in different ways to new audiences. But this also bedded in the exponentially growing trend of misinformation, leaving traditional media scrambling to adapt. And, in a world first, social media giants Facebook and Google were compelled to pay traditional news organisations for content, when the Australian Parliament passed groundbreaking legislation known as the News Media Bargaining Code.

Other questions were thrown up as well. Questions of trust, truth and our contract with the community. What was our role in shaping public opinion during a public health crisis? How should we interrogate facts and disseminate the truth responsibly when a story risked causing widespread public panic? What was the role of the media in countering misinformation while sustaining a respectful discussion of ideas? How could we hold politicians and authority accountable when trust in all institutions was decreasing? How could we motivate our team to keep digging when we'd separated them from their colleagues (sometimes, from their families) and they were struggling under enormous stress?

Big questions. Hard questions. Not necessarily answerable, even now. But by asking ourselves what we did well and what we could have done better, we give ourselves the chance to learn and improve, to perhaps guide future journalists around some of the pitfalls and steer them to safer paths so that we emerge from this crisis better equipped for the challenges ahead.

INTRODUCTION

To tell this story, we asked representatives across all of Australia's major news organisations to share their personal reflections. This collection considers the incredible, heterogeneous range of personal and professional experiences journalists had during the early COVID years.

In these pages, you will hear from hard-nosed reporters trying to hold our leaders to account in an environment where the truth was slippery, misinformation was everywhere, and facts changed fast. There are raw, personal stories of abuse and even death threats on social media from an increasingly distrustful and frustrated public. Journalists tell stories of finding renewed purpose and resilience (or throwing it all in) in the face of the moral injury of COVID reporting, and how politicians around the world used the emergency to control messaging.

Editors and producers provide insights into how the audience upended the old order and seized control of the daily news agenda, and experts explain what it was like to be thrust into the glare of the spotlight. We examine the rise of data as a tool to explain the curve, the complicated and the complex, and discuss the rise and rise of TikTok, an unashamedly non-news platform that became an unlikely news town square.

Pandemedia is the story of all this and more. It is the collective experience of a diverse handful of journalists, editorial leaders, commentators and media academics who care passionately about their craft and want to give something back. In these pages you will find the good, the bad, the funny, the poignant and the ugly. It is the story of how we now stand as an industry: still a little shell-shocked, but also hopeful about the future and humbly changed.

If journalism is the first draft of history, then this is the first draft of how a global pandemic changed the lives and work of the storytellers. And how, in doing so, it forever altered how we bring stories to the public.

COVID Timeline

2020

25 Jan — Australia's first recorded case

1 Mar — Australia's first COVID death, in WA

2 Mar — First local case of community transmission reported

11 Mar — World Health Organization (WHO) declares coronavirus a pandemic

13 Mar — Australian F1 Grand Prix cancelled

15 Mar — First National Cabinet held

International cruise ships banned for 30 days

16 Mar — International arrivals to self-isolate for 14 days

18 Mar — Non-essential indoor gatherings limited

19 Mar — *Ruby Princess* passengers allowed to disembark in Sydney

20 Mar — Australia closes borders to everyone except citizens and residents

22 Mar — JobSeeker payments increased; COVID support payments announced

22 Mar — Australian Football League (AFL) season suspended

COVID TIMELINE

23 Mar — Queues build up at Centrelink offices across Australia

Stage 1 restrictions come into effect: national lockdown of pubs, clubs, gyms, cinemas and casinos; restaurants and cafes limited to takeaway

National Rugby League (NRL) season suspended

24 Mar — 14-day quarantine begins for arrivals to SA, WA and NT

25 Mar — 14-day quarantine begins for Qld arrivals

All non-elective surgery suspended

Australians banned from travelling overseas

27 Mar — Hotel quarantine system begins for international arrivals

30 Mar — Fed. government orders Australians not to leave home unless absolutely necessary

Fed. government announces JobKeeper wage subsidy package

31 Mar — Vic. lockdown begins, first of 6 in that state over next 18 months

5 Apr — WA hard border established

10 Apr — Qld introduces 14-day quarantine for returning residents

26 Apr — Fed. government releases COVIDSafe app

19 May — Australia records 100 COVID deaths

8 July — Vic./NSW border closed for first time

23 July — Melburnians told to wear masks in public

16 Aug — Vic. announces increased lockdown measures, including 5km rule and overnight curfew

COVID TIMELINE

24 Oct — AFL Grand Final played in Brisbane, first time outside Melbourne in 125 years

18 Nov — SA announces strictest lockdowns of the pandemic after an outbreak linked to a pizza shop

24 Nov — WA introduces 'controlled border' allowing entry from states without community transmission for 28 days

19 Dec — Sydney's northern beaches go into lockdown (ends 10 Jan 2021)

2021

3 Jan — Masks now mandatory in enclosed spaces in Sydney

8 Jan — 3-day lockdown and mask mandate in Brisbane and surrounds because of virulent UK COVID strain

25 Jan — Therapeutic Goods Administration (TGA) approves Pfizer–BioNTech vaccine

15 Feb — TGA approves Oxford–AstraZeneca vaccine

21 Feb — PM Scott Morrison and Chief Medical Officer Paul Kelly receive country's first vaccines

22 Feb — First vaccine doses offered under a phased system

21 Mar — Bluesfest cancelled on festival eve after COVID case in Byron Bay

16 June — Delta variant hits Australia

23 June — Sydney's eastern suburbs go into lockdown

26 June — Greater Sydney, Blue Mountains, Central Coast, Wollongong and Shellharbour go into lockdown (ends 11 Oct)

25 June — TGA approves Johnson & Johnson vaccine

COVID TIMELINE

- **9 July** — NSW introduces 10km rule
- **24 July** — Anti-lockdown protests held in Sydney, Melbourne and Brisbane
- **9 Aug** — TGA approves Moderna vaccine
- **15 Aug** — Qld announces all vehicles at border to be checked
- **16 Aug** — Huge delays at Qld–NSW border
- **30 Aug** — Australia records 1000th COVID death
- **22 Oct** — Victoria's 6th and final lockdown ends
- **27 Nov** — Omicron variant reaches Australia
- **16 Dec** — Cricketer Pat Cummins ruled out of Ashes test after a COVID restaurant scare

2022

- **16 Jan** — Tennis player Novak Djokovic deported and banned from Australian Open because of vaccine stance
- **21 Feb** — Australia reopens international borders to fully vaccinated travellers after almost 2 years
- **1 Mar** — Morrison tests positive for COVID
- **3 Mar** — WA's hard border ends after almost two years
- **16 Mar** — Full crowds return to AFL matches in Melbourne
- **21 Apr** — Labor leader Anthony Albanese tests positive for COVID during election campaign
- **3 July** — Australia records 10 000th COVID death
- **18 Sep** — US President Joe Biden says, 'The pandemic is over'

COVID TIMELINE

22 Sep — WHO Director-General Dr Tedros Adhanom Ghebreyesus says, 'Being able to see the end does not mean we are at the end'

14 Oct — End of mandatory COVID isolation requirements

8 Dec — China eases COVID-zero policies

2023

4 Jan — Test cricketer Matthew Renshaw tests positive for COVID but allowed to play

9 Jan — Australia introduces mandatory COVID tests for visitors from China

NB: Public records can differ on these dates because many of the changes came into effect at 11.59 p.m. or midnight. When that occurred, we've recorded the date as the following day.

PART I
MORE THAN THE HEADLINES

The Storytellers' Story

Tracey Kirkland, Continuous News Editor, *ABC News*, Sydney

There was a morning, well into the third year of the pandemic, when everyone gathered in the newsroom to have a discussion about whether we should still be broadcasting the daily COVID death numbers. It was a lively debate, as discussions between journalists often are. On the one hand, numbers were as high as ever, with the death toll still peaking at around thirty a day. On the other hand, we knew the audience was fatigued: discontented, disbelieving, tired of bad news and switching off in droves.

We had been broadcasting the death numbers for more than two years. Sometime after the first wave we'd added infection and hospitalisation numbers to the tally, in the hope it would explain to our audience the scope of what was happening. We now know that there is only so long a person can be bombarded with the daily reality before it either becomes white noise or anxiety takes over.

With the advent of widespread rapid antigen testing, the infection numbers had become skewed, so they were the first to go. So, what to do with the data? How helpful was it to repeat the tally of hospitalisation and death numbers every day when they were freely available on the various health department websites? How did it serve the Australian community? What was our responsibility to our audiences? Was the dogged pursuit of truth a justification when there was concern the reporting could be causing psychological harm?

This was not the first ethical dilemma we faced during the pandemic, and it would not be the last. Some we got right, others we could have handled better. There is always much to learn.

A Global Story

While the story of COVID feels very personal to most people, it is a global one. When Australia first heard about the novel coronavirus, Donald Trump was in power in the United States—a powerful, charismatic yet unreliable character. Xi Jinping had taken China to new economic heights yet was widely distrusted outside his homeland. Boris Johnson had just pulled off his controversial and divisive Brexit win, withdrawing the United Kingdom from the European Union. Into this global setting, a mysterious virus emerged, quietly killing people as it spread. Australian journalists, already exhausted from months of blanket bushfire coverage, watched on, at first with curiosity, alert but not yet alarmed, as COVID-19—short for 'coronavirus disease', with the number indicating the year it was first reported—made its way through China, Italy and the United States. It appeared this deadly virus was spreading through human-to-human contact. As the tension built, we started to want to know more. We sought answers.

The first case of coronavirus, a man returning from Wuhan, reached us at the end of January 2020. A few days later, the World Health Organization (WHO) declared it a public emergency and the lives of journalists across the world, including in Australia, changed dramatically and suddenly.

The Australian Experience

Before we explore how COVID-19 disrupted and changed the Australian media from early 2020, it is worth noting the many trends and changes that were already underway. They played a part in what happened in and to the media over the following three years, many accelerated by necessity.

There was already serious audience fragmentation, as more-traditional media organisations were shunned by young people with an appetite for on-demand and digital content. Streaming services were on the rise, along with platforms like TikTok, as competitive and legitimate news sources. Traditional news organisations, squeezed by rapidly falling advertising revenue, were facing serious financial pressure to adapt in this fast-changing environment. Understanding and tapping into new audiences had become crucial, along with moves to shore up revenue by offering either subscription services or, at least, pay-to-view schemes.

But there was also a change in what consumers were demanding: 24/7 updates, live streaming, more choice, more platforms. Misinformation and its politicisation were rife thanks to international campaigns. And you could add to the mix discussions with Google and Facebook about media organisations being properly compensated for their work, calls for greater diversity of talent on our screens, criticism that news had become too negative, and discussion of the journalistic work–life balance, or the lack of it.

Into all of that, the pandemic slid, slowly at first, a bewildering story that seemed more like a Hollywood movie than a news item. Journalists, like the wider community, were forced to learn fast as COVID began to rip through Australia with little regard for borders, age, status or wealth. It infected everyone from cruise-goers and international travellers to those living and working in aged-care homes. It was brutal in its impact, forcing us all to stay indoors, and calling on us to co-create, or at least begrudgingly abide by, a raft of new social rules.

Being so isolated, late to the party and able to effectively lock down its borders, Australia has a unique story. So, too, do its writers, journalists and other storytellers, as an entire industry was turned on its head virtually overnight.

For most journalists, the standard workday changed instantly, forcing us to stay in our homes and find ways to tell this story from our bedrooms, lounge rooms and studies. It was something we were not prepared for, especially as we became a frontline workforce caught up in the unrelenting wake of a global crisis, pushing both our own limits and those of the work environment just to do our job. It meant we were removed entirely from the synergistic environment of daily editorial meetings, serendipitous hallway chats and ad-hoc brainstorming sessions. Still, as the country's storytellers, we committed ourselves to explaining, unpacking, warning, debunking and telling human stories in the hope that, by sharing them, we could help make sense of a complex, frightening and rapidly evolving situation.

For those still in the newsroom, the fear was palpable. Mask-wearing became compulsory, the gaps between desks were measured, workers were spread out, and many teams were divided into groups that didn't see each other for months on end. Together yet separated, we were forced to find ways to tell the same story, over and over, every day—a story we were all living through.

Interviews could no longer be done face to face. Interview 'talent' was banned from television news studios and morning show couches, forcing us to innovate and learn quickly—Zoom, Skype and FaceTime became necessary staples. To our surprise, the audience accepted the dramatic drop in broadcast quality without complaint.

Added to this disruption, audiences and readers now had a seemingly insatiable appetite for every crumb of information in order to make sense of what was going on, with their lives literally dependent on us getting it right. Television and radio news audiences, website hits and newspaper sales all soared, halting then reversing the long trend of decline in traditional media consumption. Audiences devoured every piece of content we offered on this single story that just kept giving; hardly any other news broke through.

Then prime minister Scott Morrison called together a National Cabinet in mid-March and we diligently reported on its decisions. Less than a week later, the *Ruby Princess* cruise ship docked in Sydney and infected cases were carelessly sent on their way, into their own communities, many later dying. This is, I think, when the fear went up a notch. It felt different. Reporters were sent to the docks but asked to keep their distance. Still, we committed ourselves to disseminating as much information as possible: how did the virus spread? How long did you need to be in a room with someone before it was contagious? Did it spread on surfaces? How did you make a mask? What were the isolation rules? Who was most at risk?

A comprehensive study of news reports between January and November 2020, by researchers from the University of Canberra, separated stories into four categories: information, experience, impacts, and conflict and blame.[1] It showed information-based stories were the most common form of journalism produced by Australia's media organisations across the board—by year's end, they made up more than a third of all stories published. Basically, journalists took it upon themselves to ensure the Australian public knew exactly what was going on and how to keep safe.

Naturally but somewhat unexpectedly, this led to the rise of the health expert, on whom we relied to explain, dissect and simplify complex scientific information. According to the University of Canberra study, with 'news coverage reflecting a consensus between political leaders, media editors and health experts [this] arguably led to the Australian public's trust in health advice and the success of its response'.[2] It seemed as if a new age of science was emerging.

Thanks to social distancing and mask-wearing, journalists had to rethink how they gathered and told their stories. There were no more public meetings due to growing fears in the community of being near others, including camera operators and journalists, as well as a stigma related to sharing COVID stories, and literal barriers preventing contact with aged-care residents and those who could tell us what was going on. Journalists also lost those social gatherings which are so important for nurturing and gaining contacts, and tossing around story ideas. Opportunities for younger journalists to watch their older peers in action dried up. Reporters started new jobs without ever meeting their colleagues and bosses. Studio audiences were banned. As a community, we were disconnected and isolated. The ubiquitous daily editorial meeting moved to videoconferencing mode—a massive change to newsroom culture and protocol, compounding the feeling of working in isolation rather than as a team.

Because so many of us were relegated to our homes, fact-checking and video verification took on a new level of importance as media outlets made use of user-generated content (basically social media posts) to paint stories when cameras were not allowed access. Who will forget the vision, taken by ordinary citizens, of toilet paper arguments, empty shelves in supermarkets and long Centrelink queues?

If we knew then what we know now, we may have not set off at such a cracking pace, and the subsequent incidents of burnout and fatigue may have been eased. Of course, when there are questions to be answered (and there were so many in those early stages), journalists are hungry to answer them as soon as possible. It's hard to change down gears when you feel the story may be getting away from you. But this turned out to be a punishing marathon we couldn't have foreseen and weren't set up to run.

The Pressure to Get Answers

Our role is to question. We ask, we process, we analyse, we write—even when, like at the onset of COVID, there are so many new words, concepts, faces and theories bubbling up all at once. We are fast learners, adaptable and agile. But we are also real people. While we were seeking answers, our parents became vulnerable, our children were sent home from school and needed homeschooling, and we were cut off from our interstate families. And yet it was our job to tell the stories of Australia, no matter how harrowing—stories about overwhelmed nursing and aged-care homes; struggling schools, and children left behind by inconsistent access to technology and learning opportunities; hospitals in crisis; ambulance ramping; continually changing guidelines; a country divided by borders. The daily press conference became our best option to question the government and the various health officers; it also became essential TV viewing.

The University of Canberra data for the second half of 2020 shows most media reports fell into the broad category of conflict and blame.[3] At the time, it seemed everyone was in disagreement. Premiers went their own way, in many cases abandoning a national consensus. Early scientific papers and theories began to be superseded. Arguments erupted between health experts. The science was doubted. The concept of 'truth' became less about facts and more about subjective experience, which meant inaccuracies and conspiracy theories found unhelpful traction. Journalists were left to try to make sense of it all on the public's behalf.

As 2020 rolled into 2021, the media focused attention on the economy, new variants, lockdowns, travel restrictions and potential vaccines. The audience remained voracious but it was a community divided by political polarisation, confusing health messaging and rampant conspiracy theories. This culminated in the ugliest of confrontations at Melbourne's so-called 'freedom rallies'. Journalists and camera operators were targeted—spat on, attacked, abused—and eventually it was not safe for them to attend. Online, journalists were subjected to rampant, unrelenting harassment and abuse just for doing their job.

At the start of 2022, Omicron hit an already overstretched and weary media workforce, and newsrooms were decimated by staff shortages and sickness. It was not until social restrictions eased that audience attention finally wavered and petered out. Ironically, 2022 saw the highest number of infections and deaths but the lowest audience interest in the story. The annual Edelman Trust Barometer added an additional blow, showing trust in the media, which had increased during the first year of the pandemic, was now again in decline.[4] Not only was the media 'the only institution in Australia distrusted by the majority of the population', it was seen as 'more divisive than unifying for society' amid fears it was 'actively trying to mislead'.[5]

Throughout it all, there was immense pressure on media managers trying to look after a workforce that was tired, anxious, isolated and burnt out. The same laments could be heard across the country, but especially in Melbourne. 'My experience of reporting on the pandemic ... was of being stuck in a one-bedroom flat live-blogging press conferences for fourteen hours a day, trying to manage pastoral care on a group of reporters who were also stuck in one-bedroom flats, while trying to buy a farm that we could not visit due to lockdowns,' says Calla Wahlquist, former Melbourne chief of staff at Guardian Australia.

At the end of the day, for many journalists it was all too much and they left the industry, looking to find balance and purpose elsewhere. Journalism can be a hard job at the best of times. During the pandemic, when we were called on to tell the same story in a million different ways, it reached new levels of tough. Usually, a journalist can step back from a story and look at it objectively, but with COVID that was much harder to do. We wrote about it, we talked about it, we lived it.

The job of a news journalist is to discover and tell authentic stories, to ask 'Why?' again and again until we are satisfied we have reached the nub of the issue. And so, during the pandemic, we did: Why didn't we order more vaccines? Why can't people see their dying relatives across borders? Why are police patrolling housing towers and stopping people from leaving? Do masks really work? Are these measures fair? Finding truth became tricky because—like the virus itself—scientific theories evolved regularly and consensus between experts could be hard to find. In this post-truth world, where facts are often trumped by beliefs, which are then amplified by social media algorithms, journalists have their work cut out for them.

But we must persist in this pursuit of facts because it is through the asking of questions, the telling of stories and the understanding of other people's experiences that journalists contribute most to society.

Acting on What We've Learnt

One important lesson from the pandemic is that the Australian public still relies on the mainstream media during big news events. When something complex and impactful needs unpacking, audiences will (and do) come. But, as data consistently shows, that same audience can evaporate just as quickly once the event is over, and that presents us with a challenge. How do we maintain audience share post-COVID?

If the pandemic has taught us anything, it is that trust is still a big problem, but it is the key to maintaining our connection to the audience. In an era of increasing misinformation, disinformation and media fragmentation, our main aim must be to cultivate a relationship of trust with the community. Going forward, that means valuing facts, seeking honest answers, holding authority to account in a way that is not self-serving, writing without bias (or at least being honest about our bias), and being willing to take the time to get things right. We also need to be up-front about our mistakes, correcting them promptly, and committed to transparency and accountability.

It's obvious traditional media will need new audiences to survive, younger audiences with different viewing and reading habits, which is why most organisations are already well down the digital transformation track. We know we need to be on the platforms where new audiences are looking for their news. But how can we do it all? And what can we take from the past few years to inform these changes, many of which COVID has fast-tracked?

Here are a few takeaways.

Relevance. When we are relevant to people's lives, and explain the issues that matter in a way that is useful and constructive, audiences pay attention. It is the only way we will reach new audiences. Like any good conversation, the best way to do this is by listening. We need to find ways to tap into what the audience wants and expects when it comes to news. We need to walk among our communities, talk with them, listen to them, reflect them in staffing and talent, and offer them news that matters to them.

To combat news avoidance, we also need to be in the 'useful information' business. It is imperative we turn our hand to providing contextual, constructive, solutions-focused stories that give people a reason to tune in.

Authenticity. It makes sense that the technological advancements made during COVID allowed us greater access to a wider range of talent. We were not restricted to only those who could make it into an inner-city studio or lived in an area where we could send a camera. Suddenly, we were able to hear from Australians across a broader spectrum of cultural, socioeconomic, geographic and ethnic backgrounds. With that breadth came more authentic storytelling. We need to build on this.

For some organisations, that might mean setting diversity targets; for others, it will be a vital part of their overall strategy. According to the latest international newsroom survey by the Reuters Institute, experimentation is happening.[6] The *Financial Times* in the United Kingdom, for example, uses bots to track the gender diversity of experts and sources. Swedish Radio analyses its news divisions to identify staff gaps. And CORRECTIV in Germany runs a youth program for those from diverse backgrounds. Whatever newsrooms try, the main point is recognising the substantial benefits of a diverse workforce and fostering inclusive workplace cultures, as well as establishing pathways for entry and continued support.

Connection to audience. The pandemic was profound in that it brought journalists closer to our audiences than ever before, because we were living the same story. It forced us to think deeply about what we could offer and how we could answer the many questions that arose. It supercharged the greater utilisation of audience engagement tools and data analysis that could, in real time, identify exactly what the audience wanted to know.

The challenge, now that the big story is dying down, will be ensuring journalists don't slip back into old habits and forget we need to be in conversation with the audience. All the time.

Connection to community. There's no question COVID has shown us that most journalists can successfully and productively work from home—in fact, work from anywhere. And if they do not need to be in a centralised office, that means more journalists can be situated in local communities, in outer suburbs or regional areas, closer to the people, to the stories. This also enables greater diversity of staff, more flexibility and hopefully a better work–life balance.

Lots of news organisations have already taken this a step further, setting up pop-up newsrooms in outer-suburban areas and unearthing stories they may never have found otherwise.[7]

Connection to each other. While working from home during those years, we lost something. Many of us suffered from being isolated both from each other and from a thriving newsroom environment. It is something we must be mindful of as we build our future hybrid workforce. Journalists are collaborators, learners, listeners and debaters. We need each other, at least some of the time.

Newsrooms around the world are experimenting with different approaches, some voluntary, some compulsory. The Reuters Institute survey found the most common approach is a '3–2 model, with three days in the office and two at home, or the reverse'. At a daily newspaper in Germany, 'reporters only have to be in the office one day a week'. A British publication has opted for 'a minimum of two days per week, with days decided by team leaders'.[8] We need to experiment and learn from each other, but it sounds like there is a recognition that, at least sometimes, we need to work together.

Sustainability. Most journalists need to do less. Trying to be everything to everyone is just not sustainable. Traditionally, a journalist who would have written an article for the main news pages or for the evening news, is now filing for radio news, the website and continuous news platforms, and offering analysis and live-blogging—all in the same day. We need to simplify our processes and prioritise platforms and stories, which is a hard challenge given the fragmented audience demands.

Support. Media managers need to be better trained to help and support their teams when things get tough. Most mid-level managers are former journalists, with little to no experience recognising, let alone assisting with, mental health issues that arise in a team.

∼

We need to take all of this on board, because one thing COVID did not change is that journalists are the creators, sharers and sometimes shapers of Australia's stories—and this is a privileged position. We are storytellers at heart. We want to move people. What we do as journalists is vital for a robust, democratic society, and we need the lessons from COVID to shape us and our reporting if we are to survive and thrive during whatever comes our way next.

The exciting thing is we've emerged from the pandemic with an expanded toolkit which we've learned to use in record time. What we need to do now is take those tools and build new ways of working that are sustainable, authentic, adaptable and courageous.

An Honest Conversation

Michelle Grattan, Chief Political Correspondent, *The Conversation*, Canberra

JOURNALISTICALLY, THE COVID-19 story has been an epic journey that has often taken those reporting on it into unexplored territory. It has also been one full of 'angles'. In April 2020, Matthew Sharpe from Deakin University reported on our online website, *The Conversation*, an email he'd received from a student stranded in northern Italy: 'Unable to return to Australia, they were in lockdown. The hospitals were filling up fast, as COVID-19 began to spiral out of control. Sales of Albert Camus' 1947 novel *The Plague* (*La Peste*) were spiking. Everyone was buying it.'

At a more core level, *Conversation* readers quickly became focused on COVID coughs, an interest that endured. An early piece got 1.5 million reads; a 2022 article on coughing after COVID was regularly in the top-five most read articles of the week across the site and has had some 2.5 million reads.

The Conversation is an innovative site, a little over a decade old, carrying news analysis written by university academics who are authorities in their subject areas. It has the capacity to quickly tap into a wide range of detailed, specialist knowledge and curate it for a general audience. When, around January 2020, a mysterious disease struck, about which little was initially known, the public were immediately hungry for information. They wanted facts, and they wanted guidance from experts they could trust. Here was a story tailor-made for our site. In December 2019, the last full month before COVID hit Australia, the monthly onsite audience for *The Conversation*'s Australian site was 4.2 million; by March 2020 it was 11.5 million. Between the start of the pandemic and mid-December 2022, *The Conversation* worldwide (it has multiple sites) published more than 7500 articles that mentioned COVID-19. The academic basis of the site increased the trust people felt in its content.

The elusive quality of 'trust' is essential to a well-functioning democracy. It is also vital to a healthy media. Yet pre-pandemic, trust in politicians and journalists was low. In contrast, people had faith in experts, especially scientists. The short version of the story that followed the pandemic's outbreak is that COVID-19 gave an encouraging boost to trust in political leaders and the media, but unfortunately, as the cycle turned, the air went out of this balloon. In federal politics, then prime minister Scott Morrison was a dramatic example. After attracting widespread criticism for his performance during the 2019–20 bushfires, Morrison's approval ratings revived in the pandemic's early stage, only to take an irredeemable dive later as the federal government came under fire for the slow vaccine rollout and other problems.

The public's trust in experts started high and is less volatile. A University of Canberra April 2020 survey of trust in information sources found 'scientists, doctors or health experts' topped the list according to 85 per cent of respondents, compared with just 53 per cent who said they trusted 'most news'.[1]

The experts, notably those in the health field, had their own distinctive experience during the pandemic. Suddenly, health officials became public figures, indeed household names. In one or two cases, they assumed a strange cult-figure status, with their image put on merchandise. Political leaders, dependent on their advice in scary times, took them to their news conference and deferred to their words.

Meanwhile, the media searched out and gave prominence to a range of experts outside government, from universities and research institutions. Experts whose identities had previously only been well known within the narrow confines of their specialties were soon familiar faces and voices on TV, radio and in print.

Later, the story became more complicated and sometimes uncomfortable for the experts. Unsurprisingly, the health experts—those who were employed by governments as well as those elsewhere—disagreed among themselves. 'Expertise' doesn't mean a uniform label. Dissent within officialdom was partially but not entirely kept behind closed doors. Some of the clashes outside government were robust, and some 'outsiders' criticised what officialdom was doing. Experts attached to government also found themselves embroiled in the political battle. Right-wing commentators repeatedly attacked the Victorian, Queensland and other chief health officers. The experts, or at least those giving health advice to government, later found their clout diminishing, as economic considerations became stronger, politicians seized back more agency and the community wanted to return to normal life.

Interestingly, in late 2022, when the Albanese government announced medical referrals would be required for polymerase chain reaction (PCR) tests, it said it was relying on 'health advice' in normalising the treatment of COVID. Experts differed in their reaction to the move.

The Important but Short-Lived COVID Trust Spurt

The surge in trust that COVID initially produced was crucial in managing the pandemic in the most difficult times. As people looked to government and leaders, they were disposed to accept the messaging, and tolerate restrictions that were not just tough but sometimes prolonged and extraordinary. Trust was helped by the substantial bipartisanship that marked the pandemic's early phase.

Conspiracy theories and the promotion of fake treatments mostly arose later, as did partisan scrapping over mismanagement.

While adversarial politics is a vital part of our democratic system, hyper-partisanship and 'shouty' politics have been among the factors, along with inequality and social media, taking their toll on trust, which has been in long-term decline over decades in Western democracies generally. The media play a part in this, highlighting and sometimes exacerbating conflict in society. There is a fine line between the media's role in holding power to account and ensuring the very necessary airing of grievances, and contributing to a weakening of the fabric that binds a community. Social media is the obvious example of this double-sided coin: it has been a wonderful channel for connecting people and their society, but because of its free-for-all nature, it also has been destructive for individuals and communities.

The 'snap back' in trust after the spike was quick and decisive. The Edelman Trust Barometer for 2022 found

> sharp declines in trust across all Australian institutions, eroding the record-high levels of public trust recorded in 2021. Only 52 per cent of Australians say they trust government to do the right thing (-9 points year-on-year) and 58 per cent trusting each business (-5 points) and NGOs (-4 points). Media, which saw a notable surge in trust in [the 2021 report], fell by 8 points to 43 per cent, making it the only institution in Australia distrusted by a majority of the population.[2]

The Media in Flux

Today's media struggle. Technology has dramatically broadened the ability to communicate. The media can transmit events from virtually anywhere in the world in real time. The consumer can directly tap into an array of sources that would have been unimaginable even a few decades ago. And activists and everyday interested citizens can be their own 'publishers' on social media. Of course, individuals' circumstances will vary greatly but, in the main, Australians can't complain about a lack of either information or opportunities for a say. Yet more is not always better. As well, there is the separate question of journalists being forced to do more with less.

The digital age has seen the media fragment, destroying the business model of the traditional media. Once, the media, especially the major newspapers, were unifying 'town squares' in their communities. Those days are long gone, as people obtain their news and other information from more diverse sources, and often exist in silos, tapping into only what reinforces their established views and prejudices. Traditional media's revenues have tightened, so there has been a squeeze on the funds available for spending on journalism, especially serious journalism. The pursuit of clicks has, at least to an extent, distorted the choices made in news coverage. Knowing how particular stories or analysis pieces 'rate' can be corrupting, because it can affect what is covered or given prominence. In the extreme, it can skew how a journalist works, encouraging attention-seeking over balance and fairness. The growth of lifestyle and infotainment journalism, catering to changing public tastes and pitched at attracting advertising as well as audience, has meant fewer resources for specialist journalism; for example, about health policy. For a while, COVID notably refocused attention on the very serious. It also brought communities together as they tapped into information. Later, the issues of vaccination and treatments led to divisions between the majority and the relatively small but vociferous minorities protesting against lockdowns and vaccinations.

Over the years, styles in journalism change. This reflects technology and the transformations in how people live, work and entertain themselves. A hundred years ago, those seeking to understand the politics of the day had only newspapers, with serious newspapers mostly seeing themselves, at least in part, as journals of record. Fast-forward half a century and the rise of television transformed politics and the way people obtain their news. Move ahead another half-century and we see today's cluttered landscape.

Maybe people have always distrusted journalists; we don't have Newspoll or Morgan to tell us about attitudes in the distant past. But if we look at distrust in modern times, a few things are obvious. Many people think journalists don't get things right; some think they are biased; others believe they're often unethical. How valid are these criticisms? Certainly, there is a fair bit of sloppiness in our journalism, and this has been exacerbated by two unfortunate developments. Subeditors have been reduced or eliminated on cost grounds, so fewer pairs of eyes see stories before they are published. Secondly, many journalists are turning around more copy in a shorter period of time. Added to this, there is a great deal of 'opinion' journalism today (in print and on radio and TV), and more journalists who insert themselves into the centre of the story. So the public's scepticism is not surprising. (It is, however, selective; for example, the ABC has rated strongly in public confidence over a long period.)

Integrity has become a central issue in recent years, as we've seen with the debate around, and then legislation for, a national anti-corruption body. It is a rather under-discussed issue in contemporary journalism, yet it is one that deserves more attention from the profession. Issues include whether journalists adequately disclose conflicts of interest, what limits media should observe in intruding on people's privacy, and the circumstances in which journalists are justified in lying. The latter is not always an open-and-shut matter—the complexities are examined in the recently published *Undercover Reporting, Deception, and Betrayal in Journalism* by Andrea Carson and Denis Muller.[3]

Circling back to COVID, for a while the media landscape became more dominated by the strictly factual and informative. And a good deal of the commentary was explanatory, often written by, or drawing on, those with relevant qualifications. It was exactly what the public wanted in uncertain times, and indeed what people say they want all the time. Whether, in fact, more straight-up-and-down reporting and less opinion would improve people's trust in the media in ordinary circumstances is an open question. It may be the 'low trust' target is too firmly attached.

COVID Becomes Yesterday's Story—up to a Point

In 2020, the media fell on COVID in a feeding frenzy. As 2023 began, it became yesterday's big headline. The pandemic had receded, most people were vaccinated, antiviral drugs were available and effective. Lives were still being lost in substantial numbers and it remained a major problem in aged-care facilities. But there was no longer a big appetite in the community for COVID coverage to get great prominence; it was as though most things had been said and most voices had been heard. Reflecting the public feeling, in the media COVID became a somewhat routine story.

That's the macro picture, but not the full one. Politicians have now taken to referring to 'living with COVID', and in the minds of many people, this means forgetting COVID. But there is still debate about how the long and unpleasant 'tail' of the pandemic is being handled. We've recently found readers of *The Conversation* are most interested in specifics: risks, those coughs, long COVID and the like. They are less interested in policy. There is low interest in specific vulnerable groups such as the elderly and people with disabilities or complex underlying conditions. That, of course, is where the obligation of the media comes in: to report on what still matters and what affects certain parts of the community, even when the clicks are relatively few.

Covering crises is a central and highly demanding role for journalists. But crises come in many different forms. We most often think of wars and natural disasters. Not for a century, since the days of the Spanish flu, have we faced a crisis in the form of a pandemic. This has been another kind of war.

We quickly found that covering COVID-19 well imposed a formidable range of demands: getting across unfamiliar subject matter; rigorous attention to detail; an ability to tap into, and gain the confidence of, experts and report their information and views accurately. Crazy theories and conspiracies could not be completely ignored because they were part of the news, but responsible journalism required they be properly debunked. At the same time, serious differences of opinion had to be given proper and proportionate airing.

In wartime, journalists report on life-and-death struggles. The story of the pandemic has been as much about life and death as any shooting war. It, too, has had its front line, and a central part of the narrative has told of how health and aged-care workers bore up under strains they had never before encountered.

The coverage of COVID has underlined the importance and responsibility of the media in a crisis. There's been sensationalism and some poor coverage. But for the most part, we've seen a great deal of true 'public interest' journalism in bringing this complex, ever-changing story to a community facing extraordinary stresses. The challenge now is to see the story through to its end.

The Daily Presser

Andrew Lund, Head of Communications, Melbourne Airport; former state political reporter, Nine Network, Melbourne

'What time is Dan?' may well have been the most commonly asked question in Victoria during the pandemic, as Premier Daniel Andrews's press conferences became a must-watch daily event. These briefings could veer from informative and important to combative or cajoling, and at times downright frustrating. I know because I went to almost as many as he did.

The news was often grim but, with a huge and highly engaged audience, these press conferences were also the stuff of political dreams. They provided a way to speak directly to hundreds of thousands of people who were hanging on every word.

While Gladys Berejiklian in New South Wales adopted a standing 11 a.m. briefing, in Victoria the timing would vary. Early in the day usually meant low case numbers and good news. The later in the day the briefing was held, the worse things were. The press conference announcing the introduction of Stage 4 restrictions for Melbourne on 5 August 2020 was held at 4.15 p.m.—about as late as possible to be turned around for the 6 p.m. news. It was stressful—I say that not just as a journalist but as a Victorian. And it was stressful every day.

In a phenomenon repeated around the country, the premiers' regular jostles with journalists suddenly went from being clipped to just a ten-second grab on the nightly news, to being broadcast live in their entirety across multiple TV channels as one of the top-rating shows of the day. Like pop stars, Gladys, Anastasia and Dan no longer needed surnames. For perhaps the first time, they were recognised around the country. People would tune in to find out first-hand what new restrictions they'd be subjected to, how case numbers were tracking, or what the premier thought about the various situations facing other states.

The community had no idea how the pandemic would play out, so the daily press conference provided it with clues about what might lie ahead, an opportunity to air grievances, and hope that the crisis would one day be over. For both journalists and the public, it also became the only forum in which to ask questions about the virus, health advice, case numbers and how the government was responding. But it also provided the premiers with a new platform to speak directly to voters, and most used it to full advantage to help build their profile. As the old adage goes, never waste a crisis. Standing alongside their chief health officers, the premiers often gave lengthy opening 'remarks', knowing they were going out unfiltered, unedited, and uninterrupted by questions from journalists.

The pressers began to take on a regular format: an announcement of the day's case numbers followed by the number of deaths, then an update on where the trends were heading, some context from health officials and some form of government announcement. All this before a single question was asked. Often, the announcements reflected a decision that had been made quickly, and which was confusing, so the journalists' job became a game of trying to confirm details so as to accurately inform people about how their lives would change. Sometimes that information was contradicted two or three times in a day as public servants told us different things.

As more people tuned in, the TV networks added extra cameras and sound engineers to ensure viewers could hear the questions and see the people asking them. It gave the public a window into the often transactional, sometimes combative and occasionally ugly world of political press conferences.

The fishing expeditions for new information.

The frustrated attempts to hold power to account.

And the less noble but just as important questions to get a succinct seven-second grab for the evening news.

It resulted in an unprecedented level of scrutiny for those of us in the political press gallery, as social media gave viewers an opportunity to provide real-time feedback to those asking the questions. Some of that feedback was kind but some was vile. Suddenly, journalists were being judged on their questions rather than their stories. It reminded me that, sometimes, it's better not to see how the sausage is made.

In some cases the feedback was helpful, as doctors, nurses and business leaders chimed in to suggest, or occasionally demand, certain questions be asked. And there were so many questions. Daniel Andrews made a point of taking every one (whether or not he answered them is another issue), so as not to be seen to be hiding or shirking on issues at a time when livelihoods were being crippled.

The Victorian premier famously fronted up for 120 consecutive days during the state's lengthy lockdown in the second half of 2020. Some of his press conferences ran close to two hours—the record was one hour, fifty-four minutes—as the premier, his ministers and health experts were peppered with queries about the pandemic, their policy and the politics behind it. The result was that Andrews and his North Face jacket became synonymous with Victoria's battle to contain the coronavirus.

A combination of Melbourne's unpredictable weather and security concerns resulted in most of the premier's events being held in a small theatre in the bowels of 1 Treasury Place. The room was always uncomfortably cold, to the point that those of us sitting in it would often bring woollen jumpers and extra puffer jackets to use as blankets. Reporters and camera crews were told the chill was because of an air-conditioning malfunction, but more than a few wondered if it also had something to do with the Premier's propensity to sweat when under pressure.

With its grim atmosphere and brightly coloured background, the theatre was quickly dubbed The Purple Wall of Doom by my Channel 9 camera colleague Tim Furness. The name stuck. The dark mood was amplified by what was happening outside it, and our inability to escape the story.

Unlike other major news events, there was no way to distance yourself from what was happening. Instead, we would all leave the press conference and then live what we'd just been reporting on. It was personal, it was gruelling, and it was repeated every day. So, when some media outlets decided to use the press conferences to push their own agendas, it grated. A handful of outlets parachuted their big names into the pressers for a day or two, so they could be filmed asking questions to power. It may have made for a nice shot, but very rarely did it achieve anything for the public good. To those of us who had been there day in and day out, hearing the same old questions and answers repeated ad nauseam felt like a waste of time and energy. Given the critical role the press conference played in disseminating information, it seemed pointless to be spending so much time going over old ground when it was clear a detailed answer, or the answer being sought, would not be forthcoming in that forum.

Practice makes perfect, and through the course of the pandemic, some of the premiers became masters of deflection. At times, the adversarial nature of the exchanges felt uncomfortable. Sitting at the back of the room, the premier's media advisers would grit their teeth and occasionally fire off a text message venting their frustration to a friendly journalist.

While the premiers and some journalists courted and basked in the fame and attention, those standing alongside them were often somewhat less enthusiastic. The chief health officers were thrust into the spotlight early in the pandemic and quickly became household names. Once known only for the occasional alert on food poisoning, these public health officials were now guiding an entire nation through a once-in-a-lifetime pandemic. Their knowledge and presence gave credibility to the political decisions being made, and they were able to give important context to the case numbers and virus progression.

Given the magnitude of what was occurring, it was critical for the public to have access to these decision-makers through the media to understand the reasons for what they were being asked, or ordered, to do. But the chief health officers were often subjected to the same level of hostile questioning as the elected politicians with whom they shared the stage. Overall, they handled the pressure incredibly well, and any disagreements they had with their political masters were usually kept well hidden. Which is just as well, because it's unlikely many other public servants have been subjected to such intense focus and public assessment of their capabilities. South Australian Chief Health Officer Nicola Spurrier was ridiculed after telling AFL fans to 'duck' instead of touching the ball if it flew into the crowd during games. Victoria's Brett Sutton, on the other hand, found himself becoming an unexpected sex symbol, with his face emblazoned on tea towels and coffee cups. In Queensland, such was the trust in Jeannette Young that she was subsequently named the state's twenty-seventh governor, an appointment unlikely to have occurred had she not been in the public eye.

The press conferences were gruelling for everyone involved, but the unsung heroes were the Auslan interpreters who would diligently stand alongside the premiers and chief health officers to simultaneously translate their words into sign language, giving hearing-impaired viewers access to critical information. To prepare for these lengthy endurance tests, many interpreters would listen to talkback radio or chat to journalists in the minutes before the politicians started speaking, to get a feel for what might be asked and what words they may need to know.

In Western Australia, Auslan interpreter Fiona Perry became a minor celebrity after struggling to contain her laughter alongside

Premier Mark McGowan over a question about whether people could be arrested for going for a run and then eating a kebab. In among the worry and uncertainty, these lighthearted moments were a gift.

While draining, these briefings were also essential. The premiers and their health advisers provided reassurance, rallying cries and hope. In Victoria's case, by leading from the front at his purple wall, Daniel Andrews became the face of the pandemic and the lockdowns used to contain it. Many Victorians hated him for it, but there were just as many who were quietly impressed.

The strain this placed on Andrews was clearly visible in the rare emotion he showed while announcing the state would finally be reopening at the end of 2020. With fatigue etched across his face and a croaking voice, he reflected on the sacrifices the people of his state had made to achieve the national goal of COVID-zero: 'Why it's emotional today is because people have given a lot. People have done amazing things. Extraordinary acts of kindness, extraordinary acts of commitment and courage. None of this has been easy, but Victorians have shown what they are made of.' At times he appeared close to tears, while some of his advisers were already in tears, as they felt the heavy burden of lockdown and the daily press conference lifting from their shoulders.

The use of the press conference to deliver the day's key information guaranteed the premiers a huge audience and helped suck oxygen from state oppositions. From a political point of view, tying themselves so tightly to daily case numbers meant they had a vested interest in securing a good outcome at the end.

For the public, the pressers became a trusted source of information at a time when the internet was abuzz with crackpot ideas and conspiracy theories. Although it didn't provide people with total transparency, it did give them the opportunity to hear directly from the decision-makers, albeit while watching the political ducking and weaving first-hand.

For the media, the briefings provided a guaranteed story, sometimes multiple stories, and a crucial opportunity to bring questions to power.

For journalists, at a time when so many people were confined to their homes, even being allowed out of the house to attend these press conferences was a privilege. Asking questions felt like a proper public service, and in most cases it was.

But the relentlessness of the news cycle and the public scrutiny took a toll. My former Channel 7 colleague Laurel Irving remarked to me: 'I don't think it's a coincidence it was the last big story I did before I left the media. It was brutal, and I don't want to go through that again.'

It's no coincidence I've also left the media. And purple is never going to be my favourite colour.

Breakfast Television

Lisa Millar, Presenter, *ABC News Breakfast*, Melbourne

THE GREEN LATEX gloves are still in the car. Something is stopping me from throwing them out. When I toss in a pair of sunglasses or grab a mint from the glovebox, I see them and baulk. Every single time.

Everyone has a 'moment'—when the pandemic moved from being a global health crisis of unknown ramifications to something utterly surreal. The phone call had come from one of my bosses in Sydney. The request was polite but firm. He wanted me to stop getting a taxi to work at 3.30 a.m. and drive myself, to avoid being exposed to the virus during the short trip. He also asked that I wear disposable gloves as I made my way from the bowels of the ABC car park in Melbourne's Southbank to the first-floor make-up room and through the green room where our interview guests had once waited.

I followed instructions. For a day or two at least. It felt slightly foolish but who were we to judge?

The gloves stay in the car because I want that jolt each time I see them. The further we are from those early days and then later, the long lockdowns, the more we ask ourselves, did that really happen?

Months later we began using taxis again. Our regular drivers, desperate to keep the few customers they had, would sanitise seats and leap out to open doors for us, to eliminate chances of contamination. Journalists and medical staff were their only passengers. They would ask if we had our signed work permits with us and tell us if the police were out in force on any given night, stopping cars outside of the 8 p.m. to 5 a.m. curfew. On dark, desolate streets, the blue flashing lights would direct cabs to the kerb. Questions would be asked and documents sighted before we were released into the night. Simply getting to work and staying safe and well became the first challenge each and every day for our team.

In the beginning we shared a sense of purpose. There was a job to do and we had to find a way to keep doing it. The pandemic was taking hold in countries to our north and Australia was heading into its first lockdown at the tail end of March 2020. Executive producers Emily Butselaar and Tyson Shine made a decision to split both the production and presenting teams. Co-host Michael Rowland, our weather presenter Nate Byrne and I stayed in Studio 38 on the ground floor. Nate's computer was moved into the studio so when he wasn't on air, he stayed within the bubble of our team.

Our finance presenter Madeleine Morris moved to a smaller studio upstairs. Paul Kennedy, then our sports presenter, broadcast mostly from home, initially on Zoom or Skype and then with professional equipment called LiveU that offered a better-quality signal—we didn't see him in person for almost a year. Viewers became obsessed with his background choices. What was the picture on the wall? What was the book on the shelf? They started sending their own—a picture of the MCG, a book they recommended for lockdown reading—hoping PK (as all our viewers knew him) would give them a moment in the spotlight.

Each team was desperate to never cross paths, to remove any chance of contamination if someone got sick. Staying on air at all costs was the goal.

Casual make-up artists were culled and the number of staff who had any direct contact with us could be counted on one hand.

Mads was asked to do her own hair and make-up in a dim upstairs area, to keep her movements contained. She's the first to admit she's no expert in that critical role and endured polite viewer concerns about her complexion or less than perfect hairstyle, or why she was puffing (she would often run up the stairs from the newsroom after grabbing the latest financial news off the wire).

Before COVID, Michael and I would start our mornings at computers in the newsroom, chatting about story ideas and checking details with producers, before going into the studio after 5.30 a.m. Now, the producers would text or email their thoughts as Michael and I sat in our dressing rooms on laptops, isolated from our colleagues. We would then rush through the newsroom, our masks tightly fitted, offering a quick wave of the hand and the briefest of hellos, fearing that too many moments spent transiting through the same airspace as our team would leave us vulnerable.

The producers were split as well, working one week on and one week from home. As the Melbourne lockdowns dragged on, those weeks at home for many of the young producers became almost unbearable. Before COVID, they'd shared loud and happy homes with friends who'd spend their weekdays planning the weekend, and who slumbered while their housemate crept out after midnight to begin their *News Breakfast* shift. But those friends ditched the city, as so many people did, returning to the security of family homes in regional Victoria, leaving behind a near-empty five-bedroom house filled now with the loneliness of its sole occupant.

For the older producers, who had families at home, it became a challenge to find a space away from children where stories could be subbed and conversations had before the rest of Australia, and their own households, woke up.

Chief subs also worked from home, trying to calculate the delay between what they were watching going to air and what was on their laptop, unintentionally hitting 'save' on an intro as we were reading it, causing the autocue to refresh and the words in front of Michael and I to suddenly change.

We are lucky to be working at all.

We are lucky to be working at all.

If we repeated it often enough, we could convince ourselves of its truth on those days when the heaviness of the news left its weight on us long after we'd left the studio.

Viewers sent messages asking why we were encouraging people to keep their distance when Michael and I sat so close together. They were right. We separated the couches, moved our chairs apart at the desk, and the studio lighting above us was adjusted. We spoke to our audience on social media explaining what we had done. Our commercial competitors followed suit within days.

Happy with our separation, viewers settled into a routine with us. There was a similarity to the messages they sent—their worlds had been turned upside down, and switching on to see the familiar faces of the *News Breakfast* team each morning was all that was getting them through the crisis. They told us of parents who had died in aged care, of children struggling with homeschooling, of jobs lost. The grief was tangible. They were still seeing us, hearing us every morning, and they wanted us to hear their stories too.

On air, we tried to find a way to laugh. I cut up socks to make face masks. We revelled in our kitchen failures, happily broadcasting the cakes that could have been, should have been. If only any of us could cook.

Guests were no longer welcome in the studio. Few people were leaving their homes anyway. Jo, our floor manager, no longer directed people in and out of the studio like a maître d' at a busy restaurant.

Some of our 'talent', as studio guests are called, adapted to the new remote technology. Others found it bothersome. Singer Daryl Braithwaite leaned forward mid-interview to fix the settings on his desktop, presenting fans with a close-up view of his nose.

We were always trying to create content. Michael and I did an Instagram Live, him baking bread in his kitchen, me mixing a martini. Nate picked up an idea from the BBC and got us playing makeshift instruments in our homes to the tune of the *Breakfast* theme music. The arrival of Tony Armstrong added another note of levity. He inserted a clip of *Jurassic Park* into the screen behind him and spent his sports segment pretending to run from dinosaurs. COVID forced us to find creative ways to keep the two presenting teams connected despite our physical separation.

Off air, those same young producers who had had their own worlds up-ended and who fought back tears of tension and stress, worked hard to protect the camaraderie. There were fancy footwear Fridays, silly hat days, and a guac-off as they challenged each others' skill with an avocado. All of it made it to air in one form or another. Our behind-the-scenes lives became fodder for television as we tried to find a balance with the grim news we delivered each day.

Broadcasting from a city with the heaviest restrictions in Australia but reaching a national audience presented a daily challenge to hit the right tone. How could you have a program that was relevant to all parts of the country when Melbourne was going through such a different experience? We expanded the program's footprint and in turn our audience numbers. Suddenly, all Australians were possible guests, not just those near an ABC studio. Our viewers adapted to seeing live crosses occasionally drop out and they rolled with it. They saw the funny side of children and pets making appearances.

None of us were prepared for how we would feel when restrictions eased and our first outside guests would walk back into that studio.

Singers Vika and Linda Bull had told us we had helped get them through the many lockdowns, when they'd wondered if they would ever restart their shattered careers. At 8.54 a.m. on a Friday morning, 22 October 2021, they brought us back to life, belting out 'Lover, Don't Keep Me Waiting' live from our studio floor. If you look back at the footage, you'll see Tony, Nate, Michael and me clapping and rushing to high-five them. We look giddy with excitement. It had been twenty long months.

Michael waves to the robotic camera and calls out over our chatter, 'That is beautiful. Back Monday folks!' And as the shot fades to black we shed tears from the sheer relief of it all.

The Economic Pandemic

Patrick Durkin, Melbourne Bureau Chief, *The Australian Financial Review*, Melbourne

It was two days before the Australian Formula 1 Grand Prix was supposed to kick off in Melbourne in March 2020, and I was at the racetrack as part of the coverage for *The Australian Financial Review*. I had the incredible opportunity to experience two laps in a Minardi two-seater F1 car, speeding around the track at over 280 kilometres per hour. It was one of the most terrifying experiences of my life, but the day also stuck in my mind for another reason. When I arrived at the track and met a fellow journalist, I stuck out my hand in the usual greeting. 'I'm not shaking hands at the moment,' they told me. 'You know, coronavirus.' The small gesture was the first time the virus had directly impacted my own life.

The GP proved a stand-out COVID event for other journalists, too. *The Age*'s then breaking news reporter Paul Sakkal recalls the chaos while reporting from among thousands of racegoers standing outside the gates on Friday 13 March, waiting to be let in. He had been sent out by his news desk around 7 a.m. because the BBC was reporting the race could be cancelled due to the emerging coronavirus crisis. 'There were hours of confusion, then some reports of drivers already at the airport,' Sakkal recalls.

At around 10.30 a.m., a track official emerged with a megaphone. 'The AGPC [Australian Grand Prix Corporation] has been informed by Formula 1 of the cancellation of the race,' he declared.

'We want our money back,' one racegoer called out, amid a smattering of heckles, jeers and boos.

Cancelling the $150 million race was big news. More than 300 000 fans had been expected to attend over the weekend, and 600 suppliers and 12 000 staff had to be stood down overnight. But most Australians had no idea it marked the start of more than two years of unprecedented lockdowns and health restrictions. It changed the way we lived, the way we worked, and in turn, the way the media reported.

'It's Not a Race'

On the morning the race was cancelled, AGPC chairman and Melbourne billionaire Paul Little bounded past a television reporter declaring, 'The race is still on!' It later emerged there had been a crisis meeting between drivers and Formula 1 at Crown Casino the night before which had run well past 2.30 a.m. The meeting had been called after news broke that one of the McLaren team had tested positive to the virus and the team was pulling out of the race.

World champion Lewis Hamilton had already lit the fuse on the debate on the Thursday, declaring he was 'very, very surprised we are here' and complaining, 'Cash is King.' The public taunt triggered headlines across the world and started what soon became a heated public dispute, often pitting health against economics. The following morning, multiple reports emerged on social media that F1 drivers Sebastian Vettel and Kimi Raikkonen had already flown out of Melbourne Airport as early as 6 a.m.

Amid the morning's confusion, Victorian Premier Daniel Andrews was doorstopped as he strode into a crisis meeting with then prime minister Scott Morrison and other state premiers in Sydney. 'There will be no spectators at the Grand Prix this weekend if a race actually happens at all,' he told reporters.

Victorian Chief Health Officer Brett Sutton later admitted he couldn't sleep in the days leading up to the Grand Prix as the COVID cases began to climb from just a handful to more than thirty. Sutton said he felt sick about choosing to keep crowds out, but that Premier Andrews had told him to 'just make the decision and we will back you'.

The dramatic events marked a significant change in the way the newsroom reported, and my work personally.

At the onset of the pandemic, our newspaper had introduced live, blog-style, online coverage of breaking news events. It had quickly become apparent COVID was as much an economic crisis as a health one. This meant financial journalism would be crucial to making sense of what was going on, as well as keeping the government accountable for its response.

As the Grand Prix was facing cancellation that Thursday night, I was up past midnight posting breaking news about the race. When the sun rose, the news continued at breakneck speed and seemed to continue that way for the next two years. The blinking red light marking breaking news on the blog became a permanent fixture on afr.com and all the major mastheads, with much more reporting over the weekends than before. Readers could not get enough information quickly enough.

A month before the GP was cancelled, I had attended a business lunch in Melbourne with Reserve Bank of Australia (RBA) Governor Philip Lowe. At that time, Lowe rated the pandemic at about the same impact as the summer bushfires, creating only a potential speed bump in the growing economy. 'I don't think the virus fundamentally changes [the] outlook, but it does mean, right at the moment, things are going to be softer than we thought,' Dr Lowe told the Australia–Canada Economic Leadership Forum, using his speech to focus, instead, on climate change.

Then federal treasurer Josh Frydenberg says it was not until a week later, when he and Lowe found themselves in Saudi Arabia for the G20 meeting of finance ministers, that the size of the crisis began to register. 'Both Phil and I were struck by comments from the Singaporeans at the meeting about how the coronavirus would weigh heavily on their economy,' Frydenberg recalls.

Back then, the word of the RBA governor was considered almost infallible. Lowe told the same Australia–Canada audience, 'We're going to be in this [low interest] world for a long period of time,' adding that low interest rates could be around 'for years, possibly decades'. Lowe later went further in telling consumers the RBA did not expect rates to rise until 2023 or 2024. When inflation eventually took hold in the wake of the pandemic, those predictions turned out to be horribly wrong. 'I'm sorry that that happened. I'm certainly sorry if people listened to what we'd said and then acted on that,' Lowe said more than two years later.

You could similarly point to Daniel Andrews claiming in February 2020 that fear over the pandemic was being driven by racism towards China, as he lit up Melbourne in the colours of China's flag to show the city's support. And, of course, later in the pandemic, Morrison repeatedly responded to criticism about the slow vaccine rollout by claiming, 'It's not a race.' Those words were powerfully used against Morrison when Labor successfully campaigned using the PM's plummeting personal popularity at the May 2022 federal election.

I highlight these comments to show how quickly things evolved, and that misjudgements were made. It's a reminder of the media's often heavy reliance on these institutions to report the news, and the need for more universal financial literacy within media ranks to enable journalists without economic experience to be able to fully challenge those making these decisions.

Add to that, facts were changing rapidly. As journalists, we had to make sense of often unreliable information as well as grapple with outright mistakes by institutions we have traditionally held sacrosanct. Most often it was not malicious or intentional, but the media still had to call them out, serving a legitimate role in holding such institutions to account. Clearly, the media faced similar challenges to political leaders and got a lot wrong itself. It needs to carefully learn the lessons of its own systemic failures.

Part of this was the media's tendency to lean into the shock value of new strains and outbreaks of the virus. That was a trap I fell into reporting one Sunday, when South Australia's chief health officer (CHO) fingered a man in his thirties for going on a shopping spree and putting the state at risk. Mainstream reporting put a strong spotlight on the man's behaviour, including releasing maps of the shops he had visited, triggering widespread public outrage. By the next day, the CHO had apologised and revealed that the man had not actually broken any rules.

The public's shock at watching the confrontational nature of the daily press conferences with our political leaders also hit home. It's a process which many viewers had never witnessed so closely before and it sparked questions and criticism about whether journalists were properly serving the public interest. It made us, as reporters, reflect on how we should behave.

Australia's First Recession in Decades

National Cabinet had met late into Sunday, 22 March 2020, to impose the first of the unprecedented emergency health restrictions. The government's decision to immediately close pubs, clubs, gyms, cinemas, nightclubs, casinos, restaurants and cafes in a series of measures was like nothing the country had seen since the Spanish flu a century earlier. A $60 billion support package, adding to a $17.6 billion stimulus rolled out a fortnight before, was announced, with Treasury predicting two million Australians could be left unemployed.

A day later, the country woke up to images of the public snaking down streets and around blocks near their local Centrelink office to register for unemployment benefits. After close to thirty years of uninterrupted economic growth, it brought to mind images from the Great Depression. The share market was in freefall—the benchmark index dropped by more than 20 per cent that month, its largest fall on record. People began fighting over toilet paper in supermarket aisles and stockpiling common household goods, as panic over the coronavirus peaked. It was a modern variation of a run on the banks, and it was clear something more would be required of the government.

In other ways, the economic turmoil felt very different to the global financial crisis (GFC) which hit soon after I joined the *AFR* as a young lawyer. The focus of the pandemic was always, rightly, on health and the rising death toll, particularly among the elderly. This meant the economic impacts of the crisis were often overshadowed. The *AFR* ran a front page with a dramatic graphic on 15 May, with a red line running down the right-hand side showing a 4.6 per cent drop in employment—eclipsing previous recessions dating back to the 1980s. It was clever newspaper editing but also memorable because not much attention was being paid to the economics of the crisis. There was also an enormous public expectation—partly because of the bailouts and government interventions of the GFC, and partly because the pandemic restrictions were being imposed by governments—that governments should and would step in to provide financial support.

Josh Frydenberg vividly recalls the lead-up to his $130 billion key policy announcement on 30 March: 'Before I announced JobKeeper, I rang [former PM] John Howard and I said to him, "John, I'm about to announce an economy-wide wage subsidy ... not exactly what I was expecting to do as a Liberal treasurer." He said, "Josh, at times of national crisis there are no ideological constraints." That was an important green light that we were doing the right thing in the circumstances.'

Frydenberg also rang business leaders, including Mecca Cosmetica founder Jo Horgan, Wesfarmers CEO Rob Scott, Richard Murray from JB Hi-Fi and retailer Solomon Lew, who was reportedly in tears on the phone after being forced to stand down his 12 000 workers.

Treasury had been examining the UK wage subsidy—paying workers 80 per cent of their wages—but argued it was unnecessarily complicated. Instead, it proposed three different options for fortnightly payments: $1000, $1200 or $1500. Frydenberg chose the $1500 figure, describing the decision as a 'break glass moment'.

JobKeeper ran to September 2020 before it was extended for another six months in a tapered-down form. The government did reintroduce COVID-19 disaster payments, but it resisted calls to reinstate JobKeeper when the Delta variant swept through Sydney and then Melbourne in mid-2021, before the Omicron wave hit in 2022.

Across the pandemic years, the economic crisis stressed and tested businesses big and small. And because so many businesses were affected, it stretched journalists' ability to both humanise the stories and explain their broader impact and context. Like Victoria's snap five-day lockdown in February 2021, when $36 million worth of flowers was tossed out that Valentine's Day by the state's florists—each one had its own story to tell. Another $100 million was estimated to have been lost by the pubs, clubs and restaurants that make up the hospitality industry, and $20 million in fresh food and produce had to be dumped.

The health of big businesses presented a different reporting challenge. Many, if not most, emerged from the pandemic healthier than ever. The role played in that by JobKeeper, originally intended to help companies which faced losing more than 30 per cent of their turnover, became a key story. The biggest beneficiaries of JobKeeper included Qantas, which received $726 million in payments yet by the end of 2022 was on track to post a $1.45 billion interim profit. In contrast, Virgin Australia went into voluntary administration on 20 April 2020, owing 10 000 creditors more than $6.8 billion. The airline, hit hard by border closures, was eventually sold to a private equity firm.

Reporting on JobKeeper required journalists to navigate competing claims by politicians and business about who benefited, or didn't, the most. There was often a lack of reliable data or financial transparency to assess that. But, according to Treasury, 'Small business accounted for $12.1 billion (88 per cent) of JobKeeper payments that we made to businesses that had increased turnover.'[1] Even so, the amounts paid out to profitable bigger businesses was still eye-watering. Governance firm Ownership Matters found that of the top sixty-six ASX companies that received JobKeeper in 2020, fifty-eight of them still reported positive earnings.

Staying Grounded

Financial journalists are often the first to sense a change in the wind as they analyse economic and socioeconomic data. The COVID story was no different. The uneven nature of the pandemic playing out in politics, with vastly different experiences across the different states, was plain to see.

Veteran business journalist Robert Gottliebsen at *The Australian* saw the uneven economic impact of the pandemic much earlier than most. And his experiences helped shape this advice to journalists: always speak to those on the ground and don't rely on our institutions as gospel alone. In my view, this is perhaps the most important lesson for the media from the pandemic. Gottliebsen's view of the impact of COVID emerged over his long walks and phone calls with middle managers during the lockdowns, which he spent at his holiday house on Victoria's Surf Coast.

In late May 2020, Gottliebsen wrote his first column about the fact that, despite Australia being on track for a recession, there was actually an economic boom underway in sectors connected to household improvements—appliances, furniture and lighting. 'Jubilant managers in some of the store chains such as Bunnings, JB Hi-Fi/The Good Guys, Harvey Norman and other homeware and lighting operators are experiencing sales jumps of 10–30 per cent,' he wrote.[2]

JobKeeper meant much of the economic risk and damage had been transferred from the private sector to the state. Economic data later showed households and businesses had squirrelled away $360 billion in extra bank deposits during the COVID crisis—money many people happily spent. Gottliebsen says the economic data being reviewed by the RBA was six months out of date.

'I'll never forget those beach conversations,' he says. 'These middle managers couldn't believe what was going on. The market had completely fallen to bits but there were just signs of activity after Easter. Nobody took much notice of it, but it started to get momentum. Then it became huge.'

An Economic Pandemic

COVID was both an economic story and a health story, the themes intertwined. Decisions justified by government to protect the community, like lockdowns, had a profound impact on individual businesses. When business spoke up against any of the health measures they were often attacked or threatened with boycotts by the public. It made me realise we needed to tell the story of business in new and innovative ways and present a very human side to the economic cost.

For me, this meant pushing beyond the usual suspects—complaining CEOs, big business groups—and highlighting the economic cost through very real examples. Like those dumped Valentine's Day flowers, or the seafood wholesaler forced to throw out 150 kilograms of live marron and over 70 000 oysters. We spoke to those who had cancelled their weddings, and to farmers and harvesters about the impact of the restrictions on food supplies. We recorded the daily battles small businesses faced in finding staff once the tap for international workers was turned off, and the problems and inconsistencies in accessing government grants.

At the same time, I received countless messages of support for helping give business owners a voice, or simply for helping to facilitate fixes. One small example was the front-page story we ran in August 2020 which forced the Victorian Government to back down on the restrictions that had crippled Australia Post's parcel delivery services, which were in greater demand than ever before. Then CEO Christine Holgate wrote to us to say they couldn't have fixed it without us.

The media faced constant criticism for the way the COVID story was covered, with accusations of bias, unfair questioning of government and heavy-handedness. Many journalists had their personal social media accounts inundated with abuse and misinformation. But the support for our work included voices from inside both the state and federal governments, privately urging us to help hold those in power, who were wielding unprecedented authority, to account.

It made our work in the media more important than ever. For me, it became the North Star in trying to strike the almost-impossible balance that we in the media need to find: breaking news quickly and before others in an intensely competitive arena; driving high readership and audiences; making our reporting exciting, dynamic and interesting; while never deviating from the fundamental journalistic tenets of truth, accuracy and serving the public interest.

PART II
THE CHANGING NEWSROOM

Fit to Print

Tory Maguire, Executive Editor, Nine Publishing, Sydney

It was Monday afternoon, 16 March 2020, and Paul Kelly had just thrown everyone in the deep end. The then federal deputy chief medical officer (CMO) was standing in for his boss Brendan Murphy at a press conference and had begun musing on COVID-19 modelling in the wake of estimates released by Imperial College London. The college had predicted a death rate among COVID-19 cases of 1 per cent (which we now know to be wildly overblown). Dr Kelly told the gathered journalists the Australian infection rate could be anywhere between 20 per cent and 60 per cent.

'I think Angela Merkel said 60 per cent of Germans the other night. My colleague Kerry Chant talked about 20 per cent. It's something in that range,' Dr Kelly said.

When asked how many Australians could die of COVID under this scenario in the following month and a half, Dr Kelly responded: 'Do the maths.' Not, 'We can't possibly know.' Not, 'I don't think it's helpful to speculate.' But, 'Do the maths.'

While newspaper editors and television news directors around the country were getting calls from the prime minister urging calm and measured coverage of the great unknown, the deputy CMO invited everyone who wanted to, to join in the speculation.

Our parliament-based health reporter, Dana Daniel (then McCauley), did the maths and rang me. I was national editor at the time, responsible for—among other things—our federal politics coverage across the Nine metro mastheads *The Sydney Morning Herald*, *The Age*, *Brisbane Times* and *WA Today*. According to the modelling, 150 000 people could die. I sent her back to Dr Kelly's office to check. I sent her back to check again. Embarrassingly for Dana, I sent her back a third time, saying, 'We are going to put this on the front page of both *The Sydney Morning Herald* and *The Age*. Are you sure?' And then we did.

In the week leading up to this, it had already become clear the information we were getting from our political and bureaucratic leaders was subject to change not just daily but hourly, and sometimes wasn't even correct at the time we were given it. Eight days before Dr Kelly's press conference, we'd run a print correction over the requirements for Australians returning from Italy. When the story was first filed, I thought the details didn't sound right, so I sent the reporter back to their source to check, twice. The story we ran, accurately reporting the information we'd been given by the government, was still wrong. This was not the only time this happened.

In the world of live news blogs and social media feeds, this was manageable. But newspapers are still a vital part of our service to readers, and knowing what to put in tomorrow's paper while the prime minister was holding 10 p.m. press conferences about banning barre classes was a wild ride. We didn't need to be asked to tread carefully.

In late 2020, then national affairs editor Rob Harris came across a story that sounded like it couldn't possibly be true. He'd heard that the early testing of the Australian-developed COVID vaccine—out of the University of Queensland and the venerable pharma company CSL—was returning false positive HIV results in participants. In the wrong hands, you can just imagine the headlines and the damage they would have done in the race to vaccinate the world. The story was true.

The federal government was mortified it had happened and equally mortified Rob had found out. It asked us for enough time to notify counterpart governments and prepare its communications to ward off panic, and we agreed. We resisted every adjective, every hot social sell, every urge to break our exclusive in a way that might jeopardise public health. We still broke the story and Rob still had his scoop, but we had missed the print edition—something unthinkable up to that point.

As the early months of pandemic panic evolved into the grind of daily remote publishing—fourteen newspapers a week; four websites; around-the-clock blogging, field reporting and photography; all performed by staff working under the same logistical and personal challenges of every other Australian—demand for journalism that was not subject to the violent oscillation of details-just-to-hand grew. Our digital presentation team, with help from our data journalists, built a COVID-19 data centre and then a vaccine tracker which attracted more than fifteen million visits during 2020 and 2021. In the same period, our in-depth coronavirus explainers attracted 9.4 million page views, and the work of our science writer Liam Mannix more than twenty-one million.

At the time, I was hosting our daily news podcast *Please Explain*. Whenever Liam was the guest, thousands more people than usual would listen. Our audiences wanted authoritative, impartial coverage. In total, our coronavirus coverage over 2020 and 2021 attracted just under one billion page views. But at a time when Australians were relying on journalism more than ever, some started to trust us less, and two other complicating factors emerged—both related in some way to Dr Kelly's invitation to work it out for ourselves.

∼

Sumeyya Ilanbey, a state political reporter at *The Age*, is a veteran of Dan Andrews's daily press conferences, the political and journalistic ultramarathon conducted over 2020 and 2021 as Melbourne endured the most days in lockdown of any city on the planet. The Victorian premier appointed himself chief information officer, a role he played every day for more than 120 days, sometimes spending hours on his feet, usually in his North Face puffer jacket, delivering a firehose of numbers, names, places, modelling and rules.

With the bulk of Victorians stuck at home and yearning for a glimmer of light at the end of the tunnel, the press conferences became appointment viewing, and journalists actors on a stage that before this time had drawn only tiny audiences. A broad audience was now watching the news sausage being made, and a lot of them didn't like it. Suddenly, reporters came under sustained attack online for doing exactly what they were supposed to be doing—asking questions. Or for asking the 'wrong' questions. Somehow, asking the premier for information or holding him to account for his decisions became advocating 'letting it rip' or 'doing political dirty work'. Sumeyya copped it, as did *The Australian*'s Rachel Baxendale. When the ABC's Leigh Sales turned up to an Andrews presser, Twitter lost its tenuous grip—the fact she was from Sydney only made it worse.

As Sumeyya tells me: 'The press conferences were a masterclass in being seen to be accountable while simultaneously dodging accountability. Vital questions from journalists about hotel quarantine policies were rarely answered because the premier had used an inquiry he established as a shield to stop answering questions during press conferences. Questions about the roadmap out of restrictions, too, were rarely answered because the premier deemed them either Cabinet-in-confidence or work in progress. Questions about the science behind decisions were, again, rarely answered because the premier deemed anyone who questioned the rationale as "wanting to hurt the vulnerable and the elderly".'

In the newsroom, we gritted our teeth and put it down to Twitter, but it was too simplistic to write it off as a social media phenomenon.

A small section of our own audience was also becoming less inclined to be challenged, less willing to contemplate an alternative view, more wedded to the view Andrews's lockdowns were the only path worth considering. As the realities of the lockdowns started to really hit—on mental health, education, small businesses, children's social development, family ties—raising these issues became a fraught task.

By the time of the last and longest lockdown, I was executive editor of Nine Publishing's metro mastheads and responsible for managing a newspaper based in a city I was not allowed to visit. Then *Age* editor Gay Alcorn, who had started in her job in the latter stages of 2020 and therefore still hadn't met many of her staff in person, had the task of navigating this complex set of audience expectations in Melbourne and balancing it with our journalistic value of holding the powerful to account. It took guts.

On 1 September 2021, *The Age* published an editorial titled 'Victoria Can't Go on Like This':

> There comes a point, and *The Age* believes that point has been reached, where the damage caused by the harshest and longest lockdowns in the country needs to be more seriously factored in. Wednesday's announced 'easing' was a harsh and cruel blow. Playgrounds can open on Friday (although, in true Victorian style, only one carer can attend and they cannot remove their mask even to eat or drink). Few experts ever endorsed the playground ban in the first place ...
>
> *The Age* is not arguing that we should throw out restrictions, but instead that we need to work out those that could be lifted at minimal risk to health but with maximum benefit to Victorians. 'Minimal risk' is not 'no risk', but we must shift towards a more balanced position, even a little. Health authorities and the Premier have always said that a 'package' of measures is needed and that one measure cannot be separated from others. But since we all

now agree we will not get to zero cases, the government needs to adjust the balance of that 'package', because, after six lockdowns, many people are struggling beyond the point of endurance.

The Age has also had enough of the lack of information from the state government. Such harsh restrictions enforced for such an extended time must be fully justified with clear evidence that they are effective. Victorians need to see the modelling. We need to know where people are becoming infected. How many at home? How many in workplaces? How many (as far as we can know) were infected while having a picnic?[1]

It was like a bomb had gone off. Reading through the 782 comments on the editorial from the time sums up how divided opinion had become. Many people were supportive, grateful someone had finally said it, but many more were disgusted, accusing *The Age* of some kind of barbarism. Many people cancelled their subscriptions. Fortunately, some others signed up.

In her weekly note to subscribers a few days later, Gay wrote that she'd received calls from Victorian Government ministers, and there was a change in tone at the press conference the day the editorial was published. 'Daniel Andrews flagged that a roadmap was being put together about what life looks like once targets are reached. And, thank goodness, he gave some hope to Victorians stuck on the NSW border unable to get home, suggesting that home quarantine may be a solution,' she wrote.[2]

Seven months after this editorial was published, 400 000 people turned up for the Australian Formula 1 Grand Prix in Melbourne. Looking back, it's hard to understand how such reasonable demands for transparency and information could be so controversial. It's like 2021 and 2022 weren't just different years but different planets.

As 2022 waned, we learned that former prime minister Scott Morrison had himself secretly sworn into multiple portfolios, and we were universally disgusted by this. But I wonder what Australians would have tolerated if we'd known at the time. My amateur pop-psychology theory is the lockdowns were so arduous and hard to bear that, for many people, the thought they might not have been strictly necessary was too hard to contemplate. If, as we were told over and over, 'We're all in this together,' then who dares question it?

What I learned as an editor is, even if it feels redundant, make reporters go back again and again to check the facts. And just because it comes out of the mouth of an expert doesn't make it true. Contrary to those who lament the old days of journalism, and I hear from them often, I think journalism actually came out of the pandemic in better shape than when it went in. None of us want to be told, 'Do the maths.' We all want answers, and it's our job to demand them.

Power Switch

Grant Sherlock, Managing Editor, ABC News Digital, Brisbane

I BEGAN RESEARCHING AND writing this essay in my bedroom, laptop balanced on my knees, shoulders hunched in the kind of position that results from being propped up by pillows on your bed. I couldn't get to my study because outside the bedroom were my COVID-positive wife and daughter. I could hear them laughing and playing around, watching TV and practising my daughter's reading. And there I was cooped up, trying to keep myself from getting infected so I could be a part of some long-planned work meetings in person.

The tables had turned since the start of the pandemic. People with COVID now had much more freedom of movement and, in order to avoid infection, I had retreated behind closed doors. My daughter could have been at school all week despite her positive result, as long as she was clear of symptoms and was willing to wear a mask all day. We tried that for one day but it quickly became clear her teachers weren't so comfortable with a COVID-positive student nipping at their heels. I got it—I was sure I'd feel the same. And so followed a conversation with my wife where we tried to figure out what was now acceptable. The rules might have said one thing, but were people ready for that, and was it even the right thing?

Three years into this pandemic and we're still grappling with the kinds of questions that consumed every conversation, just about every page of a newspaper's news section and countless online stories during the first two years of COVID. What even are the rules now? How many cases are there in my neighbourhood? Is there another wave on the way? Is this variant worse than the last? Am I just tired or is this long COVID?

In my twenty-plus years in journalism, there's never been more written about a single topic. Donald Trump's presidency would be the only other story in the same league, but COVID would still win out. There'd be barely a publication in the world that hasn't ended up covering COVID in some way, thanks to the fact it impinged on almost every aspect of our lives—for most, it dominated their output. That was in part because it was the biggest story in town, but it was also the greatest audience opportunity that had ever presented itself. Suddenly, there was a story everyone had to know about. For news organisations, this brought into play whole sections of society that previously had had no interest in regular news consumption. Those people could now realistically be considered a potential audience.

Regarding Trump, the story was driven by the man himself and the media. For the most part, audiences just went along for the ride, watching from the sidelines in delight or disbelief—sometimes both, I suspect. When it came to COVID, news organisations that previously had felt in control of their agenda faced a more uncertain journey, one driven by the population's thirst for information about the virus rather than simply coverage of the world's response to it.

What followed was a significant shift in how some news teams chose their stories. It was a moment when long-established rituals for determining what was important were flipped on their head. For these teams, no longer were journalists and editors the unrivalled judges of what was newsworthy. Now, readers had decisive control over both choosing what to read and telling the news teams what to cover. Some would say that has always been the case because circulation figures and page views ultimately drive decisions, but the reality is that, in recent history, COVID is unique for being the single story that everyone was interested in—every facet of it. Editors could ignore that message if they chose, but the reader would simply go elsewhere thanks to the casual consumption habits of many these days. And among news organisation bosses, there are few fears greater than the prospect of your audience shifting to a competitor.

At public media institutions like the ABC, the threat is different but similarly serious. Fail to serve the public's needs and irrelevance beckons. For an organisation committed to being a part of Australians' everyday lives, not playing that role during such a threat to public health and economic security would have represented an unforgiveable fail.

Answers amid the Noise

So, what caused this shift, and how did the media respond?

It makes sense to start by unpacking the role of 'search'. For many years, Australians have made Google searches a part of their daily existence. Whether it's checking the opening hours of their local supermarket, finding a recommendation for a restaurant, or getting the number for their GP, they interact with search in an unending variety of ways. Want to know who won in the English Premier League overnight? Head to Google when you wake up. Heard something on the grapevine about a favourite celebrity? Google will help you find out who's writing about it. While media companies would love people to go directly to them for these answers, and some do, many people just select from the range of choices offered by Google. It's a fast and effective way of breaking through the noise on the internet.

Every news organisation has by now cottoned on to the opportunities Google presents—indeed, many did so a long time ago. Some have search engine optimisation or SEO teams who do their best to ensure the company's content ranks high in Google results. Others pay close attention to trending searches and align their commissioning decisions accordingly, in the hope of reaching some of the audiences using Google. Whether they like it or not, Google delivers a portion of the total audience they rely on. For some it represents a small portion, for others their livelihood.

When COVID came along, the possibilities were clear for all to see. While those doing searches on Trump were greater in number and demographically more varied than for the average politics story, they were still people mostly interested in politics in some way. With COVID, just about everyone was interested, and as the pandemic went on, the reasons became unique to each person as they got to know more about the virus and applied it to their personal situation.

What ensued was a tsunami of questions thrown Google's way. Analysis by Chartbeat, which provides audience analytics to media companies in more than sixty countries, found reader traffic from Google searches 'grew much faster than any other source from 2019 to 2021'. Across the sites it works with, Chartbeat reported a 36 per cent growth in page views from search during that time. In the same period, visits from social media platforms and occasions where readers went directly to a news site both remained relatively stable, especially in 2021.[1] Not only was search delivering more page views to news sites, but the people coming via that route were on average spending longer consuming content than other types of visitors. In short, the uncertainty of the pandemic prompted many to seek answers, and large numbers chose to just type their questions into Google.

For those following the trends in search, each day brought another version of the question, 'What are the symptoms of COVID?' Other questions that came up with relentless regularity from early in the pandemic were those relating to exposure and symptoms—'How long am I contagious?' and 'How do I know if I have the flu or COVID?'—and the latest COVID isolation requirements. This challenged the normal editorial processes inside media organisations.

No team charged with specifically responding to online search trends could adequately cater to the demand. At the ABC, stories on topics that directly answered such questions attracted a greater readership than most others written that day.

The awakening happened fast. If journalists wanted to be read, they had to consider what audiences wanted to read. If they tried to convince audiences to spend their time reading about another topic, which was sometimes still an important thing to do, they had their work cut out for them.

Inside the ABC, this led to a joining of forces between editorial teams that normally would be chasing different stories specifically related to their patch. COVID became intertwined with politics, science, health, medical, social affairs, consumer affairs, Indigenous affairs, business, sport, arts and entertainment, local news and numerous other reporting teams in our network. Foremost in their minds was the fact Australians were experiencing a previously unthinkable moment: borders shut to the outside world; fears of a health system collapse; massive queues at Centrelink offices as firms struggled with a sudden loss of business. This was an enormous unfolding news story, yet because *everyone* was covering it, it was hard to get your own reporting noticed. And so began the greatest listening exercise the ABC has ever conducted.

The Struggle over Who Knows Best

Editorial meetings previously dominated by teams highlighting their latest find began instead with summaries of what the audience wanted to know that day. Search trends led the way in indicating the volume of questions attached to a specific seam of interest. At first, some struggled with how, yet again, people wanted to know about COVID symptoms, in all manner of detail. Hadn't we already answered that question? What more was there to say on the topic? Shouldn't we move on to covering other issues? All reasonable questions, and grappling with them represented a growth in understanding how to best serve audiences using search.

For starters, information about symptoms was changing all the time, as more became known about the virus. Then there was the fact that answering the question yesterday, for someone interested then, offered little assistance to someone searching for that information today. Anyone relying on Google to show them content from yesterday, let alone last week or beyond, when others are likely to have covered it today, would normally be disappointed. After all, Google has long made recency of publication, or 'freshness', a key ingredient in search results for news content.[2] So, teams faced the challenge of considering each day a new opportunity to serve audiences with the news and information they needed. It meant becoming increasingly creative in finding ways to cover similar topics without repeating old news. It tested our ability to think afresh on a daily basis. But the results spoke for themselves. The portion of the *ABC News* audience reached via search increased significantly during the first two years of the pandemic, helping us to reach more Australians via digital platforms than ever before. It was an important illustration of the power search engines can have in connecting news organisations to Australians, particularly those not normally in the business of reading news.

The focus on explaining COVID via a style of story simply referred to as 'explainers', which ask—and answer—a clear question and provide context on the topic, was the first step in focusing on the delivery of information as heavily as news. Take 29 March 2020, for example. It was the day Scott Morrison and then federal chief medical officer Brendan Murphy announced a dramatic cut to the number of people allowed to gather in one place, from ten to two. The *ABC News* story on the topic was titled 'Gatherings Restricted to Two People to Slow Spread of Coronavirus'.[3] An explainer published the same day sought to help people understand this development,[4] and it performed significantly better (1.4 million page views versus 826 000).

It was a pattern that would be repeated as the months rolled on. Time and time again, people chose information presented simply and based on a burning question over the more traditional delivery of written news. With reader analytics delivering a clear message, the focus shifted to ensuring explainers were always part of the content mix.

While search offered a way to monitor mass trends in the information being sought, other measures helped to inject the voice of the reader into conversations normally reserved for journalist and editor. Some were new, while others simply came into their own when the time was right. In the latter category are audience call-outs, a basic way of building a connection. The ABC has used the premise for decades in local radio and brought it into the digital space several years ago. More recently, call-outs have been used to shape commissioning decisions by encouraging readers to let editors know the questions they want answered by filling in a form embedded in stories. The belief is that, if we want to stay relevant, we need to stay connected.

The technique has been used across a variety of topics, often resulting in hundreds of questions flowing in. And then came COVID. ABC News Digital launched its COVID questions project in March 2020, just as the virus was beginning its domination of the headlines, by asking people what they wanted to know. That month, the seventy most-read stories on the *ABC News* website and app included only one that wasn't about the coronavirus—there'd never been a month like it. So, when we offered people the chance to tell us the exact thing they wanted to know, they responded immediately. That first month, 45 000 questions were submitted. Another 15 000 questions came in April, followed by a further 10 000 in May. By mid-June, the total had reached 70 000. It seems incredible to me now, given the pace of developments at the time, that we had members of the team reading each question as they came in, categorising them by theme—health, travel, government support and education—and providing updates to editorial teams considering which angles to cover next. By September

2020, we'd reached 100 000 questions—a tally we'd never imagined and barely had the resources in place to manage.

The project continues to this day, with Widia Jalal having led the project throughout. More than 310 000 questions have been submitted, and updates on key questions readers want answered continue to be provided to editorial teams—see the graph for a breakdown of the most common queries. After reaching the 100 000 mark, Jalal and

Most common audience questions

Category	Count
Health (e.g., symptoms, masks, personal health, mental health)	38818
Other	26992
Travel and immigration (e.g., borders, interstate travel)	14812
Science (e.g., vaccines, virus)	20368
Government support (e.g., supplements, restrictions, lockdowns)	7390
Communication and technology (e.g., misinformation, contact tracing, apps)	6498
People and pets (e.g., families, pets, state, specific cases)	4754
Business and economy (e.g., businesses, industries)	4054
Education (e.g., schools, universities, teachers)	4109
Work (e.g., working from home, work restrictions)	2996
Public spaces and events (e.g., events, public spaces, transport)	3031
World (e.g., WHO, other countries)	1129
Personal finance (e.g., financial issues, tax, super)	534

Accurate as of 31 January 2023, 1.45 p.m.

colleague Neryssa Azlan wrote an update for readers, saying: 'Often, we'd arrive at work at 6 a.m., log on and there'd be 3000 questions from just the past twenty-four hours demanding to be answered.'[5]

Jalal believes it has played an important role in giving ordinary Australians a voice during the pandemic. 'The call-out is a great way to connect with our audience and at the same time get feedback on what we do, beyond quantitative measures,' she says. 'It gives us access to people's raw thoughts, questions and experiences in real time, and helps us to find ways to create value out of those for them in return. Real value comes from listening to what people have to say.'

In some instances, our efforts to build a stronger connection with Australians helped them form a stronger connection with each other. When two casual workers contacted us separately over concerns about the announcement of the end of the pandemic leave payments scheme, a viewer who saw their stories got in touch to offer financial support. It was one of a string of occasions when people found ways to help each other. A different forum, the daily live blog, became a place where readers offered each other, and the ABC bloggers, support via kind words and tips for coping. They were all in it together as they watched yet another daily press conference. For some, the blogs became an addiction, enabling them to take part in a quasi-watch-party for press conferences from the state and territory premiers, the PM and health officials. Regulars became part of a community, giving them a sense of togetherness during a stressful period.

Information over News

Those uncertain times also brought rapid change to somewhat ingrained thinking about what constitutes news coverage. Before COVID, the appropriate way to cover a prime minister's press conference would have been to distil the main points, attach the appropriate context and include relevant additional views. Of course, this continued during COVID, but so exceptional were the circumstances and so significant were the developments during many of these press conferences, that the *ABC News* team took to simply publishing a transcript. Despite the video being available, people invested time reading the announcement line by line. Context continued to be crucial, and it was provided in many other forms, but the speed of developments was so fast that new ways needed to be found to enable people to soak up what was happening at their own pace. In these situations, we felt it was vital to ensure people had access to the information.

That need brought greater prominence to forms of content focused on information over news. In August 2020, when Daniel Andrews told Victorians they had to stay within a 5-kilometre radius of their homes, with only a few strict exceptions, *The Age* and the ABC were among those to publish a tool allowing people to calculate the zone they could travel within.[6] Why? Because soon after the premier announced the restrictions, Google's trends tool showed spikes in searches for '5km from home', '5km radius from home' and 'my 5km radius', content that had to be provided.

Similarly, regularly updated lists of exposure sites served a basic function. King among these information formats for the ABC was the 'Charting the Spread' presentation of the latest COVID numbers around the country. It was created by our Digital Story Innovations team in response to a clamour for the latest COVID numbers in each state and territory from early on in the pandemic. During the busiest news period for the *ABC News* website and app, being the past three years, 'Charting the Spread' was the most-viewed individual article. It's likely our most-read story of all time: twenty-eight million of its thirty-three million page views were recorded in 2020. Incredibly—a reminder of the panic in the air at the time—13 per cent of the total views came in the first seven days. Each year, search contributed a significant slice of the total audience to 'Charting the Spread': 39 per cent in 2020, 37 per cent in 2021 and 44 per cent in 2022. A similar tracker for the Australian vaccine rollout was the most-viewed page for the ABC in 2021.

Throughout those first years of the pandemic, 'traditional' news coverage continued and performed well as an overall heightened state of anxiety drove people to seek out all kinds of updates. But from the *ABC News* experience, the content that stood out, and often performed best with audiences previously averse to news consumption, tended to be that which focused on the simple delivery of information over commentary and debate, enhanced by being able to listen to the audience in a more direct way.

COVID presented an opportunity for journalists to see the benefit of involving the public in determining what to cover. Previously, many journalists would have considered it communicating with their audiences. In reality, it was audiences communicating with their journalists, helping them understand where to look for the next story. Ultimately, in a world where information is available via a quick search, even during a crisis, the power lies with the reader. The need to remain relevant applies as much to investigative and specialist journalists as it does to those simply summarising that day's events. There's an essential balance between responding to that audience call and uncovering important things the audience doesn't yet know about. The risk of not doing the former is that, if audiences don't feel listened to, they likely won't stick around to find out what else we have to tell them.

Nightly News

Max Futcher, Presenter, *Seven News*, Brisbane

Most of the world's big news stories happen suddenly. An event of global significance will often take us by surprise. That's why everyone remembers where they were when they heard momentous news. We remember where we were when the planes flew into the World Trade Center on September 11, and when we heard Princess Diana had died in a Paris car crash, because those are the moments that caught us completely off guard. But do you recall where you were or what you were doing when you first heard about a strange virus making people sick in Wuhan, China?

It's a safe bet none of us paid much attention in the early stages of the pandemic. We'd seen avian flu and swine flu come and go. It was a foreign crisis affecting foreigners. However, as the cases mounted, people started dying. Videos emerged of men and women dropping dead in the streets of central China's Hubei Province. It was a relatively slow burn, but fear mounted as the virus spread into Europe and the United States. We knew it was coming. It was just a matter of time.

I do remember when COVID-19 came to Queensland. We'd finished our nightly news bulletin and I was driving home when a close friend who worked for the state's chief health officer, Dr Jeannette Young, rang me. 'Maxy, he's a confirmed positive,' he said, having just gotten word that someone who'd arrived on a flight from China had tested positive at Gold Coast University Hospital. He was Queensland's patient zero. COVID was here.

I turned the car around and drove back to the studio to prepare news updates announcing Queensland had its first case of the virus. Little did I know that the way we did our job would change from that night: the way we gathered news, the way we interviewed people, how we interacted in the newsroom—and most importantly, our priorities and news agenda, which would be transformed over the next two years. Now, as we begin to emerge from the global pandemic, many things are returning to the way they used to be, but in the news game there are some elements that are forever changed.

Tuning in

Queensland's first COVID-19 case was confirmed on 29 January 2020 and it became clear in the ensuing week that the public's appetite for information was voracious. Most of our bulletins were devoted to the pandemic. Nightly rundowns were structured to cover the situation across the state, where a public health emergency was quickly declared. Just as crucial was the response from Canberra, with then PM Scott Morrison establishing a National Cabinet. The most shocking images came in from Italy (specifically Milan), which overtook China's COVID death rate in March, and later from the United States, Spain and the United Kingdom.

Most of us viewed the news from the Northern Hemisphere as a horrifying glimpse into Australia's future. The scenes through March and April were especially bleak, from mass graves being prepared on Hart Island in New York, to the Spanish military discovering the bodies of those abandoned in a nursing home in Madrid.

What should Australia do? How should we prepare?

Searching for answers, Australians went looking for reliable information. It's true that recent decades have seen traditional media lose audience to the internet and social media, but in this time of crisis, that all changed. Social media was awash with misinformation, disinformation, self-appointed experts and conspiracy theories. The wildest dark fantasies were spreading like wildfire, usually riding shotgun with crazed QAnon tropes about Satanic cabals ruling the world. In mid-2020, I was receiving several carefully typed letters a week advising me I was peddling lies and, on a day of reckoning, I'd be hung in the town square. Thankfully, this was the extreme fringe—most Australians were looking for the facts. So-called legacy media became the main source of information and, in the case of television news, viewer numbers inflated further as major centres went into lockdown.

A PwC report studying media trends in 2020 found television news viewers increased dramatically in the first year of the pandemic. 'Television grew as the primary medium for news consumption amongst Australians during COVID-19, with 51 per cent citing the medium as their main source of news,' the report stated, up from 39 per cent the previous year.[1] Data from IPTV provider Fetch showed free-to-air news viewers increased by 200 per cent in mid-March that year. The highest-rating news show in that period was a *Seven News* 6 p.m. bulletin that attracted 1.38 million viewers nationally. Oztam survey figures reinforced this, with an average 1.06 million viewers watching *Seven News* each night of 2020, up from 940 000 over the year before. Television literally had a captive audience, but while the nightly bulletins gave a comprehensive picture, another show emerged as must-see TV.

During lockdown, aside from homeschooling, bingeing Netflix and home-baking sourdough bread, there wasn't much to do. Increasingly, Australians got into the habit of tuning into the morning press conference featuring their premier and chief health officer. In a time when all sport was cancelled, here was a morbid way of checking the score. Every morning, Dan Andrews, Annastacia Palaszczuk and Gladys Berejiklian held court in their respective states, and viewers waited in suspense for the all-important numbers. How many new cases? How many hospitalisations? How many in an intensive care unit (ICU), and of those, how many on ventilators? How many people had died, and later, how many had been vaccinated?

Initially, the usual morning programming would be interrupted to take the start of each press conference, but as it became obvious how crucial this information was, most networks began running the entire thing. Andrews's North Face jacket became famous, as did Palaszczuk's 'double doughnuts' hand signal if Queensland had had a good day without new cases or deaths. At the peak, we even had anchors introducing the morning address and then summarising the main points at the end. It was raw information, straight from the source, and in the context of that time, in its own way, it was gripping television.

Behind the scenes, there was careful choreography of reporters and camera operators. Masks were mandatory, and camera crews had to space their tripods a safe distance from each other. Operating safely at press conferences was one thing, but news-gathering in a pandemic involved difficulties no-one had previously considered.

Trial Separation

A fundamental part of journalism is interviewing people. You can't avoid it; you can't report the news without speaking with those affected. Newspaper and radio reporters can do this over the phone, but television requires the camera operator and reporter to hit the street and interview people face to face. This presented a huge challenge for television newsrooms during the pandemic. A single interaction with the public could leave the news crew infected and they could quickly spread the virus through the newsroom, shutting down the entire news operation. The risk was scary. Recognising the importance of information flow, the state government designated those in the news team 'essential workers'. But still, how were we to do that job safely?

'All of a sudden we had to adapt faster than ever before,' says *Seven News* Operations Manager Craig Dyer. 'We went through a really steep learning curve in a very short period of time.'

The immediate challenge was staff safety. 'We were buying masks, we were buying rubber gloves, we bought as much hand sanitiser as we could, and then we started manufacturing our own hand sanitiser because we couldn't purchase enough,' says Dyer.

The news team was divided in half. We had a red team and a blue team, each with their own toilets and kitchen. 'Readers weren't sitting near each other, make-up artists only did certain people,' says Dyer. In fact, for many months, some did their own make-up—often with questionable results.

Conducting interviews required some lateral thinking. 'We went to Bunnings and we bought 3-metre paint-roller extension poles,' explains Dyer. 'We drilled through the roller end so we could adapt a microphone onto them. That was so the crews could stand the required 3 metres away from the talent.'

Often, though, even a pole wasn't good enough, such as when the person was in hotel quarantine or isolating at home. Dyer says: 'We were shooting people standing on balconies on their mobile phones and recording the phone audio through the camera, while they were on the seventh floor. Crews were in a front yard shooting interviews with people at their window.'

Sometimes even those measures weren't enough, and so we witnessed the advent of online video interviews. Many people became adept at using Zoom or Skype or FaceTime, and the media was no different. Prior to COVID, such interviews would have been deemed to be of inferior quality, but the extraordinary times meant they were not just acceptable, they were essential.

'We couldn't have got through without it,' says Dyer. 'It changed the face of broadcasting, because now, no matter where you are, you can talk to someone.'

The first time I tried one of these online interviews was in the saddest circumstances. Des William was eighty-five when he and his wife Bev went on a cruising holiday from Sydney to New Zealand. When they got back, they were among the 2700 passengers who disembarked the *Ruby Princess*. Des was one of the 440 who tested positive to COVID-19 and he became the fourth Queenslander to die from the virus. I interviewed his stepson, Craig Blackburn, on 3 April 2020.

'He was healthy, nothing wrong with him at all, so we thought he would come through it fine, but it just decimated him,' Blackburn told me. Cruelly, Bev also tested positive and was forced to isolate even as she mourned her husband of twenty-three years. The family couldn't even give her a hug. 'My mother's alone, basically, sitting there crying, and we can't do a thing,' said Blackburn. 'We've just basically lost one family member and staring down the barrel of doing it again.'

So-called 'death knocks' are always a terrible, awkward part of being a reporter. Interviewing someone who is processing such grief and loss is never easy. Some people value the chance to pay tribute to their loved one; others find it cathartic to talk about it. I've always found it the hardest part of the job, and the use of online video technology doesn't alleviate this. In person, there are a few moments after an interview where you can share some small talk, sometimes receive a quiet smile as the interviewee shows you photos and tells funny anecdotes while the camera crew packs up their gear. The encounter is sad, but it usually ends organically with a handshake and a warm smile. That's missing with the Zoom call—the interview ends with the finality of a phone being hung up. I find it cold and empty, but it is an interview method that's here to stay.

At *Seven News*, separate computers have been set up that are devoted to online interviews. 'It's an everyday tool now,' says Craig Dyer, adding: 'It's expanding our ability to cover a story better.'

Backlash

In covering the pandemic, news broadcasters became a major conduit for the information people were receiving, and sometimes this resulted in negative feedback. I put this feedback into two categories.

The first category comprised rampant conspiracy theories about the virus and the vaccines. Social media accounts would attack the mainstream media for supposed lies about COVID-19, the individuals behind them convinced it was a hoax. The abuse from these people could be venomous and threatening online, but in person they could be truly intimidating. Any crew attending one of the frequent 'freedom' rallies would encounter harassment and abuse, so much so that our network had personal security guards accompany them. Leaders of the marches would encourage protesters to surround the media and chant 'Tell the truth'—whatever they believed that truth to be. On one occasion in Brisbane, police were forced to intervene to protect reporter Ned Balme and his camera crew. At a Sydney rally in July 2021, Seven reporter Robert Ovadia was mobbed and had his phone stolen. Two months later, at the height of the Melbourne protest, reporter Paul Dowsley was assaulted, sprayed with urine, and on another occasion he was struck in the head.

The second category of critical feedback involved those concerned about the constant negativity. Our reporters would be approached and told we were sensationalising the pandemic and stoking fear in the community. In this regard, the media has been judged in many different ways. Some might say there was too much coverage. But there was so much information to disseminate. An hour-long news bulletin needed to include vital information on the current status of the virus, the latest restrictions and lockdowns, as well as the latest developments interstate and overseas. The community expected to know where the government-declared hotspots were, and the locations involved in contact tracing, so graphics and maps displaying this information were unavoidable. In hindsight, broadcasting the premiers' daily press conferences in their entirety may have heightened anxiety in a population trapped in their homes, but the media would have been slammed if we hadn't broadcast those vital addresses in full.

As a news anchor, I was seen by some sections of my audience as the face of this coverage. I didn't encounter much of the second category personally. A trip to the supermarket was more likely to result in multiple conversations about the daily facts and speculation about what would happen next. There were a couple of times when members of the first category would engage me, questioning why the media wasn't telling the truth. They'd point me to certain 'experts', who always ended up being a discredited scientific outlier. They'd encourage me to do 'research', which mostly meant listening to the same circle of online conspiracy peddlers.

Time has passed, and the prophecies of millions dying from the vaccines haven't eventuated, but I think it's a mistake to ridicule the believers. Both categories were responding to fear. People were scared, with no sense of control over what the future might hold for them and their families. Some found empowerment by joining a cohort who believed there was a sinister plot to oppose, while others didn't want to hear about it. For both categories, the media was an easy target.

Lasting Impact

The pandemic moved through many different phases over the past three years, with so many dimensions to the narrative. Jobs were lost. Businesses shut down. State borders closed. Each element required significant resources to report. Journalists spent many days at border checkpoints, interviewing families kept apart by a plastic barrier. Parents taught children at home. Toilet paper was raided. New terms entered the vernacular. There was the UK variant, then Delta, then Omicron. Slowly, though, the temperature went out of the story. As vaccination rates increased, the fear eased, and appetite for the story waned exponentially. I remember a producer quipping late in 2020, 'Can you imagine a time when we don't have COVID in the news? One day, it'll just cease to be there.'

At the time, it felt like news bulletins would be infected by COVID forever, but even the biggest stories run their course. Soon, the pandemic will make the inevitable transition from news to history, but it will have left an indelible mark on the television news industry and the way we bring the big news stories to our audience.

A Media Newcomer Bringing Hope

Anita Savage, News Director, 103.2fm, Sydney

WHEN I WALKED into the radio station in Sydney's west in the second half of 2019, work was underway—literally hammering and sawing—to build a newsroom, the long-held dream of community radio station 103.2fm. *Hope News* launched in November that year, just in time to be thrown headlong into covering the fast-moving, deadly Black Summer bushfires, and then seamlessly into reporting on the equally fast-moving, but tracking an unknown path, COVID-19 pandemic.

Our team was few in number: two experienced journalists and a trainee, to be precise, all trying to make inroads into a robust media environment. We were aware knowledge of *Hope News*'s existence was limited to a loyal audience and a handful of others who might have seen it advertised on the back of Sydney buses. *Hope News* was not a priority among the newsmakers. Getting people to return our calls was a massive challenge. When our reporter turned up to a news conference, the media minders would sidle up to him, a fresh face among well-known journalists, and regard him as a curiosity. Who are you? Where are you from? *Where?*

As newcomers, we had to work out how to get traction in an environment dominated by the well supported, traditional media players.

A MEDIA NEWCOMER BRINGING HOPE

It's no surprise that it came through consistently turning up. Being engaged. Making contacts. Breaking news. By the time the Omicron wave hit and the second lockdown was declared, we'd had a mic flag made so that 'Hope News' was on daily display along with the NSW premier, health minister and a revolving door of health officials. For many, it was a purple-and-white curiosity amidst a sea of imposing, high-profile television and radio station insignias, like a *Where's Wally?* scene. While recognising the seriousness of the situation, it was also thrilling for the radio station's staff and supporters to see that, despite all of the pandemic's sorrow, stress and anxiety, there was Hope.

Those press conferences were a godsend for our cadet reporter's learning curve. About a decade's worth of experience was gained in those months of daily reporting. The trajectory was steep, but he rose to the challenge of synthesising a lot of information to meet tight deadlines. It was also an opportunity to ask authorities questions that were pertinent to much of our audience, a large proportion of whom are of Christian faith, such as what restrictions and lockdowns meant for corporate worship, meeting together, and communion.

What is now known as Hope 103.2fm started broadcasting as 2CBA (Christian Broadcasting Association) in Sydney in 1979. However, it wasn't until forty years later that listeners, keen for reporting they considered trustworthy, banded together to raise the funds to support their own newsroom. While it sits in the framework of a Christian radio station, *Hope News* is not a Christian news service. News is news. However, it was set up with the aim of providing a wider variety of voices and balance within news coverage.

Community radio stations like ours played a vital role during COVID, transmitting pandemic information to those of different cultures. The government knew it, too, harnessing respected community leaders to take to the airwaves to encourage people to heed the health advice. It was a smart move, with around 360 community radio stations across the country boasting more than five million listeners each week.

As with the broader society, so, too, were the responses to the pandemic from people of faith. *Hope News* reached out to influential church leaders—Catholic and Protestant—to provide thoughtful, steady words of wisdom, encouraging people to trust the health authorities and government officials, reassuring them that faith wasn't limited by steeples, stone walls and heavy church doors.

As the virus spread, and restrictions and lockdowns were introduced, all except those on-air were cleared out of the radio station to work from home. I loved the quiet of the corridors, streets and skies—a reprieve from the otherwise non-stop news noise. Like all journalists, I carried a letter from my employer just in case I was stopped by police on my way to or from work, to let them know that I was an 'essential worker'. That seemed to me a grandiose description, as I certainly didn't consider myself essential in the way of healthcare workers on the front line, day in and day out fighting the virus and its unknowns, saving lives.

But to our listeners, we were essential. Essential to inform them of what was happening. Essential to provide balance. Essential to present a calm, reassuring voice amid unprecedented uncertainty. Of course, that didn't stop a passionate and vocal minority of critics who levelled accusations that we were only reporting the government's line, that we weren't reporting other sources, accompanied by a plethora of links to research papers on alternative treatments such as Ivermectin, an antiparasitic medication for horses. Conspiracy theories were treated as gospel truth.

'We report on the facts,' I respectfully wrote to one complainant.

'I prefer truth over facts,' came the reply.

The unknown parameters of the pandemic made decision-making difficult and necessarily fluid. Was it risky sending our reporter out? Yes. But it was a calculated risk, involving masks, hand sanitiser (lots of sanitiser) and careful screening of reporters at NSW Health press conferences. Improvisation became our friend, such as when caught out interviewing people standing in line for COVID testing, realising it might be better next time to put the handheld microphone on a long pole. Or wiping door handles when someone tested positive, realising in retrospect that it probably would have been wise to have worn gloves.

Maintaining a healthy news staff was paramount because without the three of us, there would be no *Hope News*. We tried as best we could to stock up on by now hard-to-find disinfectant wipes. Not only was it a safety precaution, it was also a respectful way of caring for our colleagues.

Despite all of this, COVID hit our staff, one by one. There were daily roster changes, adaptations. Then came the day when all our journalists were out either with COVID or because they were isolating as a 'close contact', or because of family members with the virus. It was inevitable for such a small team. An outsourced backup news had to be run. From the start of the pandemic, contingency plans had been in place. *Hope News* had been on standby to be the backup network news service should the community stations' network hub be forced to shut.

The development of vaccines heralded a new hopeful stage of the pandemic, although reporting the panaceas unleashed another round of phone calls and emails to the newsroom from listeners trying to correct our 'misinformation'. Often, the correspondence would begin, 'I'm not an anti-vaxxer, but ...' Having faith doesn't mean letting go of intellect and critical thinking.

We had the added challenge of colleagues and family members who treated COVID-19 and the vaccines with scepticism. There was personal grief and concern amongst my staff about unvaccinated loved ones, about colleagues self-isolating from unvaccinated parents who questioned the information we were reporting in the news. Hope FM had chaplains on call, caring, listening, praying. Their care continues now and will do so into the future.

Our journalists were conscious of not wanting to add to the hysteria and panic in the community. Our aim was to inform, not alarm.

Knowing the power of language, every word we wrote and aired was carefully chosen. There was no 'COVID crisis'. For us, the daily statistics of positive tests, hospitalisations, ICUs and deaths weren't simply numbers. We made a deliberate choice to never say 'COVID deaths' but instead to talk about 'people with COVID' who had died. Every statistic was a human being, someone's loved one, a person with a heart and soul.

Never in my three decades as a journalist, both here and overseas, have I experienced such a non-stop, exhausting news cycle—physically, emotionally and mentally. The risk of burnout was real.

Talk about a baptism of fire! As a newcomer, *Hope News*'s launch coincided with the COVID-19 pandemic, but our processes have been refined and strengthened, and our listeners, critics and competitors have confirmed our credibility as a news source. Perhaps the true reflection of our legitimacy is that the newsmakers are now ringing us or returning our calls for interviews. In addition, while many media organisations are shrinking, we've expanded, having recently hired another journalist, hopefully proof of a positive future.

As a journalist, travelling down the bumpy, uncertain, coronavirus-corrugated road, charting the ever-evolving journey in an untested news service, aiming to be balanced and trustworthy, I wouldn't have wanted to be anywhere else.

Kohler's Book Stack

Alan Kohler, Finance Presenter, *ABC News*, Melbourne

I CAN'T REMEMBER WHOSE idea it was for me to do the finance reports from home during the COVID pandemic, but I was all for it! Just going upstairs to my recently set-up home office instead of schlepping into Southbank every day sounded like a good idea to me.

Peter 'Droughtie' Drought was assigned to supply me with the equipment. On the appointed day, he lugged the lights, tripods and a very large rolled-up sheet of green something-or-other up the stairs. My office has a chimney that goes through the middle of it, from a fireplace downstairs. Droughtie decided the studio should be placed on the door side of the chimney, green screen against the wall, two lights pointing towards the white ceiling and the camera over near the coffee machine, which, as it happens, was on a bench that used to be a make-up station.

'Where's the camera?' I said, suddenly alarmed he'd forgotten it.

'Right there,' he said, pointing to my phone.

Huh?

He took my phone and downloaded an app called LU-Smart, which was to be my daily companion, and lifeline to the world, for months. The app would connect me directly to the ABC studios in Southbank, so they could record my work.

Yes, the phone was to be my camera, perched on a tripod behind a metal platform on another tripod that was to hold my laptop for the autocue (no, I can't remember the 90 seconds worth of words I recite each night). It was both rickety and very cosy in that tight space between the chimney and the door.

We practised. After doing my make-up next to the coffee machine, I had to turn on the lights, open the LU-Smart app on the phone, connect it to the studio, and speak to the director in Southbank to see if they were ready to record (oh yeah, I forgot—I had to buy a second $50 prepaid phone so I could talk to Southbank while using the camera on my phone), then get the autocue going on the laptop, dance back to the spot in front of the green screen, and ... GO!

I admit it took a while to get it right, but eventually the operation was a smooth machine and we were ready to do it for real. And it wasn't live, so if I stuffed up, no problem. Just do it again. And again. And it was fine. In fact, I doubt the audience even noticed.

But I did. I hated the way it looked—a bit blurry and a bit amateurish, I thought. And it was really awkward doing the set-up and running back to perform. So, after a few weeks of this innovative new process, I asked if I could do it sitting at my desk instead, on the other side of the chimney. Sure, said the boss, let's see what it looks like.

I had an old, white trestle table as a desk and my wife Deb gave me a Chinese money plant as a prop. The camera and the metal platform holding the laptop rested against the chimney, and I draped a doona over the tripod to help deaden the sound. Everyone at the ABC agreed it looked fine, so it was decided from now on, I would present from the desk.

Deb did two other things that changed my life for a while: she offered to start the autocue for me each day, so I didn't have to run back around the desk, and she suggested I put some books on the desk as another prop, so it didn't look like a big empty space.

And so began Alan Kohler's Book Club, which was the name of a new Twitter account started by a very nice woman living in Gippsland, a yoga teacher as it happened, who enjoyed tweeting about my books. I started changing the books on the little stack in front of me every night, then tried to do themes. On International Day for the Elimination of Violence Against Women, I even went down to Readings and bought a couple of related books—although I already had, and admired, Jess Hill's *See What You Made Me Do*.

Sometimes I sent subversive messages using the book titles. On Leonard Cohen's birthday, I featured his books. On another day, a few of my PG Wodehouse first-edition collection made the cut. And on another, it was kids' books that I'd been reading my grandchildren—probably that day.

It was a lot of fun, I must say, and I spent happy hours searching through our bookshelves for inclusions in each night's stack, and—with a glad cry!—coming up with something funny, or meaningful, or just silly. The problem was, of course, the viewers were so busy peering into the TV set to see what the books were that no-one was listening to my pearls of wisdom. I mean, everybody seemed to be having a good time, and there was plenty of excellent chat on Twitter about it, but the day's finance goings-on were being vastly ignored. So, when that first big Victorian lockdown ended in late 2020, and the ABC powers-that-be said they wanted me back in the studio, I readily agreed.

There was some talk about bringing the books into the studio, with Sydney suggesting they could appear on my desk, but I don't think there was a lot of enthusiasm for that in Melbourne. And anyway, I could imagine getting into an awful mess lugging books into Southbank every day and then forgetting them.

So, we just returned to the old set-up in the studio, with that weird background of a stylised stock exchange; Mel, Tamara and Christine alternating on autocue; Eliza and Peter operating the cameras and lights; and me driving into Southbank, trying to find a park, and then standing and delivering. Despite the fact it's all come full circle and we've returned to exactly the same format, what we've learned is what's possible, if we ever need to pivot again.

I do miss those days of doing the finance at home with Deb as my all-in-one make-up artist, studio director and autocue operator; picking the books selection; and heading downstairs in time for a glass of red and dinner. But I also really enjoy going into Southbank every day and chatting to Sue and Harriet in make-up and joining the team in the newsroom.

Maybe in 10–15 years, when Deb and the kids take my driver's licence off me, I'll get the lights out of the cupboard and set them up on the other side of the chimney again, and creak upstairs to do the finance reports in my dotage—if they'll still have me.

PART III
THE TRUST EQUATION

A Question of Balance

David Speers, Presenter, *Insiders*, ABC, Melbourne

It was early in the pandemic, somewhere between major sporting events being cancelled and full lockdowns being imposed. One of the then prime minister Scott Morrison's press secretaries called to raise concerns about the *Insiders* panel line-up we had promoted ahead of that Sunday's program. There was a problem with one panel member specifically, who had been critical of glaring inconsistencies in some of the government's recent health advice about whether to shake hands or go to the footy, or why arrivals from some countries were banned and not others. The press secretary suggested this panellist should not appear on the program on the grounds they might undermine trust in the official health advice. This was not, I was assured, an attempt to stifle criticism of the Morrison government. Heavens, no! This was about maintaining confidence in the expert advice behind critical decisions, which required a level of compliance to be effective.

I politely declined the suggestion. Editorial advice from a politician's office is always met with immediate suspicion. And after all, this had come from a press secretary, not any health official. This was, however, an early indicator we had entered a new dynamic with the arrival of the pandemic, where any questioning or criticism of the 'expert advice', and the decisions based upon it, was problematic, given what was at stake. Before long, state governments each went in their own direction, making difficult decisions to close borders and lock down communities. They, too, required strong public trust and compliance for the measures to work.

This dynamic presented a challenge for the media, particularly those with a role in scrutinising and analysing decisions of government. Were we to comply with the pressure to uncritically explain what the government was doing based on 'expert advice', in the interests of public safety? Or were we to test that advice against the opinions of other experts, expose contradictions and highlight consequences, all while avoiding any misinformation or exaggeration?

The pressure on the media wasn't just coming from federal and state governments. It was also coming, increasingly, from sections of the audience, understandably anxious about COVID and already shifting their viewing, reading and listening habits. The fracturing of the media landscape and the declining trust in media were well-established trends before the pandemic hit.

An Ipsos Global Survey published in June 2019 found Australians to be more trusting of news sources than the global average, but in line with the international drift, the number of Australians who trusted the news 'less' was rising at about twice the rate of those who trusted the news 'more'.[1]

As for the splintering of audiences, COVID arrived after two decades of upheaval and transformation in the media sector, a process which is still underway. The digital shift to online news sites, social media and streaming platforms has already caused enormous disruption and taken its toll on journalism. In 2021, the Media Entertainment & Arts Alliance estimated there were fewer than 10 000 'recognised journalists' serving the Australian community, a number that had fallen by around 5000 over the past decade.[2]

Alongside this rapid decline in the number of journalists has come the added pressure of an audience empowered by access to primary-source information online and the tool of social media, where they're able to engage directly with journalists and let them know what they think of their work. Often, this pressure is a force for good—calling out dodgy journalism, inaccuracies, and areas of much-needed improvement—and journalists shouldn't be so stubborn as to completely ignore this feedback.

On an episode of *Insiders* in mid-2020, one of the topics discussed was the Black Lives Matter protests in Australia. None of our panellists were Indigenous and the condemnation on social media was swift. As was correctly pointed out, the program had not featured an Indigenous panellist since going to air in 2001. We lacked diversity and were called out for it. Rightly so. On the following week's program, we owned up to the failure, apologised, and pledged to do better. *Insiders* now features a regular rotation of Indigenous panellists and more diversity generally. It is a better program for it, and we continue to look at how to bring both political insight and lived experience to our analysis of different issues.

The feedback from social media, however, isn't always a force for positive change. Too often, it can have damaging impacts on journalists and their work. Partisans can provoke pile-ons of disproportionate abuse, and sexist, racist and homophobic attacks occur all too frequently.

Plenty of academics, commentators and others have explored the impact of social media on journalism. I don't seek to do that here. In the context of how COVID impacted journalism, however, it's simply worth noting this background of the rapidly evolving and challenging landscape confronting news organisations when the pandemic hit.

∼

The arrival of the virus drove an immediate and extraordinary demand for information from both social media and traditional news outlets. In March 2020, Meta (which owns Facebook, WhatsApp and Instagram) noted that 'in many of the countries hit hardest by the virus, total messaging has increased more than 50% over the last month'. Users were spending 'up to 70% more time' on the social media giant's apps.[3] Google searches on anything to do with the coronavirus similarly went through the roof, as did ratings for TV news and current affairs programs.

The hunger for information was unsurprisingly intense, given the impact this event was having. People needed to know the risks they faced from COVID and how to protect themselves and their families. They needed to know what the rules meant. Could they see loved ones or go to work or school? Could they even leave their homes? Audiences needed accurate information, and plenty of it.

Data journalism took off as we all became experts in virus reproduction ratios and the need to flatten the curve. The ABC's Casey Briggs led the way in delivering detailed and digestible explanations of how COVID was spreading and what strategies were proving successful.

Viewers demanded to see every minute of lengthy press conferences with health officials and political leaders, along with the questions being asked by reporters. It wasn't just news channels carrying these press conferences live. Free-to-air networks broke into daytime programming to show premiers and CHOs announcing new clusters, containment strategies, and eventually lockdowns, school closures and even (in the case of Victoria) a curfew.

Epidemiologists and other public health experts were in high demand. They were interviewed throughout the day, pressed for any new insights or analysis they might offer about the nature of this virus, how it was spreading, and whether the various government responses were appropriate.

Accurate information was in high demand. As with coverage of any emergency or natural disaster, the public looked to the media to deliver it as quickly and comprehensively as possible. Unlike a bushfire or flood, however, the COVID disaster rolled on and on.

And because this crisis involved a highly contagious virus, the need for public cooperation was heightened. There was a legitimate fear that any lack of cooperation would only contribute to faster transmission of COVID, putting more lives at risk.

Journalists, who would often question and critique the response to a bushfire, flood or storm event, were under pressure not to do so during an ongoing public health emergency. This put journalists in a difficult position, particularly as there were plenty of questions that demanded answers. Different state governments were responding to the same virus in very different ways. Indeed, the expert public health advice also appeared to differ from one jurisdiction to the next.

The way lockdowns, school closures, mask rules and border closures were applied depended upon which state or territory you were in. It was legitimate to ask why this was the case and point out how the pandemic was being managed in different states and around the world. It was fair to question how decisions were being made and how much consideration was being given to the impact on livelihoods, wellbeing and mental health.

Clearly, some journalists, commentators and publications did more than just question the COVID rules and restrictions. Some were highly critical of any business and school closure. The *Herald Sun* in Melbourne took a typically tough line towards Victorian Premier Dan Andrews, with front-page headlines including 'Dan-Made Disaster', 'Don't Trust Dan' and 'Premier's Grab for Absolute Power', and regular references in its opinion pages to 'Dictator Dan', a label born on Twitter before crossing over into print.

Which brings us to Twitter. The platform's role in shaping media and public discourse has also been well traversed elsewhere, but it is worth noting how it was particularly weaponised by opposing sides of the COVID debate in Australia. This is not to suggest equivalence between those who thought COVID was a hoax and those who thought lockdowns were the only answer. But there were some similarities in the online behaviour from the two ends of the spectrum.

According to a study conducted by researchers at Queensland University of Technology (QUT), 'the first tweet containing the #DictatorDan hashtag was authored on 3 April 2020 by an anonymous fringe account (@CCPIsWatching, 2020), but received no engagement'.[4] The tweet was later deleted, but the label came back to life the following month thanks to then Liberal MP Tim Smith, who 'arguably set off the viral dynamics of #DictatorDan on Twitter' by asking whether 'Dictator Dan' or 'Chairman Dan' was a better name for the premier.

A competing #IStandWithDan Twitter campaign sprang up around the same time. It was a response to the attacks on the premier and proved to be even more highly circulated than the anti-Dan sentiments. The two hashtags battled it out online and both sides regularly targeted journalists, who they accused of being on one 'side' or the other.

Interestingly, the QUT analysis showed that 'with respect to active contributions, #DictatorDan and #IStandWithDan [were] similarly concentrated around a hard core of participants: the top 1% of most active accounts posted some one-third of all tweets with these hashtags (34% for #DictatorDan and 32% for #IStandWithDan)'. The study found nearly three-quarters of all #IStandWithDan (74 per cent) and #DictatorDan (72 per cent) tweets came from just 10 per cent of those in the opposing hashtag armies.[5]

In other words, a small number of highly prolific and motivated partisan Twitter warriors were predominantly responsible for the raging online debate that regularly targeted journalists and sought to influence what was being written and broadcast.

For some journalists dragged unwittingly into these online brawls, the abuse involved not only constant criticism of their work but also, in some cases, threats of violence. Journalists certainly aren't perfect, and they should be held accountable. Their work is often the subject of robust debate and, as mentioned earlier, critical feedback and audience engagement can be helpful. It can lead to constructive change. But the level of abuse directed towards journalists during COVID was extreme.

Sadly, the attacks from one end of the spectrum weren't limited to online aggression. Reporters were physically attacked while covering anti-lockdown and anti-vaccine-mandate protests in Melbourne in late 2021. A Seven Network reporter was grabbed by the neck, spat on and hit in the head with a drink can.

Yet, despite all the aggro from a noisy and relatively small section of the community, trust in the media rose considerably during the first year of COVID. According to the Edelman Trust Barometer, trust in the media in Australia rose to an all-time high during 2020. It fell over the course of 2021 and 2022 but remains higher than pre-COVID.

~

So, what does all of this tell us? How should journalists balance the need to provide essential public health information during a crisis while also asking necessary and critical questions to highlight problems? And how should journalists remain open to valid audience feedback, advice and criticism while navigating a noisy and at times toxic environment on social media? For my part, there are a few lessons I've taken from the experience, mainly reminders of the fundamentals of good journalism.

The first is to remember what comes first in covering any emergency: delivering accurate information that's relevant to the audience. It sounds like a simple statement of the obvious, but the pandemic has been a powerful reminder that audiences crave the facts. Data, evidence, expert analysis, details of whatever steps are being taken in response—these must come first. Audiences have a greater appetite for detail than many give them credit for. It's no coincidence the prime minister and state premiers shot to their highest levels of popularity when they were delivering detailed daily updates on

COVID and announcing decisions while standing alongside public health officials, grounding every move in 'expert advice' rather than political ideology.

The second (and related) lesson is to ensure any questioning of the decisions being taken is equally grounded in evidence. Decisions made during a public health crisis obviously rely on strong public confidence, but they should be robust enough to withstand questioning. Journalists have an important role to play in asking questions and highlighting concerns during a crisis, as long as they're based in fact.

Indeed, this is a lesson that doesn't just apply to a crisis. Political interviews never venture far beyond spin unless an interviewer is thoroughly prepared with accurate information. Much of that information and research may never come up during an interview, but it needs to be on hand. An interview isn't about 'winning' or 'losing' an argument; it's not about getting bogged down in a contest over who knows more. A good political interview is about drawing out new and accurate information for the audience, exploring motivations, and calling out any misinformation or selective quoting of facts aimed at blatant self-promotion.

The third lesson is to keep an eye on valid audience feedback, both positive and negative, while keeping it in perspective. Relatively small numbers on social media can make a lot of noise. The volume doesn't always equate to where the broader audience is at, the information they're after and the questions they want asked. Many viewers and readers are open to having their views challenged and hearing different perspectives. As always, it helps to have a strong team of journalists and editorial leaders around to discuss the best approach to an issue, particularly during a public health emergency.

At times during the pandemic, journalists have faced competing demands to either be 'team players' disseminating information or to question and challenge government decisions. This journalistic conundrum isn't unique to the pandemic, but it was more sharply felt during the events of 2020 and 2021. The whole experience underscored the importance of some basic journalistic principles: facts, accuracy, putting the audience first (and remembering who the audience is), and holding the powerful to account with questions based on evidence.

The best approach was summed up by an unnamed Wisconsin-based journalist who told a US study on pandemic reporting that to be a journalist during COVID-19 is 'to stump for the truth and to stump for critical thinking and to try to teach the importance of those things'.[6]

Stump for the truth and stump for critical thinking. It's a good rule of thumb for journalism generally.

Public Backlash

Rachel Baxendale, Victorian Political Reporter, *The Australian*, Melbourne

THE OTHER DAY, a political contact sent me what he evidently thought was a considerate private message on Twitter. He hadn't liked something I'd written, and had tweeted, repeatedly, to that effect. But he wanted me to know that he hadn't tagged me in the tweet, 'because I don't want reams of misogynistic rubbish on my timeline'. Apparently, it subsequently occurred to this bloke—whose political organisation lists gender equity as one of its top priorities—that someone other than him might also be affected by such abuse. He added, twenty minutes later, '… and of course I don't want you to be subjected to that'.

How selfless of you! I thought, and laughed, because really, what else could I do?

As a journalist working in 2022, I don't get a choice. Online abuse is a vile but unavoidable part of the job—even for reporters without social media accounts. Like so many of my colleagues, I've been subject to death threats, rape threats and attacks on my family. While I suspect much of this is a natural consequence of the social media age, the pandemic has undeniably made things much worse.

I can pinpoint the moment my negative online mentions exploded to August 2020, when COVID case numbers soared and the second, and harshest, of what would be six Victorian lockdowns totalling 262 days was in full swing. Daily, my press gallery colleagues and I filed into the cold, dark room we came to jokingly call The Purple Room of Doom—Melbourne's Treasury Theatre, adjacent to Daniel Andrews's office, at 1 Treasury Place. For at least an hour, the premier would reel off the day's COVID statistics and any adjustments to lockdown rules before taking questions in front of a purple wall with the slogan, 'Staying apart keeps us together.' On the day in question, some of us began questioning the premier over his government's role in the hotel quarantine and contact tracing failures that led to that second lockdown. My phone almost blew up with abusive messages, many with the hashtag #IStandWithDan.

I'd always seen my role as a journalist as being one of constructive criticism—of exposing the failures and acknowledging the successes of those in power in the interests of good and democratic government. I still do. But a noisy, cult-like, online minority had absorbed the premier's 'You're either with us or against us' rhetoric and taken it upon themselves to portray anyone who even questioned, let alone criticised, the Andrews government's decisions as an enemy of the state. When I asked an utterly unremarkable question about the medical efficacy of mandating face masks outdoors, in regional areas, where there had not been a single COVID case and people's contact with others was limited (a law being enforced by police at the time with $200 fines), the premier snapped back, 'What's the issue, Rachel? Seriously, what's the issue? Why is it such a massive issue?' His online fans got the hashtag #WhatsTheIssueRachel trending—as it did for months hence, every time I asked a question they didn't like—and I was depicted as some sort of nutjob who valued personal freedom over human life.

The reality is a little more boring—and perhaps less useful for a premier attempting to cast his critics as villains. I believe now, as I did then, that lockdowns and border closures saved lives as we waited for as much of the population as possible to get vaccinated.

But I believe at least as strongly that those benefits came with costs. All of us know families with children and young people whose mental health suffered profoundly due to their inability to socialise during the pandemic. I've had spouses and children of dementia patients shake with anger as they've told me of their relatives' sharp decline when they were denied visitors for months on end—in situations where, had they been faced with the stark choice of a lonely but physically healthy longer life or their last days surrounded by loved ones, they would have chosen the latter in a heartbeat. My journalist colleagues and I owed it to those people to ask questions on their behalf. It was our duty to put the onus on the government to explain and justify restrictions on people's freedom where the epidemiological rationale remained unclear at best, such as a ban imposed on the use of children's playgrounds, and nightly curfews which were imposed upon Melburnians for months at a time.

Some have sought to portray the premier's treatment of me and other journalists as bullying. And he is a politician who's had years of practice looking down the barrel of the camera, choosing his words exceptionally carefully, and knowing exactly what effect they're likely to have on the other side of the TV screen. But I ask my fair share of provocative questions and I'm not interested in seeing myself as a victim. How dare I, when the reality is that I hold an immensely privileged position which must be valued and never abused or taken for granted—that of almost daily opportunities to speak truth to power and ask questions to which Victorians deserve answers. If politics and journalism are both functioning as they should, it's always going to be a robust exchange. If I wasn't annoying those in power and their one-eyed supporters, on both sides of the political aisle, I wouldn't be doing my job.

As for dealing with the online backlash, I'm still learning, but I've developed a thick skin. The only times the online portrayals of me have ever really hurt have been when they leached into real life—when I met someone whose entire impression of me was based on a hashtag, or worse, when someone I'd known for years appeared to have altered their view of me after reading something in some dark corner of the internet. I almost never block anyone on social media because I believe very strongly that part of being a good journalist is being willing to be confronted by opposing viewpoints. But I liberally mute and otherwise limit my exposure to content that crosses the line into pure vitriol, and I report the really nasty stuff. I also constantly remind myself that Twitter is not reality—in fact, only 6 per cent of Australians describe themselves as frequent users.[1] And I have one social media–free day a week, when I turn my phone off for a while and re-engage with non-screen reading.

For all the negatives, the pandemic also presented some remarkable journalistic opportunities. Never before had hundreds of thousands of people tuned into state political press conferences. Never before had so many taken such an interest in the work of state political reporters, and never before had that work had such a bearing on people's daily lives. Most of the time for better, and sometimes for worse, viewers of the pressers and readers of my work knew where to find me, and I thrived on much of the engagement, particularly when I was able to inform my questioning and coverage with information from people living the pandemic—whether that was families stuck at home, or doctors and nurses, bureaucrats or small business owners, teachers or truckies. I hope I was able to do their trust in me justice and that I'm able to carry the many lessons learnt in the strange, febrile, compressed couple of COVID years with me as I continue my career.

The Role of the Expert

Prof. Raina MacIntyre, Professor of Global Biosecurity, University of NSW, Sydney

IN 2020, THE general community learnt the term 'epidemiologist'. Suddenly, there was a raft of new faces on our television screens and it seemed everyone was an expert.

Although epidemiology arose from infectious diseases, with the investigation of a cholera epidemic in 1854 by John Snow in London, it has since expanded to underpin every area of medicine. Epidemiology underpins drugs and vaccines, all of which have to undergo the epidemiological design of randomised clinical trials before they can be widely used. It underpinned the discovery that smoking causes lung cancer. It is a methodology used in all areas of health, including chronic diseases.

Now, almost overnight, we saw media commentators with no substantial experience in pandemics, but other areas of epidemiology, waxing lyrical to the media about COVID-19. What most people fail to appreciate is that infectious diseases is also a very broad field. Being an expert in one area of infectious diseases doesn't necessarily mean you have the requisite knowledge in pandemic or epidemic infections. Yet we saw many people eagerly representing themselves as pandemic experts, despite having very little background in the field.

THE ROLE OF THE EXPERT

Terminology like 'elimination', 'eradication', 'epidemic' and 'endemic' was widely misused during the pandemic, including by so-called experts. A true epidemic disease occurs in waves, just as we see with COVID-19 now, and as we see with measles and influenza. It rises and falls in short periods of time. Epidemic potential is defined mathematically by how contagious an infection is, or how easily it spreads from one person to the next. There is a formula we use to calculate the required level of immunity (from infection and/or vaccines) needed for herd immunity, a concept that arose from vaccination programs. No infection has ever controlled itself through 'letting it rip'. And yet we had experts thrilled by the idea of the Great Barrington Declaration,[1] spruiking herd immunity through natural infection. The same experts were misusing terms like 'eradication' without understanding what they meant.

We then saw the politicisation of the pandemic response, with some genuine experts in this field perceived with hostility by some politicians because we weren't eager to be political mouthpieces. Journalists, too, became partisan, ridiculing some of us and elevating others. Instead of public communication, much of what we saw was simply propaganda.

By mid-2021 I had mostly stopped doing media, as I did not feel there was anything to be gained by either joining the fray or raging against the machine. Instead, I sadly sat back and watched the transition from public health to public disease. From having one of the lowest burdens of COVID-19 in the world in November 2021, we went to one of the highest in a period of three months.

Along with that came disinformation, with so-called experts and commentators telling the public that getting infected to prevent infection was a great thing, and you might as well get infected today to prevent infection tomorrow. That was the twin propaganda of herd immunity through natural infection and immunity debt, a new phrase conjured up during COVID-19. Immunity debt is akin to telling people to smoke as much as they like now and get their coronary bypass over and done with sooner, or drink and don't wear their seatbelt so as to have their car accident sooner. The entire meaning of public health seemed to have been lost among the favoured experts of government and journalists, pushing personal responsibility onto a community left to fend for itself, yet unable to get a fifth-dose booster if they wanted to exercise that responsibility.

From where I stood, the era of investigative journalism seemed to be well and truly dead, with some journalists now taking on a role as propagandists for the state and other interests. Few questioned the unprecedented excess mortality seen in Australia, while the community kept getting fed the lie that these deaths would have happened anyway and were a form of 'reaping'. The message was sent over and over again that deaths were only occurring in people who deserved to die anyway. It was only a short step away from officially declaring a policy of eugenics. The risk of long COVID was clear from studies conducted as early as 2021, with more and more evidence accruing of substantial long-term effects on the lungs, heart, brain and immune system—in the first twelve months after COVID infection, the risk of having a stroke, heart attack, cardiac arrest, pulmonary embolus and a range of other cardiovascular events is just about double.[2] And yet the unexplained rise in cardiovascular deaths during COVID-19 has been ignored, as it is inconvenient for the happy narrative that the pandemic is over and COVID-19 is not as bad as was feared.

All of this occurred against a background of unprecedented disinformation, a form of information warfare that trickled out of the United States and United Kingdom to other countries all over the world, including Australia. In the United States, vaccination rates were low and anti-vaccination sentiment high. We saw a convergence of right-wing extremists and alternative lifestyle groups, energised by a common agenda of anti-vaccination and anti-mask sentiment. Fortunately, in Australia, our historical cultural mindset of being civic-minded prevailed, and the concerted effort to get vaccination rates up worked well in 2021, with Australia achieving among the highest two-dose vaccination rates in the world—over 95 per cent of people aged sixteen years and over.

Then, however, the propaganda began in earnest, with the pandemic declared over and officials scratching their heads as to why the rates of third-dose and fourth-dose vaccination remained suboptimal. Of course, if we tell people the pandemic is over, we cannot expect them to go out and get their boosters. This left Australia even more vulnerable in 2022, because two vaccine doses barely protects and their effectiveness eventually wanes substantially. In addition, in the latter part of 2022, we saw an unprecedented Omicron variant mix. The newer variants are highly immune-evasive, leaving the vaccines even less effective.

Added to this new agenda of widespread infection with very little effort to mitigate transmission, there were plenty of experts who were willing to be slavish cheerleaders for government, with an equal number of journalists of the same mindset. Together, they told us COVID was mild. Many experts called themselves 'centrists' and labelled people like me, a public health physician with an interest in preventing disease, 'extremists'. The deliberate use of such terminology branded people like me as dangerous enemies of the state, whereas these self-proclaimed centrists were the go-to experts for politicians and media alike.

Then we had the dropping of the last bastions of COVID control: isolation, mandatory reporting of a positive test, and daily reporting of COVID data. The net effect of these policy changes included increased transmission and decreased transparency, with obfuscation of data. Actuarial data, for those who care to look for valid information, show a rise in excess mortality in 2022. And yet media was not reporting on this, except for a few lone journalists now and then. Nor were they reporting on the lack of vaccination for children under five in Australia, when research shows the risk of long COVID in children is higher for those aged zero to three years than for older children.

So, what lessons have we learned? Very few is my guess, having witnessed the 2009 influenza pandemic. Some of the lessons the government should have learned then included the importance of stockpiling masks, medical supplies and equipment. We failed badly at this pre-COVID, despite having an opportunity to restock masks after the bushfires of 2019. Sovereign manufacturing capacity for vaccines, drugs, masks and medical equipment is something we should invest in more. The importance of non-pharmaceutical interventions such as masks, testing, tracing, quarantine and isolation were not well appreciated early in the pandemic and had to be learned on the run by expert advisers.

The role of airborne transmission was denied for much of the pandemic and very few journalists called it out, with plenty of experts willing to promote non-evidence-based dogma and ideology. Professor Lydia Morawska of QUT led over 200 scientists in a successful challenge of the WHO around airborne transmission of SARS-CoV-2, and was subsequently named among *Time Magazine*'s top 100 influential people of 2021. Yet little interest was shown by the Australian media, government or experts in highlighting her expertise or bringing her to the table to improve Australia's control of COVID-19.

Face masks became politicised, strange for such a simple, non-invasive intervention that is proven to reduce transmission of SARS-CoV-2. The importance of testing was also downplayed in 2022, when COVID-19 rates were so high that testing infrastructure could not keep up. The cost of a constant supply of rapid antigen tests is prohibitive for most people in the community, and yet a test is needed to benefit from the COVID-19 antivirals that are available today. Over and over again, we seem to be cutting off our collective nose to spite our national face.

Social media was probably the only place where information was not censored or filtered as it was in the mainstream media. For me personally, social media was a very important source of rapid information on the latest medical research. By following trusted medical experts who were tweeting about COVID-19 research, I was able to keep across the latest research in a way that would have taken much longer if I'd had to search for it case by case. The problem here is obvious. It is difficult for a layperson to navigate the vast volumes of both disinformation and valid information on social media. We also saw the same polarisation of experts on social media as we did in the mainstream media.

Community members, too, became polarised and quickly identified which experts to follow for their news about COVID-19. It was shocking to me to see professional colleagues become internet trolls during the pandemic. Some of them acted like swaggering schoolyard bullies, working in packs, singling out individuals to ridicule them and encouraging others to troll and harass them. I was surprised they would behave in such a way on public forums like Twitter but keep themselves looking respectable on LinkedIn.

In 2021, certain legislation was used, as well as the Australian Health Practitioner Regulation Agency (AHPRA), to silence doctors who disagreed with government policy on vaccines. I write about this in more detail in my recent book *Dark Winter: An Insider's Guide to Pandemics and Biosecurity*. But here, we saw the ugliest side of the polarisation of experts. Many good doctors I know were reported to AHPRA by other doctors who were stalking and trolling them online. I, too, was attacked, with the trolls hanging off every single word I tweeted, quick to pile on the abuse at the slightest perceived weakness.

This ugliness, the unveiling of the nasty nature of many academics and doctors, was one of the saddest realisations of the pandemic. I believe many people are still grieving for the world we lost in 2020, and part of the normal grieving process is anger. That anger is directed at truth-tellers who refuse to take part in the misleading narrative that COVID is mild and the pandemic is over. It's a form of shooting the messenger when the message is unpalatable.

We live in an information age when many sources of information, often conflicting, are available to consumers. Information is both an opportunity and a threat, depending on how it is used. How we navigate this landscape to ensure the best interests of Australia and Australians in the future is a major challenge.

Behind the Hard Border

Peter Law, former political reporter, and Josh Zimmerman, Political Reporter, *The West Australian*, Perth

'We'll be turning Western Australia into an island within an island, our own country.'

With those words, outside Parliament House in West Perth in early April 2020, Premier Mark McGowan set the course for WA's response to COVID. The border would open and shut to different states at different times, but it would be 697 days before WA welcomed back all of Australia and the world. The state's unique pandemic experience over those two years—Perth was locked down for a total of twelve days—would reshape Australian politics long after the health emergency passed.

In March 2021, McGowan's popularity propelled WA Labor to the biggest electoral victory in any Australian jurisdiction in more than seventy years, all but wiping out the Liberal opposition. The following year, the federal Coalition was punished for its initial support of Queensland billionaire Clive Palmer's border legal challenge, delivering Anthony Albanese a majority government. The WA premier reaped the political benefit of remarkable success in keeping the virus out, but he actually had to be nudged into making the move. It was WA Liberal leader Liza Harvey who first raised, in parliament, the merits of imposing restrictions on interstate travellers after a push from a group of senior hospital doctors.

As almost all quarantine-free travel into WA ground to a halt in the spring of 2020, so, too, did the spread of the virus. The feared first wave never arrived. Cases in the community dwindled to single figures as WA Health Department contact tracers worked around the clock to tell people when they'd been exposed. Restrictions on work, school and play were removed faster than anywhere in the country and celebrated by a grateful—perhaps even proud—public.

While premiers and health authorities in other states—notably Victoria and New South Wales—came under increasing media scrutiny for the failures of their hotel quarantine systems and the ensuing lockdowns and restrictions, it was a very different story in WA. Watching Gladys Berejiklian front reporters demanding answers about the *Ruby Princess* disaster, or interrogating Daniel Andrews about locking down entire apartment towers, felt like a different world.

Outdoor press conferences in WA began to be interrupted with cries of 'I fucking love you McGowan' from passers-by, and the 'State Daddy' was immortalised in tribute tattoos and TikTok videos. Journalists who questioned the finer details of the ever-changing COVID rulebook—and the glaring inconsistencies—were mocked mercilessly on social media.

A telephone call *The West Australian* received in late May 2020 soon elevated McGowan-mania to new heights. Clive Palmer had been denied permission to enter WA and revealed he would use his immense wealth to fund a High Court challenge on the constitutional validity of the border closure. *The West Australian* leaned into the enhanced state pride with a poll showing one in three West Australians wanted the state to permanently secede from the rest of the nation. Palmer was variously depicted as a cane toad, a cockroach and Mike Myers's Dr Evil when it emerged the United Australia Party leader had attempted to sue the state for $30 billion in damages over a stalled mine project. By contrast, McGowan and then treasurer Ben Wyatt were portrayed as 'Captain Westralia' and 'Iron Ore Man' in the newspaper's 2020 state budget coverage, which boasted that WA's economy was recovering faster than anywhere else in the world.

An otherwise dull state election campaign was thrown a curveball when a leaky hotel quarantine system plunged Perth into a snap lockdown in February 2021, exposing the secretive nature of the government's COVID decision-making. In opposition, McGowan had promised 'gold standard transparency', but attempts to obtain the minutes and documents of the two decision-making bodies chaired by the premier during COVID were deemed exempt from freedom of information.

McGowan's commitment to transparency ahead of the 2017 election had long ago been relegated to something of a running joke within media circles, but it was taken to a new level in the wake of the pandemic. An early promise to provide a breakdown of cases by council area, as became standard in other states, never materialised. Extracting even basic information from WA Health, such as the number of patients on a ventilator, could take weeks, even months.

Most opaque was the G2G Pass system operated by WA Police that decided who got into the state and who didn't with the tap of a keyboard, leaving distraught families separated by the border to approach the media to plead their case publicly. Almost exactly one year into the pandemic, West Australians went to the polls and delivered their verdict on McGowan's COVID elimination strategy. By that time, just eight people had died in the state from the virus.

Arguments could be mounted about the dismal condition of the WA public health system and the questionable morality of the strictly enforced hard-border policy, but neither had much cut-through with the public at large, especially when being prosecuted by a near-impotent Opposition. That was evidenced by the result of the March 2021 election: an historic bloodbath that handed Labor fifty-three of fifty-nine seats in the Legislative Assembly.

McGowan promptly responded by completely overhauling Upper House voting to remove the pre-existing system that ensured half of all Legislative Council MPs were selected by regional electorates—a reform that heavily favoured his own party's metro-centric voter base. Parliament was effectively sidelined as an institution to hold the government to account. Unlike other states, there was no parliamentary inquiry into the government's pandemic management. In Question Time, half of the frontbench who sat opposite McGowan were MPs from his own party.

Because of the premier's popularity and power, the role of the media in WA during COVID was unlike anywhere else in Australia. The media became the default Opposition, taking the COVID debate out of parliament and turning to businesses and families directly impacted by the border closure to give alternative perspectives of the impact of McGowan's decision-making.

On 20 January 2022, the premier convened a late-night press conference to reveal his government was backflipping on its commitment to reopen the state to the rest of the world on 5 February. It was a defining moment in WA's pandemic journey. For the first time, a significant chunk of the adoration for McGowan fell away and a blindsided media accused him of 'cowardice'. He attempted to justify the move by claiming the emergence of Omicron had 'changed everything', and that more time was now needed to achieve a higher third-dose vaccination rate. But his failure to provide either a new reopening date or nominate a vaccination target meant the state was in limbo and the reunion plans of hundreds of thousands thrown on the trash heap.

After almost two years, on 3 March 2022, WA's border finally reopened—to the vaccinated, at least. By that point, the once near-universal support for Mark McGowan had fractured, but at the federal election ten weeks later, the political legacy of his COVID response was secured. Four of the net seven seats that secured Labor a majority came from WA, and, against a national 0.5 per cent primary vote drop for the party, WA Labor secured a 7.4 per cent increase.

The biggest challenge journalists in WA faced over those first few years of the pandemic was transitioning from their main task of informing the public of the government message as accurately and quickly as possible, to interrogating and then casting doubt on that message as the extent of the threat became better understood. This was a precarious balancing act in a state where questioning the premier and his 'health advice' was tantamount to putting lives at risk.

Having attended too many COVID press conferences to count, we had a front-row seat to witness McGowan's transformation from a consensus-building first-term premier whose hands appeared to shake during moments of high stress, into a tough-guy politician complete with hands-on-hips superhero pose and a determination to never give in to 'whoever's complaining the loudest'. By the end of 2020, McGowan 2.0 had arrived.

Reporting on the premier elicited polarising reactions from our readers and on social media. There was one vocal group that used the hashtag #IStandWithMarkMcgowan and another that posted memes depicting the WA leader as Adolf Hitler. In the middle of this divide were reporters for whom abuse became part of the job.

This divide reached its deepest point when WA's no-jab, no-job vaccine policy was in effect, when protesters against the mandate would regularly protest outside Parliament House. Reports on how WA's vaccine rollout was tracking, or the merits of high immunisation rates, inevitably sparked accusations we were doing the government's bidding. On the flip side, a front-page story on a healthy WA woman who suffered a debilitating stroke after receiving the AstraZeneca jab resulted in a torrent of outrage on Twitter.

In the months following the 2022 federal election, COVID quickly faded into the background, allowing a much higher degree of scrutiny to return to the day-to-day running of government.

And the virus that once dominated the daily news cycle has now been replaced by a broader range of issues, including the ever-increasing cost of living, a power grid whose stability is threatened by the rapid transition to renewables, and the parlous state of an overstretched public health system.

But COVID's legacy lives on in two opposing groups of West Australians. There remains a substantial cohort of McGowan cheerleaders who shower every post on his now 489 000-strong Facebook page in likes—their enduring support slammed into place at the same time as the hard border. At the other end of the spectrum is a smaller but perhaps even more vocal band of detractors, forever convinced the entire pandemic was an elaborate scam designed to consolidate power among the 'elite'. While both groups continue to demand 'truth and transparency', what they really crave is confirmation of their existing biases. And there is no shortage of that in the echo chambers they inhabit.

Thankfully, the majority of West Australians remain somewhere in the middle. They're the ones you never hear from on Twitter or in the online comments sections, instead reserving their judgement for the ballot box.

The Slippery Truth

A Q&A with Rick Morton, Senior Journalist, *The Saturday Paper*

Q [Tracey Kirkland]: When we first talked about this, you said to me: 'Although I have much I would love to sit down and chew over about the last three years, I am also of the view that if I ever have to write about COVID again in my life, it will be too soon.' Why is that?

A: It's made me sad, genuinely, in the end. I actually did tell my editor, 'I don't want to write about COVID ever again,' and, so far, they've kept that promise. It wasn't the pandemic itself but the polarisation I kept seeing happening around it. Across the three years, every time I wrote something it became increasingly fractured. It was very hard to get to what I considered an approximate truth. I really like being able to do that in my day-to-day journalism and I found I couldn't do it with COVID.

I had all these competing interests that I couldn't square in my own mind in terms of people in the population that were really concerned about their health, but equally scientists and public health experts who were saying, 'Look, this is always going to become endemic, we need to deal with it and here is a smart way we can do that,' and then people from every side being completely and utterly unhelpful and, in the end, I just didn't want to deal with it. I definitely feel traumatised by COVID but I can't point to why. I don't think I was equipped for this level of public scrutiny.

Q: So, we've got this huge public health crisis and there are a lot of voices, some of them very loud, and a lot of competing interests, and we, as journalists, are trying to find the nub of truth in all that. How challenging was that?

A: With an unfolding natural disaster like an earthquake or a cyclone, you've got misinformation that comes out during the first few days, maybe the first week, but it's quickly corrected and you very quickly arrive at a story that did happen, that is true, and that is an account of something real. With COVID, not only is the virus changing so fast, but any scientific article you might have referenced, even if it's been peer-reviewed in March 2020, would be completely out of date by November that year and then twice as out of date by March 2021. Then you've got all the other variants and so much is changing in-between.

I think journalism is fundamentally incapable of dealing with something that is not settled for many, many years. An issue like climate change is the same. Especially in a day-to-day sense, we find it very difficult to pull back a bit and see the bigger picture because we don't know where it is going to end. And I found myself increasingly frustrated by that in my own work. I wrote a lot of things that were very perceptive that were going to happen, including that this thing might become a pandemic. And, of course, it did. But I often found, within months, my own journalism was overtaken by new developments, and I wasn't comfortable, then, that whatever I was writing was going to be true in four months and it just made me very nervous, I guess.

Q: So, in that situation, with the story constantly changing around us, what is the role of a journalist?

A: I battle with this. I've written about disability a lot in my career so I've got a lot of contacts from the disability community. And they were very worried about COVID, and they still are, even though the rest of us have adjusted—because we can, and we have that privilege.

So, I've always felt my role is to take their side, and anyone who is marginalised, against power structures and the privileged. But equally, I struggled with the fact I didn't want to alarm anyone and cause fear when there was no need to be afraid, or at least where the science was saying, 'Hey, you might be doing more harm than good if you are constantly worried about this particular aspect of COVID-19.' And if we could have some very good public health communication messaging around it, we might be able to bring people together. And so reconciling those two things has been the legitimate fear.

It's kind of like opposite ends of magnets. Those two forces were repelling and I couldn't bring them together. I still can't. I don't know what the answer is because I don't want to write fearmongering stuff and I think, accidentally, I did.

Q: You also said to me, 'I think the media failed and I think I failed, and I'm burned by the experience.' Why is it so personal for you?
A: I take my job very personally. I was trained in a different environment as an old-school newspaper reporter and I was really good at it. Then I learnt a little bit more about the world. The older I get, the more I realise I don't care about getting the front page. I like knowing things and I like finding stuff out, but more than anything I like being able to write a version of things that are happening that is as close to true as possible.

I don't like people lying to me. I get really fixated and obsessed if I think someone is trying to hide something from me or cover something up, which is a great defect to have with journalism but it's not a healthy one. I realise the distance between what is true and what is someone's deeply held belief that has no intention of harming anyone, is like the size of a gossamer tree—it's just tiny. And you're going to get stuff wrong in that environment, especially when you're reporting on COVID. And you do, and I did. And it actually hurt me. I genuinely have lost a bit of my confidence as a reporter over the past three years and I was very seriously contemplating quitting completely. And I would have, I think, but I needed the money.

If you've got a net and it's always caught a certain-size fish, and then suddenly the fish change and they're really small and they keep slipping through the net, it's a really discombobulating experience. Suddenly, what you thought to be the way the world works, doesn't, and you're not equipped for it, and that's what I felt like with my reporting. There was a certain methodology that I approached the world with, which was, if you've got a scientific paper that's highly credible, that's been peer-reviewed, in a good publication …

I've never trusted government to tell the truth but I've trusted people in positions of medical influence. I'm not saying they lied, but I'm saying there is no subjective truth in this environment. And even the science. The one good thing about this was the race to develop vaccines. I genuinely find that awe-inspiring—not the pharmaceutical side of it, though, where they're now being sold for extreme profit. But when it comes to studying the virus, we're all still figuring it out. The problem with journalism is that it's so public that when things change, it feels like you've got something wrong and it does not compute with how I was trained as a journalist, which is to try to always be right. I genuinely struggle with it.

Q: Do you think there are things we can learn from the past three years that will make us better journalists or, at least, make our storytelling better?
A: I feel like there needs to be a way for us to slow down a bit, as an industry, and learn not to update every tiny little thing. It's okay not to have fifteen-minute updates. Every four hours is fine. Give people enough time to interpret the information they are receiving.

I don't think the human brain was built to be in an alarming situation 24/7 while also filtering all of the information itself, which is what happens in a 24/7 news environment. You report every single update because that's 'your job', to report things as they happen, but you're not actually providing analysis or context at the time and so the public—and us at the same time because we are the public—are interpreting this information without the full tapestry. Personally, I genuinely believe it's a recipe for madness. We didn't evolve to do it and COVID has become the perfect example where we report every tiny little thing.

I'm proud of the stuff I wrote about aged care and nursing homes. I'm proud of the stories I wrote about vaccine procurement and the hospital system more generally. But that became so political it was a nightmare anyway, because there were people in management positions telling me everything was okay, but every single person we spoke to who was a worker, a doctor, a nurse, anyone, was saying, 'No, this is really bad,' and it's like you're being gaslit constantly. But I'm proud of those stories because they meant something. But I could have cut my production by about a quarter and had the same effect in terms of quality journalism.

My hope is in the Zoomers, generation Z, that they are rebelling against some of the silly decisions we've made.

Febrile Nation

Prof. Mark Kenny, Australian Studies Institute, Australian National University, Canberra

IT IS EASY to forget now, but the early months of the COVID pandemic were gripped by widespread anxiety. Little was known about infection modes, treatments, survival rates and the longer-term implications of contracting the virus. No vaccine existed, and there was no realistic expectation that one would be found. Governments were in uncharted waters. Clueless, political leaders deferred to the best technical advice available, which saw chief health officers pushed to the fore. Mainstream media, particularly the news channels, became the principle modes of official messaging, and of conveying direct advice from medically trained scientific experts, from microbiologists and infectious diseases experts, to epidemiologists, health economists and other specialists.

With the population confined in their homes, the traditional media became instruments of government policy as state and federal leaders communicated daily, the nation grimly hanging on each day's infection, hospitalisation and death numbers. But the technology which made this the first genuinely digital national health emergency also stoked the growth of bespoke and alternative media, catering to sections of the population who resented stay-at-home health orders, compulsory testing, curfews, and the expectation to be vaccinated once that was possible. An early rise in trust in governments eventually yielded to a collapse as misinformation and disinformation flowed through these non-mainstream media channels, catering directly to conspiracy theories, and validating grievances.

~

When the Victorian premier slipped on some steps at a holiday house on the Mornington Peninsula in March 2021, it was widely reported nationally, the shock felt beyond his state. Daniel 'Dan' Andrews had actually fractured his back and broken several ribs in the freak incident and it was initially feared he might not walk again, much less return to his very demanding job. How long would he be out of action? Who would take charge at this perilous moment? Simultaneously, the media carried and amplified these broader public anxieties, often quite consciously.

Andrews was just one of many figures in politics, health and academia who had gone from obscurity outside his home state to national prominence. For better or worse, people had got to know him. Elevated by the creation of a National Cabinet, all state premiers had become more prominent, more present, in the lives of Australians, but Andrews was perhaps the first among equals on that score. Despite his government's disastrous mishandling of hotel quarantine,[1] which helped lumber Victoria with the toughest and longest-running lockdown rules of any state in Australia, Andrews was lauded for his forthright health messaging and generally front-footed approach to the pandemic threat.

Part of the attraction was that, more than any other government leader at the time, Andrews seemed to be willing to apply a moral/ethical overlay to unprecedented government intervention and the requirement for total community compliance. Known for his plain-speaking clarity, Andrews also affected to speak directly to citizens over the heads of reporters to explain lockdown rules—in his 22 March 2020 press conference, he famously said: 'You won't be able to go to the pub because the pub is shut. That doesn't mean you can have all your mates around to [your] home and get on the beers, that's not appropriate.' This resonated with middle and centre-left voters because it was consistent with the medical advice flowing freely through mainstream media channels, and perhaps because it revived an idea which had become unfashionable in the era of market-oriented small government and neoclassical economics—that of the active community. It turned out there was such a thing as society and it amounted to more than a mere aggregation of individuals in a market, all maximising their own advantage.

But Andrews was also the poster boy for conservative criticism of government overreach, with right-wing media and even senior federal government ministers (usually Victoria-based) condemning the state government over its aggressive pandemic management, and its readiness to curtail fundamental rights of movement, association, and political protest.

These were extraordinary times. Acting on health advice, liberal democracies around the world found themselves suspending basic freedoms in order to stave off the viral threat. Through sustained periods in 2020 and 2021, Melburnians themselves were required to obey night curfews, to stay at home at all other times (except for a small number of tightly defined purposes), and to avoid gathering outside with more than one other person. But lockdowns of various configurations and durations would be enacted in all Australian jurisdictions at one time or another, and the movement of citizens between states and territories would be made either difficult or impossible.

Border communities were particularly hard-hit. Regional centres like Tweed Heads on the NSW–Queensland border and Albury–Wodonga on the NSW–Victoria border struggled under differential rules applying in each state, causing huge problems for people who travelled daily across the border for work, education or medical treatment. The media reported cases of patients refused permission to attend regular dialysis, chemotherapy and other necessary therapies because they lived near a hospital but on the other side of a state border.

Restricted to their homes, many Australians took to watching the rolling news channels which carried daily press conferences live from not merely one's own premier but those of other states as well. CMOs Dr Kerry Chant (New South Wales) and Dr Brett Sutton (Victoria) became the expert faces of the emergency response, as they articulated the key public health messages, and exercised strong influence on their elected governments. Around this quotidian theatre of fear were many other players who themselves would become familiar if not household names—epidemiologists such as Professor Mary-Louise McLaws, Professor Raina MacIntyre, Professor Catherine Bennett and Professor Brendan Crabb.

Bennett told *The Guardian*'s Donna Lu in July 2021 of the personal change brought about by the blanket news coverage of the virus emergency, which propelled her from relative obscurity to national prominence:

> While it happened progressively, it's still a very strange thing. As a researcher at a university … you want to actually make people's lives healthier and safer. But you rarely get to hear from the public in the way we are now. It's a mark of how strange these times are, but at the same time it's the bit that reinforces your drive to contribute.[2]

McLaws agreed:

> People will come up and say, 'Thank you very much for talking to us apolitically,' or, 'You make me feel calm about what's happening' … When I'm asked for opinions in Australia, I have been criticised that I'm not considering the economy or mental health.

But I try to remind the listeners or the readers that that's not part of an epidemiologist's responsibility—that's leadership.[3]

∼

Everything felt different, including time. A new pragmatism took hold across the workforce and society, as 'what was best' yielded to the more prosaic 'what was possible'.

Those fortunate enough to be able to continue their jobs from home were generally able to adjust quickly. Internet-facilitated video-conferencing platforms like Zoom and Microsoft Teams went from being used by a tiny minority of mainly business types to everyday use by millions of people.

With near-saturation media coverage of the emergency, talk among friends and colleagues was often dominated by the latest numbers, with eyebrows raised when discussing where and when the epidemiological modelling suggested the outbreak would peak. Global, national and local death rates were the biggest preoccupation.

For those such as this author who had weekly live broadcast slots which had only ever been done in studios with professional-standard lighting and sound-recording conditions, these, too, migrated to the lounge or study. Visually, this provided a dramatic diminution of established standards that was at times jarring. Interview guests—known in the business as 'talent'—would appear on national news and current affairs broadcasts from their lounge rooms, kitchens or home studies.

For continuous news broadcasters like Sky News and the ABC's News Channel, the need to keep the show rolling, and to provide expert analysis of developments regarding the pandemic and other fields like politics and sport, flipped long-held production-quality requirements on their heads. Correspondents, scientists, former politicians and academics beamed in from their own lounge rooms to those of their housebound audience.

Many of the interviews put to air were hard to watch and difficult to hear, whether through excessive roominess (echo), lack of volume or poor connection. Dogs barked, leaf blowers and mowers blared, and sundry other sounds of domestic life intervened. Internet connections failed, pictures pixelated and sound was chopped up or dropped out. Still, the interviews proceeded. In a medium where basic production values such as picture composition and background and a level eyeline to the camera had been universal broadcast prerequisites, all were observed in the breach—sometimes in the same interview.

Yet this dramatic drop in standards brought other advantages. One was the sudden broadening of the available talent pool. A relatively small number of professional commentators who were familiar with television standards and protocols was significantly widened. What's more, once there was no longer an expectation of having guests attend the studio for interviews, contributors could be literally anywhere there was an internet connection. As a result, it became just as practical for program producers to attract 'talking heads' in another state, or even another country, dependent only on time zones. This technology-enabled democratisation of news media was probably in train before the pandemic, if only because newer generations have become conversant with presenting and performing to screens, but there's no doubt it was accelerated further and faster by COVID.

On the demand side, larger forces were at work. Consumption was fracturing. The internet, with its mysterious and opaque market-optimising algorithms, was inviting citizens to go around the 'elite' silos of so-called legacy media, to find alternative flows of information—some of it reliable, much of it not.

∼

While public health experts and government leaders used the media to broadcast their messages, resentments were brewing over the social and economic hardships of pandemic restrictions. Bitterness towards elites was a particular factor. Lockdowns and other disruptions had brought asymmetric effects depending on the types of work people did and how much they earned doing it. Public servants and other office workers employed securely in the information economy were able to easily adapt, but those in lower-paid physical occupations much less so. Yet these citizens had typically had less access to the mechanisms of government and the discourses of power.

Whole communities disproportionately affected by lockdowns—which is to say, communities where employment was more typically precarious—felt the restrictions more keenly. Some of these employees in occupations like hospital services, cleaning, wholesale food deliveries and a variety of self-employed service roles, were left severely out of pocket, struggling to meet living costs, and/or forced to work in difficult conditions. For these communities, the absolute nature of lockdowns, masking and testing, and the constant messaging about the virtue of physical separation from others, may have felt discriminatory and disenfranchising. Heavy-handed policing designed to ensure community compliance with health orders added to the sense that working-class and multicultural communities were treated more harshly than those in wealthier areas.

For those disproportionately affected by stay-at-home orders but ineligible for the federal government's temporary but generous JobKeeper wage subsidies, surviving the dark days of the pandemic became extremely difficult. This fed a sense at the bottom of the income and power scales of some being forgotten, leading to brewing outsider disenchantment.

In an already disrupted media landscape, where surveys had shown people increasingly getting their information not from free-to-air television but from other sources, the pandemic turbocharged this sense of distrust of the extent to which governments and 'old' media treated all people equally.

Social media platforms enabled the rise of personalities peddling 'alternative facts', to quote Trump aide Kelly-Anne Conway (in

January 2017, Conway explained the then president's plainly false claim of a greater inauguration attendance than for his predecessor by declaring Trump had used 'alternative facts'). These included claims vaccinations led to more deaths than the virus; that it was connected in some way to a plan for mind control using the 5G network, and that the individual rights of the people were being permanently withdrawn. Conspiracy theories took hold, and groups proclaiming sovereign citizenship took to the streets—particularly in Melbourne, resulting in direct clashes with police. Media covering the events were attacked as they had been in the United States and other places where such demonstrations were also on the rise.

It was one of the more glaring ironies of the COVID emergency: the pandemic threat saw the revival of scientific expertise in government decision-making, if for the simple reason that the kind of populist posturing that had passed for policy would have been immediately exposed. Governments in Australia (at least) correctly concluded that rejection of the medical advice would have been immediately measurable in hospital overloads and fatalities on a colossal scale. They turned to their medically and scientifically trained specialists because there was no other response.

In the public realm, this also afforded political leaders a high degree of 'moral cover' for the exercise of what were the most draconian powers used outside wartime. The broad consistency between medical advice and government action had the twin effects of providing community reassurance and elevating community observance of public health orders. This led some observers to wistfully claim that a national trait of laconic independent mindedness had given way to a dull obedience and a deference to authority.

But this was a misreading. What it actually showed was that when the full foundations of policy are explained, and are linked logically to outcomes, citizens will be convinced. Via mainstream media, Australians were able to receive and understand the very same advice being given to governments. Scientific and medical consensus called for measures to slow or ideally stop the spread. Australians were not obedient so much as they were logically informed.

Which is not to say everybody was happy to be held in sustained home detention, nor even at ease. People were on high alert and households were in turmoil, with homeschooling and work-from-home proving stressful.

Future historians will no doubt draw conclusions about the confluence of several parallel and intersecting developments in the lead-up to the COVID pandemic—things which made certain outcomes inevitable, while others were more contested. These assessments will evaluate the emergence of supranational social media platforms such as Facebook and Twitter, the use of encrypted end-to-end messaging services within political communities, and the sophisticated use of user data for commercial gain and nefarious political purposes.

In the context of the Brexit referendum of 2016 and the election of Donald Trump later that same year—both considered major upsets at the time—these dynamics were both cause and effect in the declining public trust of mainstream major-party political norms and the accompanying media. The emergence of a new and deliberately uninhibited tantrum politics has exposed the extent to which old norms have loosened their grip.

As academics Mark Evans and Gerry Stoker noted in their 2022 book *Saving Democracy*, the role of the media as a civil watchdog, providing a conduit between governors and the governed, has been widely assumed, whereas the extent to which the media could ensure the population within a democracy remains actively engaged has attracted even less attention. The emergence of raucous if numerically small dissent over vaccine mandates, lockdowns and even mask mandates proclaims this fracture. In so doing, it may have revealed the extent of mainstream media's current reach and pointed to its likely further atrophy. In any event, there is little argument that governments and media in mature democracies face a genuine and perhaps existential challenge in rebuilding widespread confidence in their willingness to speak to all and for all.

As Evans and Stoker write: 'The widespread emergence of information that is false or misleading, that is intended to persuade or confuse rather than inform, is therefore a likely contributor to the decline of trust in media.'[4]

~

When the pandemic hit, trust in governments, institutions and the media had been in steady decline in most Western democracies for many years. For three decades, these governments had been telling their citizens that private capital was best equipped to deliver an efficient price, and that investor capital would be uniquely agile in designing the most relevant services. According to this frame of reasoning, longstanding public utilities in areas of health, water, electricity, telecommunications, banking and transport had been either privatised or exposed to competitors, as leaders of centre-left and centre-right parties spruiked a neoliberal consensus emphasising smaller government, lower taxes and an expansive private sector. In so doing, governments had vacated functions in which they had previously dominated—frequently holding monopoly power—and conducted relationships directly with their citizens. Their withdrawal, however, left taxpayers adrift and vulnerable to profit-driven decision-making by corporations.

Mainstream media, the bulk of which is privately owned, played a crucial part in valorising this shift, pushing for lighter regulations in their own sector and projecting market economics as ipso facto efficient and less of a drag on the economy. But with the arrival of COVID-19, government was suddenly back centrestage. Only governments could organise the emergency response. Only governments could agree to close the international border, order vaccines, institute new rules for travel, and coordinate a society-wide—as distinct from economy-wide—response.

In the first half of 2020, this colossal re-entry of governments—state and federal—into the lives of ordinary people provided reassurance to a terrified electorate. To say the media was crucial in this period is an understatement. Indeed, because of the nature of the threat which necessitated the physical atomisation of society to slow the spread of the virus, mainstream media became the only means for government communication. At the height of the pandemic, media access to epidemiologists facilitated a broad society-wide acceptance of restrictions otherwise completely at odds with liberal democratic societies. Meanwhile, prime minister Scott Morrison and state premiers legitimately used the cover of medical/epidemiological expertise to directly intervene in the economy, and to enact and defend social-distancing rules usually considered anathema in a liberal democracy.

But the extreme circumstances affected people in different ways. Those employed in the knowledge and information economy were often able to adapt quickly to stay-at-home orders because their work was capable of being done from anywhere. Plus, they generally enjoyed the financial resources and employment stability to remain confident. For others, however, the emergency measures posed existential challenges which grew exponentially as the pandemic dragged on.

As the strain built, and governments were seen to struggle in providing equal protection to all parts of the society, other discourses around the wisdom of government policy, the efficacy of restrictions, the science of microbiology and epidemiology, and the role of the media began to emerge. To some, legacy media came to be seen as part of a larger complex designed to extend elite control over ordinary 'sovereign' citizens. Social media platforms and encrypted end-to-end communications services became forums for the venting of these frustrations and the unleashing of outlandish rumours, feeding a mounting distrust—although the rise of misinformation and disinformation as pernicious sub-discourses was partly an international phenomenon, consistent with the nature of the internet itself.

After the Morrison government had failed to secure early vaccine contracts, nor even accept that it had been tardy, trust in both government and mainstream media began to decline. By 2022, it was at rock-bottom. According to Ipsos research conducted for the Governance Institute of Australia (GIA), the 2020 spike in its 'ethics index' of a survey high of 52 fell back to 45 in 2021, and further to 42 in the survey of August/September 2022. Indeed, the GIA ethics index had charted a decline in all sectors, but the sharpest fall was in media where trust had tanked, dropping from an ethics index score of 18 in 2021 to just 1 in 2022. 'The Index found the media industry to be Australia's least ethical sector, sitting below large corporations and resource companies. State politicians fell to the very bottom of the ethical pile for occupations,' observed the institute's CEO Megan Motto.[5]

While generally well managed, the pandemic emergency exposed Australia's unpreparedness for an infectious diseases outbreak. But it also exposed the viral dangers of false information, particularly within sections of the community no longer reliant on traditional media outlets for their information. That is not just a health challenge for the immediate future but an issue which poses an under-appreciated economic and democratic threat.

PART IV
THE JOURNALIST EXPERIENCE

The Power of Purpose

Gavin Fang, Deputy Director, *ABC News*, Sydney

Late in 2022, I sat down with a colleague to have lunch. 'Everyone is just really angry,' she told me, 'and they don't know why.'

A few months earlier, I had been a guest speaker on a panel, called on to discuss the impact of the pandemic on the media to a group of mainly young journalists. Many of their questions had similar themes. Why would anyone want to get into journalism today, they asked, and how can I navigate the challenges of our industry?

My answer, that night and still today, is this: to survive in this business, you need to find and understand your purpose. Afterwards, several audience members approached me to talk more about this, saying it resonated with them more than anything else discussed that evening. It made me reflect on how the pandemic had sharpened the moral and ethical challenges we face as journalists.

As we examine the landscape left after this extraordinary story, it is time for media leaders to also ask ourselves: What is our purpose? Not just as an industry, but as individual journalists. Because, in more than twenty-five years in journalism, I've never had more conversations than I've had recently with colleagues who are disheartened, struggling, leaving or wanting to leave the media.

A Time for Hard Questions

When we look back over the years of the pandemic as journalists, what lessons will we learn? The audience numbers, just like those daily case numbers we all sweated over, tell us a story.

For the best part of two years, audiences swelled on television, radio and digital. More Australians than ever turned to media to help them understand this once-in-a-generation story. For big media players, and many smaller ones, the pandemic was an audience bonanza, arresting or at least stalling the seemingly inexorable decline in people turning to mainstream media to inform and interpret. And yet we all suspected, or knew, that this would be a short-lived sugar hit.

Now, as the worst years of the health crisis appear to be behind us, those audiences have left in droves. And there is no comfort in looking at the numbers anymore. Worryingly, despite or perhaps because of being at the centre of people's lives for two years, trust in the media has settled back into the mire. In Australia, retail industry giants Woolies and Coles are now among the most trusted institutions, despite the whole weird run on toilet paper that still stands as one of the strangest of the pandemic stories.

For so many journalists, it is a time for soul-searching. While not on the front line in the same way as doctors and nurses, journalists are first responders. Our job is to rush towards trouble and then tell everyone about it. As for those other first responders, the pandemic has at times felt relentless, both mentally and physically exhausting. And if all we end up with is an audience that trusts us even less than before, it is no wonder journalists are asking, 'Is this worth it?' or more significantly, 'What's the point?'

Eyes Wide Open

In the first few months of the pandemic, nobody knew how the story would play out, how it would impact our entire lives. But early on there was a moment that still stands out. And, on reflection, it was a warning about how covering the pandemic would change our industry but also profoundly test journalism's very reason for being.

In April 2020, the pandemic had not fully hit Australia's shores but was raging in other parts of the world. China had locked down and Italy was in the grip of what we now know was the first wave. In America, the pandemic had escaped into the big cities of the northeast and was hitting the most famous one, New York, like a hammer blow. In Central Park, a makeshift field hospital was up and running as the city tried and failed to keep up with the staggering toll. Dead bodies were being put in mass graves. Watching from our island fortress, Australians were scared but still feeling safely isolated.

For the media, telling the story of the pandemic in the United States meant charting a tragedy and a cautionary tale. For media leaders, there was an added concern. Could we, in good conscience, leave our people in America, and in other pandemic-hit countries, risking their lives for the story? We do that in other scenarios. Journalists, camera operators and producers have covered wars in a variety of ways for a very long time and risked being killed in the course of doing their job. But for this story, the threat seemed more insidious and harder to defend.

ABC journalist David Lipson was in Washington when the pandemic hit the United States and started to escalate. ABC correspondents around the world had been given a choice: come home, with no hard feelings—the ABC's preference—or stick it out, understanding it might mean the organisation wouldn't be able to get you home later. Many came home. Lipson, among others, decided to stay. With New York in the grip of the pandemic, he put in a pitch to travel up from Washington to cover the story. At *ABC News*, we interrogated Lipson's pitch. We did a risk assessment with a heightened sense of dread, looking at things we would not normally consider. We didn't know at that point what we now know about how COVID travels.

Would Lipson and the team be safe if they wore protective gear suitable for facing a biological or radioactive hazard? What if they destroyed their clothes? Could they safely go into New York for a few hours but stay away from the worst-impacted areas? What if they stayed out of town overnight and just drove into New York and didn't get out of the car? What if they got sick and couldn't get medical care? What if one of them died? How would we explain that to their families?

For all of us involved, the stakes were incredibly high. Was it worth risking the life of a colleague for the story? On that occasion, we said no.

In New York, people kept dying as we looked on. Lipson would later describe how he felt: 'It was reassuring that the ABC was looking out for us, but as a journalist, it was agony to watch the biggest story of the century unfolding just up the road in New York and not being able to go there to cover it.'[1]

It was a sentiment that would be echoed in different ways by journalists around the world. A type of guilt. As a journalist, if I can't be where the action is, when life and death is at stake for people, then why bother? What is our purpose?

AstraZeneca: Whose Side Are We on?

Truth underpins journalism. The pursuit of it, in the public interest, is what journalists do. But as a journalist, it is not enough to simply report the facts or the truth. Truth alone isn't always enough to meet that public interest test. And sometimes truth can harm. We must always give people context and a broader understanding of and perspective on issues, so they are equipped to make up their own minds.

Because the pandemic touched the entire community, and was about life and death, it made context in our storytelling even more critical. It ratcheted up the responsibility that many journalists felt to not just get it right but to ensure the impact of their work served the public good. It meant marking ourselves hard and asking ourselves every day: Are we working in the public interest? Have we provided more than the facts? Have we armed the public with the information they need and, if not, what is the cost? What is the media's role and responsibility in shaping public opinion?

These questions would be asked repeatedly during the debate over COVID vaccines and their safety.

On 15 February 2021, the Therapeutic Goods Administration (TGA) gave provisional approval for the AstraZeneca (AZ) vaccine in Australia, paving the way for local production. It is easy to forget how significant the announcements of vaccines were during the pandemic, and how extraordinary an achievement it was by scientists and drug-makers to get vaccines for COVID on the market so quickly. Then prime minister Scott Morrison, announcing the decision, described the approval process as full and thorough. 'Our vaccination program is on track, our vaccination program has the backing of the best medical experts ... and it is going to make a huge difference to how we live in Australia this year and in the years ahead,' he said.[2]

Health minister Greg Hunt then celebrated the approval: 'What that means is that the vaccine rollout is on track.' That turned out to be hopeful thinking. The slow pace of the vaccination campaign and uptake of vaccines would become the story of 2021. AZ was the turning point. At first, the public were firmly behind the government and the experts, but after that, trust—including trust in the media—began to erode as things went wrong.

It started to unravel in April 2021, when Genene Norris, a 48-year-old woman from the NSW Central Coast, died not long after receiving an AZ vaccination. A TGA investigation found her death from thrombosis with thrombocytopenia syndrome (TTS), known to most people as blood clots, was linked to her AZ vaccination. Just over a week earlier, the PM had staged a late-night media conference to confirm that AZ would no longer be recommended for people under fifty, after European regulators had found a link between the vaccine and the rare blood-clotting issue.[3]

Genene Norris wasn't the first Australian case of this, but she was the first death. For the media, this was a tricky moment that sparked debate about the best way to cover the story. According to an Australian Government fact sheet published in 2022, two to three out of every 100 000 people under sixty suffer blood clots from AZ. In people over sixty, the number is slightly lower, at about two people.[4] But when those early cases emerged, no-one was quite sure yet how prevalent this potentially deadly side effect of the vaccine would be. We knew it was rare, but how rare?

With Australia's borders still slammed shut, the virus wasn't claiming many lives here, but overseas it was running riot. So, when reporting on the death of Genene Norris and the blood clots, the media had to ask itself: Is going big on this story the right thing to do? Is telling the unvarnished truth the best option, when it could generate fear and potentially slow down vaccinations?

Of course we had a responsibility to report on these cases but, with lives at stake, it did force the media to be more thoughtful in assessing the impact of its reporting. It wasn't about whether or not to report it but rather how much to amplify the deaths. How many stories, how high in rundowns, how much context needed to be given?

As expected, the AZ deaths gave a good kick-along to vaccine hesitancy as an issue in Australia. In the months to come, politicians and scientists would line up on different sides over AZ. Most famously, Queensland's then CHO, Jeanette Young, said on 30 June 2021, 'I don't want an eighteen-year-old in Queensland dying from a clotting illness who, if they got COVID, probably wouldn't die.'[5]

On the same day, Dr Nick Coatsworth, who was on the government advisory panel, took to social media to say he disagreed and questioned the risk: 'Adults should be allowed to consent to an intervention with a 3-in-100 000 risk of thrombosis with thrombocytopenia syndrome and less than 1-in-1 000 000 of death.'[6]

In the media, we were regularly making judgement calls on whether a negative sentiment towards vaccination was anti-vaxxing and harmful to the public, or a legitimate concern. Mostly we got it right and reported in the public interest. But the public—on both sides of this debate—didn't all see it that way. As the months dragged on, questions over vaccine mandates, lockdown restrictions and whether or not to open up were also polarising. On those issues, the divide in the community and between opinions in the media were wide and well entrenched. But the vaccination campaign remained the most contentious topic.

The pandemic demonstrated the extraordinary power information and misinformation had, and still have, in shaping the views and emotions of the community. By February 2022, when thousands of people attended rallies around the country to protest vaccine mandates introduced by the federal government, the atmosphere was febrile. Journalists, photographers and camera operators attending the rallies were spat on, chased, verbally abused and threatened. Eventually, the outright anti-vaxxers became so hostile it was almost impossible to report on them anyway. They'd claim we never tried.

India: Bodies Are Burning

Journalism is often about tragedy—there's no denying that. A journalist's job is often to report the human cost and impact of planned or random events. Death is writ large across much of our reporting. Road tolls used to be a staple of media coverage. Holiday death tolls, in particular, were once reported as numbers, not people. Most of the media stopped doing that over the past decade, recognising that it was dehumanising. But during COVID, an obsession with death tolls returned—state and national death tolls, country death tolls and even significant global death tolls. Coronavirus updates out of Johns Hopkins University in Baltimore became a key source of information. Along with the morning media conferences with state premiers, the death toll numbers became a daily habit. In Australia, breaking news reports on COVID fatalities became a daily counter clicking over each time a life was lost. It cannot have been good for us.

India escaped the ravages of the virus in the early months, so much so that stories were written examining how this huge country was somehow avoiding the outbreak. But that changed rapidly and in devastating fashion in the second year of the pandemic. By May 2021, COVID had India firmly in its grip, and around the world, reporting on that country was dominated by stories about death. Mostly it was the funeral pyres that drew attention. The images of bodies burned in mass cremations ran on our television screens for days on end. We had become so used to stories of death that this didn't seem out of place.

It took a community event with members of the Australian Indian community to shake me out of this obsession. Why, they asked, were we not reporting more about India, and why were we dehumanising COVID in India by focusing on mass funerals?

Millions of people died during the pandemic around the world. And people needed to know that. But as an industry, we sometimes lost sight of the fact that every one of those people had an individual story. COVID reminded us that the best and most impactful stories are about people. Focusing on people forces you to care more about the tragedy you are reporting on. COVID brought that into sharp focus.

However, it's challenging to constantly bear witness to events on a global scale that also touch us profoundly and personally. Putting people at the heart of our stories—especially the tragic ones—comes at a personal cost.

The Power of Purpose

The pandemic was—and still is—like no other story. It has been relentless. It has touched all journalists personally and stretched our resilience by changing the way we work. It has forced us to re-examine how the way we present and shape stories can influence the community, and to confront the way we cover tragedy. It has laid bare the challenges we face as a profession—daily moral and ethical challenges. We must navigate and explain to the community a world where truth is different depending on your perspective, and where facts are constantly disputed. All of that in a media environment where audiences demand different story treatments across multiple platforms, twenty-four hours a day. The word 'churn' is commonly used to describe it, and it fits. It is not like being a nurse or an aged-care worker, but it is still mentally taxing.

Alongside the decline in trust and the rising demands of multiple platforms, there's rising avoidance of the media. The 2022 *Digital News Report* by the University of Canberra and the Media Research Centre found '68% of Australians now actively avoid the news at least sometimes'.[7] The percentage was even higher for people who mostly get their news from social media. The reasons given included too much news about politics and coronavirus, and the negative effect it had on their mood.

At the same time, we're being sent strong signals from the audience about the level of trust they place in our work. According to the 2022 Edelman's Trust Barometer, media was the only institution in Australia distrusted by a majority of the population.

As journalists, how do we deal with all that? Most of us have been schooled in the purpose of our profession. Holding power to account, shining a light into dark places, serving the audience, counting the cost of events—these are our mantras. But in today's environment, that isn't enough. And according to the support firm Converge, there was a significant increase in calls for mental health assistance from the media across the pandemic.

So, what can we learn as an industry, and especially as media leaders, from the pandemic and our coverage of it? It is a stark wake-up call.

I believe it is time to accept that the pursuit of bold public interest alone won't sustain journalists through the challenges to come.

They need to find or rediscover their individual purpose. As journalists, we all need to re-examine why we do what we do. Because if our personal purpose doesn't align with what we do and why we do it, then no matter how much we might support the broad ideas of journalism, the current demands of our industry are unsustainable.

That is not a call to abandon the journalistic principles that guide us but to more personally align our own passions and purpose with our work. From my experience, it is the people who have a strong sense of purpose, in service of journalistic principles, who are still thriving.

What might that look like in practice? It isn't about throwing away objectivity or bringing personal crusades to causes, and I'm not suggesting there aren't issues around the way we work that don't need separate attention. It is about doing the hard work of having personal and professional conversations between leaders and their staff about what drives them. And then finding ways to engage and align each person's purpose with our journalism.

My personal purpose is to learn and share knowledge. Applied to journalism, it means getting inspired by the pursuit of information and passing that on to others through stories. For others, it will be something totally different but equally valid.

Imagine what that pursuit of purpose might yield. A more engaged, enthused and personally connected fourth estate, more thoughtful about the ethical and moral challenges we face, emerging from the pandemic better able to serve the audience. With the audience demanding from us more authenticity, more engagement with them and more attention on the issues relevant to them, is there any other alternative?

From Moral Injury to Trauma Resilience

Dr Kimina Lyall, Deputy CEO, and Dr Erin Smith, CEO, Dart Centre Asia Pacific, Sydney

A FEW MONTHS INTO the pandemic, the Dart Centre Asia Pacific (DCAP) organised a (Zoom, of course) training session with Australian journalists. We were joined by about fifteen reporters, photographers, camera operators, producers and editors from across the country, and across news organisations. Our workshop was called 'Covering COVID—a Discussion about Trauma for Journalists'.

We are used to providing trauma workshops for journalists—it's what we do. Usually, we observe a range of emotions in such workshops: fear, distress and shame, along with anger and its variants, frustration and rage. These are all clear trauma responses, connected to the flight–fight physiological response, and the continued holding of this response in the body long after the danger or event has passed.

What we saw in the COVID workshop was quite a different response. Instead of the usual outpourings of stories and experiences connected to what is sometimes the first time journalists have learned about trauma, most of the participants stared at us from their home offices with a look of hopelessness and despair. Many described having 'had enough' and talked of colleagues they knew who, after decades of covering the world's biggest stories, had contacted their editors and said, 'I'm done.' They were all too aware COVID fatigue could kill off their careers.

'There is an amorphous endlessness to this,' said Katherine Porterfield, a clinical psychologist and Dart expert trainer, in an interview. 'And the fact that what is coming is as scary or scarier than what has already happened, that really makes people anxious.'[1]

What does this despair response mean? It, too, was a reaction to trauma. Along with fight or flight, a more dangerous and insidious physiological response to trauma can emerge: immobilisation or defeat, often presenting as hypo-arousal, apathy or depression. It was not the first time we had observed such a reaction from journalists. But they were usually at the extreme end of the trauma response, reserved for extraordinarily terrifying events, or stories that involved moral injury. Covering COVID led many journalists into that defeat.

In Australia at that time, unlike in other parts of the world like New York, India and China, few local journalists were bearing direct witness to death, body bags or violence. However, their trauma exposure did involve the threat of death: as one Pakistani journalist put it in a podcast we produced at the time, the story was harder to cover than the market bombings he was used to, and in which he'd once been injured. 'I'm worried that when I go out to cover the story, I'm going to bring the virus home to my family,' he said. Such concerns dominated journalists' fears throughout the region, including Australia.

This is moral injury: the harm that arises when trauma transgresses journalists' expectations of a just and ordered society.[2] It arises when journalists are required to intervene directly in the story, or where their personal safety is at risk. Moral injury also explains reactions by people to events that challenge their sense of purpose or moral compass.

COVID-19 did just that. Journalists had as much risk of catching the virus as anyone else in the community—perhaps more for those reporters, photographers and camera operators in the field, those who covered crises at hospitals and reported from testing queues. Others found themselves confined to their homes, contending with the lockdown's impact on their families, becoming vulnerable to long-term trauma impacts through increased stress and isolation. Another dimension that emerged involved the misinformation and fake news pandemic, challenging the trusted role of the news reporter within society. In sum, journalists were exposed to a life-threatening virus, lost their connection to colleagues and friends, and had their very role in society questioned. In other words, moral injury.

As a result of this unusually intense and ongoing trauma exposure, DCAP received the greatest number of requests for training and peer-support programs for many years. Since March 2020, we have reached hundreds of journalists and media workers from more than fifty news and journalism-aligned organisations. Unlike two decades ago, when this organisation was first formed, journalists are now willing to identify the impact of stories on their psychological well-being, and editors are increasingly aware of their duty of care to their newsrooms. In the main, news organisations in Australia stepped up to the plate.

But perhaps it was also the universal nature of the epidemic that became a protective factor. Rather than experiencing their trauma responses in isolation, for perhaps the first time in many decades, journalists' experiences were shared with each other, their editors and their audience. It was no longer necessary to suffer alone, and conversations around the impact of COVID were widespread throughout the community.

An example of this was a warning from the WHO as COVID-19 emerged—the world was in unchartered territory. Headlines such as 'Mental Illness Is Epidemic within the Coronavirus Pandemic' (from *USA Today*) warned of a new danger on the horizon, as anxiety and depression reportedly increased by 25 per cent in the first year.[3]

And while these dire predictions were largely accurate, they also underestimated the community's response. What we know from trauma research is when disasters impact whole communities, community members often come together to support each other in ways that are not needed during 'normal' times. And that aids recovery. The COVID epidemic showed us, with some exceptions, the extent of that community support. For journalists, it extended to individuals reaching out to each other and being willing to connect and learn about trauma, COVID and its impacts. As a result, despite the potential for long-term psychological damage, what we have observed across the journalism community is resilience; that is, the ability to recover from an initial trauma response—kind of like physiological and psychological homeostasis that allows the affected person to self-regulate and use available resources (such as online peer support and connection) to counter the trauma impacts.

Research—and history—have consistently demonstrated that when bad things happen, we will likely be just fine. Journalists are no exception. Those who develop post-traumatic stress disorder (PTSD)—the mental illness diagnosis often associated with trauma—are in the minority. Even war correspondents are largely immune, with only around a quarter developing PTSD.[4] Another study on photographers found the number to be only 6 per cent.[5] A more recent small study does show journalists covering COVID-19 *directly* were more likely to develop PTSD symptoms than those who didn't.[6] Yet, even so, most of that minority who develop a diagnosable trauma condition are likely to recover. In groundbreaking research, Dr Cait McMahon, the founding Managing Director of DCAP, concluded that as PTSD levels among print journalists in Australia increased, so too did post-traumatic growth, or the ability to rebound from the distress and incorporate the experience into new understandings of the self and of journalism work.[7]

~

From our decades of work and research, DCAP has concluded there are three main factors that protect against the long-term impacts of trauma exposure. This is what we call the 'triangle of protection'.

The first is physical exercise. As well as the other known health benefits of exercise, physical activity plays a specific role in trauma protection as it allows the body to discharge the adrenaline surge of trauma exposure. While on the one hand, journalists in lockdown were glued to computer screens, there was also the possibility the rules around designated times people were allowed outdoors increased the likelihood that journalists, and others, would engage in daily exercise.

The second component is social connection: both peer connection and activities involving family and friends. This is supported by research on the role of social networks during and after crises: we become more resilient when we deepen and broaden our social infrastructure, with social ties providing emotional support, information and collective action at critical times.[8]

The third side of the triangle, and perhaps the most important, is a strong sense of purpose. Having a clear reason for the trauma exposure provides journalists with the ability to withstand the psychological impact of their work.

Building—and sustaining—this triangle of protection doesn't have to take a lot of extra time or effort. Journalists in our sessions highlighted the importance of back-and-forth (or 'serve and return') interactions as simple and easy ways to stay connected with both peers and social connections during ordinary moments throughout the day. Media organisations should be encouraging staff to take brief breaks throughout their workday to engage in these protective connections.

While we have witnessed a widespread epidemic of resilience over the past two years, that resilience is indeed being tested. It is evident that journalists are also dealing with escalating violence and abuse both online and in person. But again, there is evidence journalists are countering the attacks on their profession's integrity with an increased connection to their purpose: the importance of telling stories accurately and shedding light on the truth.

For many decades, the stigma of discussing mental health ran deep among journalists who view their work as a calling. However, as our experience during our many COVID-era training sessions showed, there is increasing willingness to speak openly about both the physiological and psychological impact of trauma. The cumulation of trauma exposure, including the Black Summer bushfires of 2019–20, the COVID-19 pandemic and the Ukraine crisis, as well as dealing with the relentlessness of covering a global pandemic that may be affecting them personally, have likely contributed to a shared sense among journalists that protecting mental health is as just as important as looking after physical health.

Across the Asia-Pacific region, journalists have shared how they were actively engaging in self-care strategies, ranging from stepping away from a big story to recharge, to switching off electronic devices or leaving them in another room when going to bed. 'I don't think any of us would have been sitting around discussing our self-care plans before the pandemic,' noted one participant. But discussing the importance of self-care has increasingly become part of the normal conversation among journalists, helping to further break down stigma and shame.

The pandemic has up-ended the lives of journalists in innumerable ways. And while it has brought stressors and challenges, it has also allowed us to celebrate an epidemic of resilience. From our interactions with hundreds of journalists across Asia-Pacific throughout the pandemic, we forecast that this positive epidemic is set to continue.

About Dart Centre Asia Pacific
The Dart Center for Journalism and Trauma is a resource centre and global network of journalists, educators and trauma experts dedicated to improving media coverage of trauma, conflict and tragedy. A project of Columbia University Graduate School of Journalism in New York, the centre has international satellites in Asia-Pacific and Europe. Dart Centre Asia Pacific is the regional arm of the Dart Center.

The Great Resignation

Emily Arnold, former reporter and producer, *7NEWS*, Brisbane

I was eight years old and in Grade 4 at Mackay West State School. We were learning how to use computers and had to type up an 'About Me'.

My name is Emily Grace Arnold. I am 8 years old (turning 9) ... [Remember those days when you wished you were older?] *In the future I'd like to ... move down to Brisbane and get a job as a newsreader for Channel 7.*

Living in regional Queensland, I grew up watching Rob Brough on 7 Local News every night. At just eight, I decided I wanted to be on the tele too. Despite my early ambitions, I ventured off that path in my teens and applied for a Bachelor of Medical Imaging at Central Queensland University. But me, the girl who made her nanna film her performing Spice Girls concerts in the garage, yeah, she was never really going to like taking X-rays.

After a single semester, I dropped out. That was a fun conversation to have with Mum and Dad. I got a tattoo in the same week, and I'm still not sure which decision they were more horrified about. I call it my early life crisis. But just days after dropping out of uni, do you know what I found? That piece of paper ...

In the future I'd like to ... move down to Brisbane and get a job as a newsreader for Channel 7.

And just like that, I knew. That was the dream. And from that moment I wasn't going to let anything stop me from achieving it. I enrolled in a dual Journalism/Business Management degree at the University of Queensland.

'You're doing journalism? Oh, but journalism is dying! There'll be no jobs! You should probably have a backup.' If I had a dollar for every time someone said something along those lines to me ... hence the Business degree add-on. It was just to shut people up, really. I knew that I wanted to be a journo.

During the last year of my degree, I figured if I was going to get a job, I should probably do some work experience. Luckily, I was able to get my hands on (what I thought was) the phone number for Bianca Stone, at the time a senior reporter for *7NEWS* based on the Gold Coast. (It turned out to be her son's, but we got there in the end.) Right from that first text, Bianca took me under her wing. After a few days shadowing her, I became a regular intern and spent many hours driving to the coast, to spend many hours working, for free. It was worth it.

A couple of months later I got a call from the 7 Local News director. They had a three-week stint in the Toowoomba newsroom for me. That led to a two-week stint in Bundaberg. Then came another call: I was offered the permanent Bundaberg gig, my first full-time job as a journalist. I was stoked. But it was just the beginning. I had to get to Brisbane, become a top reporter, covering the top stories.

I spent just under three years in regional newsrooms across the state, covering court, crime, croc and shark attacks, meeting locals with colourful tales to tell, working ridiculously long hours for ridiculously ordinary money, knowing it would all be worth it when I got the job in Brisbane.

It was May 2019 when I got the call. I was in a police press conference when I saw the *7NEWS* Brisbane news director's name flash on my phone. I'd recently done a couple of casual weekend shifts, and after months of thinking about it had reached out to say I felt I was ready to make the move. He agreed. He offered me the dream.

And that's what it was for a while. I was living the dream. The privilege of that is not lost on me. I could wake up each day and feel happy about going to do a job I loved. You can imagine my surprise, then, when those feelings slowly started to change.

At the start of the pandemic, I felt fortunate to be able to play a very small part in informing people about such a significant and life-changing event. But as the days turned into weeks, into months, it just felt like a chore. A chore that often came with a side of abuse whenever a camera operator and I would leave the newsroom. 'Fucking scum! Why don't you tell the truth?!' There were also the online comments plastered on stories about lockdowns and vaccines. Comments, words, that hurt.

Just after covering the eastern Australia floods in February 2022, when the Omicron curve was starting to turn down, my camera operator and I were trapped for four nights in Placid Hills, a small community between Gatton and Grantham in the Lockyer Valley. There, we experienced the opposite of the abuse so many journalists had been copping: an extremely kind family took us in and provided us with a place to sleep, shower and eat.

That family reminded me of the overwhelming good in this world, but still, when I got back to the newsroom after that trip, it was as if two years of covering COVID, on top of everyday events like crime, crashes and court sentences, hit me at once. I was tired. Tired of the bad news. Tired of following daily infection numbers. Tired of not getting home until long after the sun went down. Tired of working every second weekend. Tired of having to say, 'I wish I could make it, but I have to work.' Just tired.

But this was the dream, wasn't it? I couldn't give it up ... or could I? I stewed on my feelings for several months, tossing and turning about what I should do. The future I had planned now looked so uncertain.

It was a Saturday night when the clarity I'd been searching for hit me. I had to work until 7 p.m. and so was going to be two hours' late to a friend's birthday dinner. That dinner also turned out to be a surprise baby announcement. I missed it. Never again, or at least, not for the same reason.

I resigned. Some people were shocked, disappointed even. 'That's a big fucking mistake' was one particular response which brought me to tears. But those whose opinions I value most—my partner, my parents—had my back. I've decided I didn't give up on my dream. I lived it. And not everyone can say that.

The dream has now changed. I've made the move to PR, or as journos call it, the 'dark side'. I once called it that too, but it's only shown me the light. I can work hard and be home by 5 p.m. I can earn more money and enjoy my weekends. I can climb the ranks and still spend quality time with my family, friends and five-year-old golden retriever. (Heck, I've even got time to write an essay for a book.)

I've found a life where I can have my cake and eat it, too. Now, that's the dream.

Editors' note: The 'Great Resignation' is a term that was coined by organisational psychologist Anthony Klotz in mid-2021 to describe the anticipated wave of post-COVID job departures. A survey conducted at the start of 2022 revealed one in five Australians had quit their jobs within the past year, and almost a quarter were considering leaving their place of employment.[1]

Making Your Way

Jess Malcolm, Political Reporter, *The Australian*, Canberra

THERE ARE FEW journalism students who are blissfully unaware of just how difficult landing a job in this industry will be. Choosing to study journalism means growing all-too-familiar with the reaction of shock or confusion when we reveal this seemingly ridiculous decision to friends and family.

'Why are you studying that if there are no jobs?' they would ask, or even, 'Do people still buy newspapers these days?' We would smile and nod our heads in the hope that, by placating their concerns, we could convince ourselves the story we were clinging to was true, that we had made the right decision, that we were going to make it. A good, healthy dose of optimism was important in the pursuit of our career goals.

When the pandemic struck in early 2020, I began to lose some of that optimism. There were widespread job losses, with regional and rural newspapers—the traditional springboards into the industry—shutting before our eyes. Advertising revenue dried up as the world headed towards an impending recession, or so we thought. Graduating with a Masters in Journalism in the middle of 2020 was not ideal timing. Many of the prized cadetship programs we had spent years working towards had been put on hold, and most newspaper jobs required a level of industry experience we did not yet have.

The trickiest conundrum for many young people starting out at that time was getting knocked back from junior jobs with feedback that we didn't have enough experience for the role, which left us scratching our heads, wondering how we were supposed to get the experience in the first place if we couldn't get our foot in the door.

∼

I was fortunate enough to land a job as a cadet at *The Australian*, which was the only journalism traineeship program in the country that was not put on hold. Five of us were hired by the newspaper and began our cadetships at the end of 2020. It was a great time to start as, at this point, we thought we were through the worst of the pandemic. Newsrooms were filling back up, restrictions had been eased in New South Wales, and life was beginning to get back to normal.

As a young person starting out in journalism, there isn't a more exciting place to be than a newsroom. We were thrilled to work for the national broadsheet, pitching stories that would reach people all over the country. We also had the opportunity to develop and learn skills from some of the best editors and reporters in the industry.

But then Delta started spreading in Sydney. COVID had been transmitted by an overseas traveller to a taxi driver and then exploded across the city. Shortly after, everyone in *The Australian* newsroom in Holt Street, Surry Hills was told to pack up their laptops and work from home for the foreseeable future. What was supposed to be a few weeks turned into five months. That period of lockdown was the hardest part of my journalism career so far. I learnt very quickly that journalism is not a job meant to be done sitting in front of a laptop alone in your bedroom.

Every day was like Groundhog Day. Daily press conferences, filing snap copy on COVID case numbers and deaths from every state and territory. Calling different GP clinics and pharmacies to see if we could tee up another picture of someone getting a vaccine. Reporting on anti-vaccination protests, business closures, and the state/territory and federal government plans to get us through the pandemic. While I was incredibly fortunate to have a job, this period was incredibly draining.

That being said, it was one of the most exciting opportunities to report on what was then the biggest story in the world. Newsrooms were empty and Australian papers were printing their papers without any editors, journalists and production teams in the office for the first time in their histories.

In that first period as junior reporters, we'd been sponges in the newsroom. Everything we learnt came from the editors and journalists around us. Watching over our editor's shoulder as they worked on our copy, listening to colleagues at their desks talking to sources, and hearing our editors converse, all allowed us to gain a stronger sense of the issues that our paper cared about. These are some of the most crucial professional experiences which help young reporters improve and develop.

Working from home took away all of this, and it also sidelined collaboration in the newsroom. Sometimes, a good story can go from okay to great by having someone drop by your desk and suggest a contact or person you should reach out to. But building new contacts and trust with people was now also more difficult, as we could not meet anyone face to face for a casual coffee.

Personally, the relentlessness of the COVID story was also overwhelming. While my friends and family could turn off the news or shut it out because it was overwhelming or exhausting, we couldn't.

∼

The pandemic generated a major thirst for news which in turn drove a massive uptick in subscriptions for traditional forms of media, with audiences turning to trusted news sources for information in a time of crisis. However, it also saw an explosion of news-related content on social media platforms such as TikTok, Instagram and Facebook, with young people able to insert themselves into the process of storytelling and content creation.

Amid a constant stream of confronting and difficult news, young people stuck in lockdown began to create content which was humorous whilst also informative. There were a myriad examples of young creators using audio from state and territory leaders' daily press conferences to make funny TikToks which went viral across the country. Some of the best included Victorian Premier Daniel Andrews's quote 'get on the beers', said during a presser before Melburnians were about to be freed from lockdown, and West Australian Premier Mark McGowan being asked about the legitimacy of a person in New South Wales going for a run and then getting a kebab.

'Explainer' journalism also thrived on social media platforms, especially on TikTok. Young journalists were innovatively telling stories to new audiences in different ways, seizing opportunities to carve out a name for themselves in a new journalistic sphere.

As a young journalist stuck in lockdown, these videos were hilarious and helped to ease the grind of the daily news cycle. However, they also brought a renewed pressure on young journalists in traditional media environments to produce audio and video content. This has been a daunting evolution, as the social media platforms previously reserved for our personal lives made their way into the professional realm. As early-career reporters, there is an expectation that we should be natural content creators on social media platforms, but in reality, for many of us this is not the case. Beyond taking the odd picture for Instagram, many of my colleagues and I have never put energy into social media in a concerted way. Now, our use of these platforms could make or break our careers.

As we emerge from the pandemic, mainstream media companies have ramped up their efforts to create content that is either dedicated to young readers or in a format they can connect with. Part of this includes greater resourcing for social media platforms in a bid to find new audiences and do journalism in a different way. The emergence of new platforms has also helped to engage younger audiences by tailoring news to them in a more conversational voice. There is a hunger among young people to be informed, but mediums such as newspapers have often neglected to engage with them, focusing instead on older audiences with well-established careers and maybe a property or two.

That said, news organisations may still face major structural challenges in attracting young people to engage with journalism and stay interested in the news. There is also a sentiment among young people that they do not want to pay for news. This is despite the fact they may be earning an income and are comfortable paying for subscription-model streaming services like Netflix and Spotify.

The good news is, while COVID was incredibly difficult for journalists and newsrooms across Australia, it did create opportunities for early-career reporters. Junior people in the newsroom were able to cover bigger stories than they ordinarily would have if there were more experienced journalists around to do it, in most instances fast-tracking our experience and setting us up for whatever comes next.

With fewer reporters in the newsroom, younger journalists are now regularly assigned major stories, such as covering world events or political policy battles. The lucky ones are sent on international trips. Some young reporters have used this unique time to carve out niches in specific topic areas, where there may have been gaps left in a media organisation's coverage of issues.

Now we're back and settled in the newsroom, we're starting to forget the hard times and remember, instead, the upsides, because in all of these circumstances, early-career reporters have found their experience accelerated through COVID. And that's something we will be banking on to set us up for robust, exciting futures in the media.

Investigative Challenges

Anne Connolly, Investigative Reporter, *ABC News*, Sydney

IT WAS 9 A.M. on Monday, 30 March 2020 when our investigations team met for its start-of-the-week story conference. Usually we gathered in the office with a coffee and some ideas to pitch. Today, most of us were in our first government-ordered lockdown, connecting with each other via video—technology which would become our godsend during the next two years and beyond. With the world still scrambling to determine how deadly COVID-19 really was, I felt as if we could be extras in the first act of a Hollywood disaster movie. Could we be working on this story until the literal end, with the inevitable scene of TV journos abandoning their posts to join the panicked throngs?

Although China, the United States and Europe had been grappling with the virus for a couple of months, for most Australians, our only crisis thus far had been an embarrassing shortage of toilet paper and the prospect of homeschooling. But we didn't need a crystal ball to see the future. In Indonesia, those who died were wrapped in plastic; in China, there were robots on hospital floors; in Italy, the dead were left in their beds, with no-one able to collect them. Later, there were the pictures of overwhelmed morgues and mass graves.

INVESTIGATIVE CHALLENGES

Our news colleagues had the mammoth and unrelenting task of responding to news as it was unfolding. Our unit now had to investigate how Australia was responding to this unprecedented crisis.

There are twenty-two journos in the Investigative Reporting Team, and in normal circumstances we would work up a story to pitch to TV, radio and digital for programs like *Four Corners*, *7.30*, the 7 p.m. news, *AM* and *Background Briefing*. We all had our 'beats', if you like, but for the next year there was only one story on the agenda. On that first day, with our unit's editor, Jo Puccini, we brainstormed crucial policy areas and potential investigations: How had the *Ruby Princess* fiasco been allowed to happen? Did we have enough vaccines/staff/expertise/ventilation equipment? Was our hardline approach stopping people from returning to Australia too much?

We needed to speak to health workers on the front line—the specialists and health administrators who had been complaining for years about under-resourced hospitals and poor emergency facilities. Using our usual databases and social media for contacts, we spoke to dozens of doctors in Victoria and New South Wales, the states which were already showing signs of being heavily hit. Though many made dire warnings off the record about a lack of personal protective equipment (PPE), workers and beds, no-one was willing to go public. They couldn't say for sure what would happen, and recognised their comments could have consequences at a time when state and federal governments were desperate to avoid mass panic.

We sent questions to ministers, health departments and the states' chief medical officers, but they often went unanswered or inadequately answered. They were dealing with an unprecedented health crisis. Our freedom-of-information (FOI) requests went on the backburner—when National Cabinet was established, it was exempt from FOI laws. As investigative journalists, we were virtually locked out.

Adding to the difficulties was the lockdown itself. Our typical method of establishing contacts was via phone and then a face-to-face meeting. People require reassurances when they are considering going public with sensitive information. Eyeballing the journalist entrusted with telling the story is part of that process. Now, that was impossible. Instead, we had to attempt to establish a relationship via phone or video screen. It meant much more constant contact via text message and regular phone calls over weeks or months. That meant our work and personal lives began to blend in an unhealthy way, leading some of us to joke that we were no longer 'working from home' but rather 'living at work'.

At the same time, we were dealing with COVID on a personal level. Some of us had partners, children or flatmates working or studying from home in cramped spaces, while those who lived alone had to cope with almost total isolation. Those of us with sick and elderly relatives couldn't visit them, and those with family overseas and interstate were cut off. I had two teenagers who needed supervision and support with their online learning and the psychological fallout of being separated from friends. In addition, each time a family member contracted COVID, the rest of us had to follow government directives and isolate. Friends and family delivered groceries to our front door and we returned the favour when they, too, inevitably succumbed to the virus.

In terms of my job, I had a very specific interest in what was being done to protect the nearly 200 000 Australians living in aged care. I knew the sector well due to a previous investigation into nursing homes which had revealed widespread neglect, abuse, and chemical restraint with antipsychotic drugs. In 2018 we were preparing to put the revelations to air in a two-part *Four Corners* series called 'Who Cares?' when the government got in early—just a day before the first episode—and announced a royal commission. The hearings were ongoing when the pandemic hit.

My first COVID investigation was into the lockdowns of nursing homes, which ended up lasting for months on end. With over half of residents suffering from dementia, family and friends who helped overworked staff by feeding, caring and comforting loved ones were banned from visiting. The federal government regulator, the Aged Care Quality and Safety Commission (ACQSC), also stopped its regular visits. No-one had any idea what was going on inside. In the end, it wasn't visitors but staff with little training in infection control who unwittingly spread the virus among residents.

When the first big outbreak happened at an Anglican nursing home called Newmarch House in Sydney's west in May 2020, *Four Corners* commissioned myself, producer Suzanne Dredge and cameraman Louie Eroglu to make a 45-minute film of events as they happened. It was one of the few times during COVID that we met people in person.

Each day, families stood outside the nursing home to highlight the hardships of their loved ones inside, while Anglicare released statements revealing the daily figures for infections and deaths. We asked some families to call relatives who were still well enough to speak and filmed them through their windows. One elderly woman said she hadn't been bathed for over two weeks. A man said he had lain on the floor for hours after a fall, despite buzzing for help. The facility was understaffed because infected carers and their close contacts had to isolate and management had trouble recruiting replacements, who feared the virus. Some families were too scared to go on camera but gave us documents, like the end-of-life forms the elderly were asked to sign on the first day of the outbreak. The families said they were being encouraged to say they didn't want any intervention.

Ironically, COVID gave us access to a direct source of official information for broadcast. Each week, Anglicare, the ACQSC and NSW Health addressed families through an online webinar, explaining how they were trying to care for residents. It was through these videos we discovered those who were infected would not be sent to hospital; the elderly were to be cared for in situ. It soon became clear the authorities feared the virus might spread from a hospital into the community, as had occurred with an earlier outbreak. They wanted COVID contained to Newmarch House.

When one family decided to take their healthy relative out before he also was infected, NSW Health said it would create a legal order to prevent it, threatening to impose a jail sentence on the elderly man if he breached it. He later contracted the virus and died. Meanwhile, infection protocols were being breached. Families drew diagrams to show that the nursing home had placed the infected and uninfected in adjacent rooms, which was against policy.

We taught families how to use their phones to film relatives when they were allowed to see them in 'window visits'. It was heartbreaking vision, seeing distraught families standing by in full PPE while their sick relative languished in bed, unable to even hold someone's hand in their final hours.

When our program 'Like the Plague' aired on 22 June 2020, we revealed the policy of keeping the elderly inside and posed the question: 'Did they die to save the rest of us?' When the next wave hit Victorian aged-care homes later that year, the sick and dying were sent to hospital in a reversal of the NSW policy.

As a new COVID strain, Omicron, spread in 2021, both lockdowns and infections got worse and the trauma for families was palpable. People with dementia couldn't understand why they didn't have visitors and felt abandoned. Some staff didn't show up when there was an outbreak, meaning residents went without meals and the necessary care.

Over the next two years, I used everything at my disposal to find out what was happening inside the facilities. Using data published by the ACQSC, I revealed its selective approach to sanctioning some nursing homes struck by outbreaks while others received no penalties. The data showed how the watchdog had stopped all unannounced visits before COVID hit. Its method for ensuring nursing homes had the correct infection policies in place was to phone them to ask—the vast majority gave themselves top scores for preparedness. At that point, more than 30 per cent of COVID deaths in Australia had occurred in aged care.

For me, Twitter and Facebook were blessings, providing me with contacts to find families who had loved ones caught up in the outbreaks. I contacted ABC talkback shows, who passed on the names and numbers of those who had stories to tell.

During my investigations, the most distressing aspect was interviewing the families who had been denied the opportunity to say their final goodbyes. One woman played me a voice message from her father in which he apologised for being so angry and told her not to worry, just before he died. Another woman had set up a live stream to keep in contact with her father during the lockdowns. When he was dying from COVID, she had to try to reassure him via video while staff clad head to toe in protective gear stood by.

Because I couldn't travel interstate, I had to ask these people to perform many technical processes, like filming their rooms, meeting photographers outside and gathering images of their loved ones for broadcast. They were gracious in providing it all despite their trauma. They bared their souls via Zoom to a journalist they had never met. They spoke up to ensure people knew what was happening to our most vulnerable behind closed doors.

Looking back, I can see how COVID has changed some of the ways journalists operate. It is now much easier to connect with people via video link and establish a rapport. The downside is we could start to see this mode of communication as being more efficient and think face-to-face meetings are now unnecessary.

For me, being a true investigative journalist still requires some old-fashioned shoe leather. Despite rapid technological change, people are more likely to divulge sensitive information in person rather than via a screen. More importantly, they deserve to have a personal connection with the journalist who is ultimately responsible for relaying their truth to the public.

PART V
INNOVATION AND NEW MEDIA

The Use of Data for Storytelling

Casey Briggs, Data Journalist, *ABC News*, Sydney

EVERYONE ENDURED THE pandemic in different ways, but there were many experiences that felt universal. Most Australians had at least one period of regularly checking the case numbers or awaiting their premier's daily press conference—for millions of people, those periods went on painfully long. This attention to numbers thrust data journalism to the fore. Where once data journalists worked away in relative anonymity in their corner of the office, they were suddenly filing the lead on the biggest news story in the world.

What was clear to us very early on was that, while there were endless angles, issues and debates to be explored, this was a story that fundamentally could not be understood without a firm grasp of the numbers. Often, those numbers were slippery and hard to hold onto, because of how they were being reported. But with a high-quality dataset, we were able to put the days' figures into their proper context, interrogate data to find patterns and trends, and talk meaningfully about what we might expect to happen.

Data helped us explain what was changing and why. It helped us identify early when outbreaks were morphing and moving. For example, we were able to quickly see when Sydney's Delta outbreak spread was shifting and becoming more challenging to control.

Data helped us uncover the fact the virus was harder to suppress in areas with larger households, and those with more people working in essential services who couldn't do their work from home. We used data to see where there were gaps and failings in the national vaccination rollout. Before we could do any of that, though, we needed to collect the data.

Domestically, each state and territory published COVID statistics once or more times a day. There were eight different sets of reports to gather, with differing levels of detail, in different formats, and on different schedules. Often, the statistics were first announced at press conferences, so getting a national picture meant closely monitoring events from up to eight state and territory leaders. Those press conferences gave us an avalanche of statistics in what is perhaps the least useful format for human understanding: a rapidly reeled-off list. And while they may have told you how many people had tested positive for the coronavirus the previous day, they often left the most important question unanswered: how is the situation changing? That's just Australia. Throw in updates from every other country in the world and it quickly became overwhelming.

In those early days especially, it was my view that the single best contribution we could make was to fill some of the gaps in this complicated patchwork of information. By helping to compile the data and surrounding it with the relevant context, we could simplify a complicated issue. We could cut through a dense wall of numbers to get to the point. In short, rather than telling people what to think, we wanted to give everyone the tools they needed to understand the situation and make up their own minds about what should be done.

I teamed up with colleagues working on a digital coronavirus dashboard to maintain a database of Australian statistics,[1] and we set about building the tools we would need to explain the data on television. With things moving at the pace they were in March 2020, we wanted to be able to update figures and share them with viewers within minutes. Commissioning television graphics the traditional way, through a team of graphic designers, was not really an option.

Enter the COVID touchscreen. It ticked all the boxes.

ABC graphics developer Ryan Kerlin set to work writing a touchscreen application, pulling together a first prototype in just a couple of weeks. It was held together with what felt like sticky tape, a hope and a prayer, but it worked. On 29 March, version 1.0 of the coronavirus touchscreen was ready, and *The Curve* made its debut on the ABC's *Insiders* program. We initially thought this might just be a weekly segment, but the audience response showed we were onto a winner, and the next day I was back on air on the ABC News Channel.

The touchscreen was running, but only just. The version we went to air with on day one was extremely simple, and we had a long list of additional features and graphics in mind. Software developers might refer to it as a 'minimum viable product', but even that might be a bit generous. Ryan jumped straight back into further development. We would often start using a new feature on air within hours of it being finished. Other times, I would discover a bug in the software while using it that Ryan would speedily fix. We were building the ship as we sailed it, but it was working.

The touchscreen helped us quickly spot trends in the data and pull out the most critical information. It helped us bring in extra datasets like transport and movement to understand the broader consequences of the lockdowns. And, importantly, it helped us do all that fast, with a set of simple and familiar graphics.

The other consequence of making the touchscreen an overnight TV star was that we soon realised we didn't have anywhere to put it. It wasn't unusual to see us wheeling it around the building looking for somewhere to plug it in. Eagle eyed viewers might have noticed COVID-19 updates from our foyer, the ABC News Channel kitchen, and an office on the upper levels of the building vacated by people now working from home. We eventually found it a semi-permanent home in the newsroom.

We weren't alone in what we were doing. In lieu of any comprehensive single source of data produced by the Australian Government, a slew of dashboards and repositories had sprung up. Some were maintained by media organisations, others were run by volunteers and independent journalists as a community service.

There was covid19data.com.au, run by freelance data journalist Juliette O'Brien, and CovidbaseAU,[2] run by who we later found out was a group of three teenagers in Melbourne. These websites became important references for many Australians, as did COVID Live,[3] run by Anthony Macali who admits he, too, was frustrated by the lack of real-time COVID-19 data from official sources. 'Initially the COVID reporting was fractured and slow to update ... this made it difficult to track the country as a whole,' says Macali.

Researchers started using COVID Live as a data source, including, at one point, the Doherty Institute team producing models and forecasts for National Cabinet. Macali recounts one piece of feedback a visitor sent him: 'Your site is the single biggest tool for managing my anxiety around COVID and for helping me understand how the country, the states and my own LGA [local government area] are truly travelling—minus any political spin.'

Other volunteer developers rolled up their sleeves to produce useful tools. Sydney data engineer Ken Tsang built an interactive exposure site map early in the pandemic. It gave people an easy way to see if they had potentially been exposed to the virus. Later, when vaccines were in hot demand, he built a tool to help people find and book vaccination appointments.

The work of data analysts and developers like these provided services that filled information gaps in official communications—although arguably, governments should not have been leaving these gaps. They saw a problem and got to work building solutions, performing a genuine public service, largely without financial compensation. They are some of the unsung heroes of the pandemic.

∼

While the word 'modelling' may once have made people think of catwalks and runways, the pandemic mainstreamed the mathematical model.

From the beginning, leaders were keen to stress they were basing their decisions 'on the health advice'. A lot of this advice stemmed from epidemiological models of viral spread and human behaviour produced both internally by health departments and commissioned from researchers in universities and research centres. Later in the pandemic, extensive modelling was conducted by several groups to investigate the impact of vaccines, and to come up with the best strategies for moving beyond the pre-vaccine response to outbreaks.

It was great to see the community take the role of scientific research seriously throughout the pandemic and look to science to help us answer many of the difficult questions we were facing. The use of modelling was, overall, a good thing. But in my view, there were several problems that emerged, and there are lessons here for journalists, the research community and political leaders alike.

No-one would seriously criticise leaders for being guided by the best available science. At times, though, it was hard for us to know if that's what they were doing. Leaders would simply say, 'We're following the health advice,' but in reality, it was never that simple. Different leaders made different decisions based on different views of acceptable risk levels. In public they would make definitive statements about what the modelling 'says', but modelling always contains uncertainties and could not possibly have been so definitive. They would selectively choose which modelling to publish, and when they did, it raised questions about political or other motivations. If modelling was commissioned and the politicians didn't like the results, we would have no idea it even existed.

Mathematical models are, by necessity, simplifications of the world that (hopefully) help us answer complicated questions. Because they are simplifications, they must make various assumptions and decisions. Different models that make different assumptions may come up with different conclusions. And the question you want to answer helps shape the assumptions you make. During COVID, it was not uncommon for published 'modelling' to be a single-page document with some charts of output, without any of the details you would need to understand how that model was produced, or how sensitive it was to changes.

Most members of the public weren't going to read detailed, mathematically dense research papers. But other academics would have, and if they'd had access to the details, we might have been able to have a much more sensible conversation about the modelling, such as how it differed from other models, and how it informed decisions being made about when we locked down and opened up.

Governments also exerted control over how modellers and epidemiologists spoke publicly, putting limits on what they could say, or even preventing them from doing interviews altogether. I think it's fair to say that most of the research community found that frustrating. There are many modellers who would've preferred more leeway to speak to the public and to journalists.

Rob Hyndman, Professor of Statistics at Monash University, has been producing weekly COVID forecasts since March 2020. Those forecasts were typically kept confidential by governments. He tells me that Australia often defaults to a 'culture of secrecy' when it comes to government data. Professor Hyndman goes on to say: 'We would always prefer for science to be conducted in the open. I think it's better for the science, I think it's better for policy, and I think it's better for public discourse if things are done openly and transparently ... But the contracts that we were required to sign didn't allow that. There does seem to be a sort of extreme risk-aversion and unwillingness to make data widely available, which is in contrast to almost every other high-income country, where data does tend to be made much more widely available.'

The suppression of much of this government-commissioned modelling, much of which made use of the best datasets, meant there was a void in the public conversation. Preventing modellers from sharing their work or speaking to journalists allowed more airtime for less reputable models. The commentary void was filled by people further removed from the actual situation, often working with inferior datasets. It also allowed misinformation to flourish in a highly contested political space.

'The forecasts and the models that were released tended to be either individuals doing the best they could with the data that they could scrounge together ... or they were models that governments chose to release for whatever purpose they had,' says Professor Hyndman. 'There's no problem with individuals running their own analysis. I'd encourage it. The problem is that they generally didn't have available the best data, because the data ... was not even released.'

There were problems, too, with the way journalists reported on models. As an industry, we failed to properly contextualise modelling and explain what it was for. Too often, news stories treated models as though they were forecasts, when the very purpose of the models was to guide decision-making that would influence human behaviour. If policies were changed, *of course* we wouldn't see the outcomes predicted by the modelling.

The fact that all modelling was just referred to as 'modelling' meant that journalists struggled to differentiate between models that were trying to answer different questions or portray different scenarios. A wide spectrum of models was produced, of varying quality, and the umbrella term used in headlines failed to explain this. Reporters also had trouble distinguishing between work by reputable mathematical modellers, and work produced by people outside the relevant fields using non-standard methods.

Modelling was critically important to understanding the pandemic in Australia, and the pandemic has clearly shown that we need more scientific and mathematical literacy in our newsrooms.

∼

There were times during the pandemic where things moved extremely quickly, particularly at the beginning of 2020 and in the early periods of each outbreak around the country. When an outbreak took hold and a state or territory government locked down regions to stop the spread, it remained the most important story each day. The pandemic was, after all, keeping everyone in their homes.

As the weeks went on, we settled into a rhythm. The pace of developments would slow dramatically. Day after day, there were incremental changes in transmission that over time, we hoped, would lead to the wave being brought under control. But with the pace of change so slow, journalists at the premiers' daily press conferences could become fixated on topics that, in my view, weren't all that relevant in terms of bending the curve or ending lockdowns: Should Bunnings still be open? What about the Reject Shop? There may have been inconsistencies in the rules, but ultimately they weren't the kinds of inconsistencies that were driving a lot of transmission. And we spent a lot of time discussing them.

The frustrating thing for me was that there were serious questions for governments to answer. In New South Wales's Delta wave in 2021, for example, the data was clearly showing transmission was occurring in essential workplaces, in areas where people had large families and lived in large households. What was the premier doing to tackle that? What were people to do if they couldn't work from home or afford to not go to work? Was enough being done to protect the people who were ensuring our supermarket shelves were stocked and our post was delivered? In parts of Sydney, a lot of people were getting sick, but it reached a point where it seemed like the government had decided there was nothing more that could be done.

These were crucial questions, raised by the data, but at times they went unasked. It allowed leaders to dodge scrutiny of their decision-making at a crucial time. As an industry, I think we dropped the ball. With too few journalists closely watching the data, important issues were neglected.

The financial state of the news industry is no secret. Publications and broadcasters are increasingly producing more content with lower profit margins, and using fewer reporters. This has forced outlets to cut back on specialist reporters and rounds-based journalism. But the pandemic has shown us how valuable it is to have health reporters and science journalists and data analysts in the room. If there had been more of them, we might have seen fewer of the issues I've outlined in this essay.

If you'd have told me in 2019 that I would soon find myself pointing at and describing graphs on live television for minutes at a time, with no other vision or talking heads, I'd have laughed you out of the room. The very concept breaks so many of the conventions of television news. Yet this has been a period when so many of the iron-clad rules of journalism have been challenged. Those segments were both a sign of the times and a signal that, for the right story and presented right, there is a real appetite for data and context in the news being consumed.

There were difficulties along the way, but the pandemic threw open the door to new styles of reporting and generating stories. My employer, the ABC, has backed our approach, and we want to take what we've learned and see how widely we can apply it—not just to events like a once-in-a-lifetime pandemic, but also the routine and the mundane. For example, we're experimenting with how we can use the technology to supercharge what we do with politics and elections. We've already used it to track politicians as they fly around the country during an election campaign, and to analyse their social media posts and ad spend. For the US mid-term elections, we used our new software to build our most flexible results maps yet.

We've used charts and maps to visualise Australia's record-breaking year of rain in 2022, and we want to see how else touchscreens and interactive graphics can help us tell stories about weather and our changing climate. We want to use the touchscreen to contextualise major events and disasters, such as bushfires, by quite literally tracking them on the map to show the devastation they bring, in real time. And we want to explore what new technology and tools will allow us to do in the future.

The future of data journalism is bright, if we seize the opportunity.

The Rise and Rise of TikTok

Lee Hunter, General Manager, TikTok, Sydney

After only a few short years of existence, TikTok's growth during 2020 and 2021 outstripped that of virtually all other platforms. To understand why, it's useful to consider what TikTok actually is. Or, more pertinently, what it isn't.

Throughout its short history, TikTok has generally been thought of by many as a social media platform alongside the likes of Facebook and Twitter. But while TikTok has social features, that's not why most people open the app. You can search for things on TikTok, but it's not a search engine. In reality, millions of Australians come to TikTok primarily as an entertainment platform. To laugh, to learn, or just escape.

TikTok has a thriving global community of more than one billion people. The platform makes it easy for anyone to create videos, to find connection and be entertained. People come to TikTok to see what culture is breaking, what trends are happening, to discover new music, to learn and be amused. The beauty of the TikTok experience for most is that it's curated for each individual. Our recommendation system delivers a personalised experience to each user, based on their preferences and engagement on the platform.

The recommendation system thrives on diversity. This, combined with the scale of our community and the varied content they create, ensures that TikTok is for everyone and is not repetitive—and, provided content and behaviours meet our Community Guidelines, that everything and everyone has a home on TikTok. With our creative community making new content all the time, the TikTok experience rarely becomes dull or predictable.

For those not familiar with TikTok, when you open the app, you're shown what's known as a 'For You Feed'. What this contains depends on what you like, and no two 'For You Feeds' are the same. They might include comedy, sports and lifestyle videos, new music or trending sounds, an occasional history lesson or interesting facts, fashion and beauty, a cleaning hack, a recipe, or anything and everything associated with everyday life. There isn't a lot of news and politics, but it's there if you want to find it. And, of course, you're encouraged to make your own content and share it with the world.

This is part of the reason TikTok has been so attractive to Australians, particularly during the pandemic and now as we move beyond the day-to-day experience that we shared during that global period of lockdowns, restrictions and other society-wide events associated with COVID-19. Our company's official mission is to 'inspire creativity and spark joy', and TikTok has been and continues to be a way for many Australians to find that joy—to inspire authentic, creative content, and to have that shared. We're proud of that. It's also a platform that focuses on discovery, delivering new content, genres, creators and styles to users who may never have sought this out themselves, and ensuring a new experience and an opportunity to learn and appreciate something different.

With the stresses of the pandemic, particularly in the early months of lockdowns and all the uncertainty that came with it, joy was relatively thin on the ground. In thousands of cities around the globe, people were suddenly restricted from socialising or mingling.

Life as we knew it had changed. In many cases, people lost work, and they were locked away from their friends, families and colleagues. Many became ill and many, sadly, lost their lives. It's no wonder people felt scared and uncertain about the future.

All of a sudden, being at home hour upon hour, week upon week, meant we all had more time and appetite for some light relief. TikTok provided that in spades. While the hashtag #coronavirus attracted tens of billions of views throughout 2020, much of this content was not necessarily focused on health information. It was often about how people were experiencing the pandemic, sometimes through comedy, or cooking, exercise or other unique ways. In Australia, for example, we saw people parody the daily media briefings of the PM and state and territory leaders. Some of our chief medical officers gained strong fan bases and videos on TikTok. We even partnered with NSW Health to live-stream those daily updates on the platform.

And while there were still dances—lots of dances—the diversity of content on the platform bloomed. Cooking tutorials were popular—everyone, it would seem, decided to learn how to make bread. Parents shared funny moments about becoming teachers; people spoke of their partners' annoying habits which they'd never noticed before; others were singing, miming to songs, and 'bored in the house' took off. We shared DIY tips, life hacks and everything in-between, with community members posting their experiences in their own authentic ways. TikTok was and is a reflection of our everyday life, but with a twist.

With so many Australians discovering and appreciating TikTok in 2020 and 2021, we knew we also had a responsibility to make sure they had access to information about the pandemic that supported their health and wellbeing, as well as providing that opportunity for entertainment. Part of how we did that was through partnering with UNICEF Australia to build a COVID-19 hub, surfacing authoritative health information and content for our community, as well as providing details about how to get vaccinated on a state and territory basis. And we donated US$2 million to the Peter Doherty Institute for Infection and Immunity to support them in their critically important work.

The very first video on the WHO's TikTok account was a relatively earnest post about hygiene practices to protect yourself and others from coronavirus. The organisation has since posted a variety of other informative videos and launched the #SafeHands hashtag, encouraging people to wash their hands—videos with this tag attracted billions of views globally throughout the pandemic.

As well as live-streaming daily press conferences, we also worked with NSW Health to broadcast a Q&A with Dr Kerry Chant at the height of the lockdowns in New South Wales. And we paired Dr Karl Kruszelnicki (Dr Karl) with Professor Sharon Lewin of the Doherty Institute, for a vaccination-focused live event aimed at dispelling myths and providing our audience with trusted, authoritative information about an issue that was very much top of mind for millions of Australians.

We knew we could support good public health outcomes by helping those reliable messages find a home in our community of TikTok users in Australia. And, of course, we stepped up efforts to detect and remove medical misinformation on the platform. As founding signatories to the *Australian Code of Practice on Disinformation and Misinformation*, we have provided extensive data on the amount of content removed in Australia during 2020 and 2021 specifically related to COVID-19 misinformation. Perhaps unsurprisingly, the growth in medical misinformation removals trended alongside factors directly related to COVID-19, including the arrival of the Delta strain, government-initiated measures to manage infections such as lockdowns and travel restrictions, and the parallel rollout of the vaccination program.

In this context, TikTok during the pandemic played two main roles: as a source of entertainment, joy, learning and creativity; and a home for content we supported to ensure Australians had reliable information about COVID-19 while they were on the platform.

∼

Where does this leave news? Of course that content exists on TikTok, but that isn't the primary reason people come to us. And when you do see news and politics on the platform, it's most often not presented in a traditional way. TikTok creators do things differently.

A Dr Karl public service announcement about the importance of getting vaccinated takes off as a techno dance craze. Trending TikTok memes are remixed to end with Victorian Premier Daniel Andrews imploring the community to 'get on the beers'. An audio excerpt of Scott Morrison getting frustrated with ABC Political Editor Andrew Probyn gets endlessly reworked with increasingly bizarre and creative dramatisations. (Probyn himself wryly noted on Twitter that his unexpected rise on TikTok was 'the only bit of their dad's "work" that my kids have taken real notice of … ever'.)

These jokes will only work if you're the kind of person who consumes news, but you're probably consuming it somewhere other than TikTok. In that sense, TikTok acts less like a news platform and more like a local pub. People might joke about the news there, and some of those jokes may even influence your views, but it's not your first stop for getting up to date with the world of news content.

Perhaps one important reason TikTok is not the go-to place for news is because, unlike other platforms such as Facebook and Twitter, it does not have a chronological newsfeed. Content is delivered to the user based on their interests, not their social network or a linear timeline.

Another reason is that our community treats news differently. Creators parody—they make highlights and explainers, and provide commentary. 'News' might come in the form of everyday people explaining their lives, their circumstances, telling their own stories, with the contextual overlay of global, national or local happenings. We've seen that with COVID-19, and with other significant events like the bushfires and the 2022 floods, where the power to tell the story of a community or individual is very much in reach of anyone with a TikTok account and a phone.

Of course, we do have some great, well-known and loved Australian media voices and outlets on our platform. They're embracing our community, and it's interesting to see all manner of Australian entities doing the same, including our politicians, large institutions and broadcasters (among many). But one of the most exciting things about TikTok is that the user is in charge of their own experience. It's their own unique preferences and tastes that guide their experience, and they make that determination for themselves through their interactions while on TikTok. This means that anybody on TikTok can take off overnight and build a huge global following. Our community loves authenticity.

The fact that there are creators on TikTok who were unknown last year but who now command audiences bigger than many major news outlets, is a noteworthy phenomenon in the Australian media landscape.

∼

So, what of the future?

TikTok is focused on continuing to pursue its mission: to be a place that inspires creativity and sparks joy. It's a place where everyone is welcome. In Australia, that means supporting our amazing community of creators and partners, building trust, and demonstrating our value and commitment. We've found the best way to build trust with our community is to be clear about our expectations when it comes to content and behaviour and enforce this through our Community Guidelines. And by encouraging and welcoming authenticity.

Personally, I feel lucky to have been part of this evolution from the early days, helping to grow an unprecedented ecosystem of creators, partners, users and businesses who come to TikTok every day. So, like millions of other Australians, I will continue to be inspired watching the country's unique and creative spirit shine through on TikTok—during challenging times like the pandemic, and hopefully in easier times, too. I'm proud of the role TikTok has played in bringing Australian communities together, and of the talent it has unearthed. I'll continue to champion the voice it has provided to creative Australians who might never otherwise have made it past industry gatekeepers.

News-makers might look to us for inspiration, or as an avenue to new audiences, but for my news, I think I'll probably stick to the real Andrew Probyn—not the remix.

Editors' note: The video-based social media platform TikTok was launched in 2016. Since then, TikTok has been downloaded globally more than three billion times. This extraordinary growth was fuelled during the pandemic when downloads of the app among 15–25-year-olds grew by 180 per cent.[1] In Australia, two out of three 18–24-year-olds now use TikTok.

Staying the Course

Claire Kimball, Founder, Squiz Media, Sydney

To explain the unfolding impact of COVID on *The Squiz* over the last few years, it's best to first explain a bit about how we emerged as a small disruptor in Australia's increasingly fragmented media environment.

In the years before COVID, I set up *The Squiz Today* email newsletter, which quickly led to its accompanying short-form weekday news podcast. It was in response to four things that, as a highly engaged news consumer and communications professional, were becoming clear and, I believed, presented a strong opportunity.

The first was that, as someone whose core work was advising politicians and corporate leaders about media management, the restructuring of newsrooms and the significant reduction in journalists, camera operators and photographers meant I was running out of 'media' to 'manage'. Finding ways of communicating directly with an intended audience was not just desirable, it was necessary. Gaining those skills by setting up *The Squiz* was, in some parts, a professional development exercise. No matter whether the business was successful, the experience would help with future employment options in my chosen fields.

The second was frustration with the increasing slant mainstream sources of media were taking. Prosecuting that argument isn't the intention of this exercise, but conversations with news-savvy friends and my employers kept gravitating to *how* our media outlets were covering the big stories and issues of the day. Regularly, that was secondary to the details of *what* they were covering. Producing an agenda-free product seemed like a smart space to be in.

The third was a commercial opportunity that I observed during my time leading communications and PR at Woolworths Group. Large companies were struggling to find ways to support initiatives related to corporate social responsibility (CSR)—or environmental, social and governance (ESG), as it's known now. But surveys, including our own, showed engaged news consumers were interested in what businesses were doing about the big issues of our time. Not only have these executions provided quality content, the approach has underpinned our revenue model.

And fourth, in the unrelenting 24-hour news cycle, I saw an opportunity for products that decluttered the environment for people who don't have oodles of hours to make sense of the information coming at them.

It seemed obvious to me educated women who are time-poor were our ideal target audience. I picked them because (1) you need to know who you're trying to connect with to make a connection, and (2) as a busy woman, I have a firm appreciation of those challenges, and it's that nuance that's part of our secret sauce. There are a few other things in our approach that highlight how we made it work:

- Being clear about our target audience dictated our tone of voice—an engaging friend talking directly to you.
- We picked the time of day we knew that audience wanted to hear from us (6 a.m.) and the channels they wanted it on (email and podcast) so we could seamlessly become part of their morning routines.

- We removed the assumed knowledge in the stories we covered in a way that didn't talk down to readers/listeners.
- We made sure the stories we picked in each email and podcast served up a balanced cross-section of news and conversation starters. The difficult and complicated news stories are there each day, but the tone is never sensational. We also ensure there's something fun—and the things our audience get a thrill out of being the first to tell their friendship groups about.

The reason to lay all of that out is when 2020 rolled around, we were already three years into building trust and, importantly, habits with our audience. We did that by showing up each day, delivering what we'd promised—to be that smart friend who helps you navigate the complex issues of the day while also leaving you with something to smile about. We also built the infrastructure for them to share us with their friends, family and colleagues who were looking for an easy way to stay on top of the news.

In March 2020, our weekday *Squiz Today* newsletter and podcast reached about 150 000 Australians each month. Since then, we have seen about 55 per cent audience growth per annum, in line with our pre-COVID expectations. What that means is COVID did not knock us off course, nor did it see us surge in newsletter sign-ups and podcast listens.

On newsletter subscriptions, what we did see was a shift in how readers discovered us. Until COVID, roughly a third came from referrals, a third via paid social campaigns, and a third from 'other sources' like media mentions. When COVID hit, that mix changed in favour of reader referrals, which allowed us to reduce our spending on paid acquisition campaigns—a welcome development given the uncertain times. However, knowing what we know now about the post-2020 Facebook algorithm changes—a big issue that's made things significantly harder for small publishers—we would have kept those acquisition campaigns going while the going was good.

Our referral system allowed us to see exactly what subscribers were saying about us to their people, overwhelmingly that we were a non-sensational/punishment-free way to stay up to date with the latest developments. For us, that was validation of our content model and it gave us the confidence to stay the course with little change to our offering.

Where we have seen the biggest growth—in audience, engagement and commercial—has been in podcasting. There is no doubt we benefited from being in the right place at the right time when we started in 2018. *The Squiz Today* was the first Australian short-form morning news podcast when it launched—a claim we're proud to make given the proliferation of products based on our format, from media outlets big and small. It continues to be the market leader, and our main source of revenue.

During COVID, our host-read ads increased as marketers shifted their budgets around. Our experience was that advertisers' budgets didn't evaporate, although it's true many reduced their spending. One major shift we saw was a reallocation from outdoor campaigns to other untried channels, like podcasts. The inverse is also true: we are just one small publisher noticing the shift back to pre-COVID marketing campaign channels, sometimes making small audience buys harder to secure.

Our model is underpinned by securing and maintaining an engaged audience. We do not want to be the biggest publisher, but we do seek to have the most engaged audience. To that end, we consider ourselves more of an engagement business than a media company.

The peak-pandemic period showed us that trust and routine from our audience will hold us in good stead as we continue to push for growth. It also demonstrated that delivering growth into the future will require the same discipline that many other publishers would consider limiting. For example, we do not pepper our newsletter subscribers with emails all day because we are very protective of our subscribers' experience and our proposition to be useful, not annoying.

In the second half of 2022, *The Squiz* conducted a survey of our audience to see how they were feeling about a range of things, including engaging with the news. Almost 90 per cent of women aged 18–24 said mainstream news made them feel anxious, 60 per cent of total respondents said they had taken steps to limit their news consumption, and 12 per cent said they felt optimistic about the state of the world. They are an alarming set of numbers that mirror other major studies, but they also underline the audience-first opportunity we have identified and started to probe.

In that survey we asked our audience why, if news is so difficult to countenance, do they come to *The Squiz*. 'I consider it a form of learning. It opens my eyes to the world, helps me explain life to my children. It helps in forming a viewpoint, opens my eyes to other views, prompts me to look into and learn more about topics and current events,' said one of the 2600 respondents.

In a nutshell, that's what we aim to do—and will continue to get up at 3.30 a.m. each morning for.

The Success of Podcasting, Corona Style

Dr Norman Swan, Health Expert and ABC Broadcaster, Sydney

I'VE ALWAYS BEEN interested in pandemics. At medical school, I liked the population health and epidemiology courses; as a trainee paediatrician, I had to learn a lot about infectious diseases; and soon after I became a journalist, AIDS hit the world. I even made a TV series on plagues and civilisation for Channel 4 (UK) and SBS. But I never thought I'd ever live to see a really big one, even though it was always on the cards.

The experience of COVID-19 was surreal and scary in the early months because you knew what was going to happen next. All you had to do was turn the page of the history book because COVID-19 was behaving as plagues had done for thousands of years.

It was the Christmas and January break 2019–20, and despite being 'off work', I was still devouring my usual diet of international news and current affairs, and health data. The stories from China were alarming, and in early January I suggested to the executive producer of *RN Breakfast* that the outbreak merited a close eye. Professor Raina MacIntyre became a regular commentator on RN's *Health Report*, and we gauged the likelihood of the outbreak turning into a pandemic by getting Raina to express her concern on a scale of 1 to 10. Raina was at 9 out of 10 well before most others.

Reporting is usually episodic, one story then another on a different topic, but COVID-19 was fundamentally different. It was continuous, a blur, where it was hard to recall what happened yesterday much less a week ago. Was this just a wee wave on the ocean or the build-up to a tsunami? Either way, we were all riding it together. I was increasingly called upon for both reporting and analysis, and developed a group of sources who had experience of outbreaks and pandemics and who understood the dynamics.

A major complication was the growing number of scientific papers that were being published without the normal peer review. The argument was that all data should be out there as soon as possible because of the frightening pace of spread. That put pressure on journalists to understand what were often highly technical reports. Public fear was palpable and not helped in the early days by mixed messages from different levels of government.

As usually happens in a national crisis, Australians came to the national broadcaster as the news source they trusted. Questions and comments flooded in. You could see it in ratings for shows like *7.30*, whose audience rose hugely. People were hanging out for every fragment of information they could get.

This was the context behind Tanya Nolan, Managing Editor of Audio News and Current Affairs, calling a meeting. Tanya brought *ABC News*'s gun podcast producer Will Ockenden with her. Will's reputation preceded him, as a digital whisperer who knew what had to be done to create and sustain a high-impact podcast. What Tanya wanted was a daily podcast covering the pandemic which answered questions being sent in by the audience. Will already had the name—*Coronacast*—and the ideal duration—10 minutes. And it would need a co-host. ABC Science Editor Jonathan Webb put forward Brisbane-based science and health reporter Tegan Taylor who, although she was in the same unit as me, I'd only met a couple of times.

A few days later we were off and running, recording Sunday through Thursday for Monday to Friday 'drops' at 4 a.m. We usually made the podcast around 4 p.m. but occasionally had to come back late at night because the 'facts' had changed in the intervening hours. There wasn't much of a plan around the format except that it be conversational, with Tegan taking the more dominant hosting role, challenging me and posing the questions. Tegan's humour, lightness of touch and everyday approach became hugely popular with the audience and a cornerstone of *Coronacast*'s success. There wasn't time for in-depth planning of each episode as we were all flat-out during the day doing our reporting for other outlets. We exchanged ideas by text, then brainstormed each episode for as long as it took prior to the recording, doing last-minute fact-checking if we'd missed something.

At the beginning, Will and I did this from the Sydney studios and Tegan from the Brisbane Southbank building, but as lockdowns approached, we kitted up to do it from home. For me, that meant doing it under a towel to give it more of a studio sound. However, before that, one day in March, Will came up to my desk to tell me he was off.

'Off?'

Back to Tasmania, Hobart, where his family was. Will and his wife, a senior international digital producer at *ABC News*, had packed up their apartment and loaded their car for a sprint through Victoria to the Devonport car ferry.

I was shocked, not by the suddenness but because it felt apocalyptic. A little packed car with a young couple driving through the night, running ahead of a pandemic. My mind was filled with the final scene of *On the Beach*, based on the novel by British/Australian writer Nevil Shute, about the end of the world after a nuclear war. A radioactive cloud has steadily wiped out the world, leaving as the last vestige of humanity only Australians, who will also soon die. In that last scene, Ava Gardner is on the headland at Port Phillip Bay as she watches the submarine captained by the man she loves, played by Gregory Peck, sail back to America and certain death.

That was what flashed before me rather than the future of our little podcast. It was one of the many times I felt as if I was outside my body, observing a catastrophe in action, knowing exactly what was going to play out in the next scene. Will makes a great Gregory Peck, by the way, but Tegan never got to stand on that beach as Ava Gardner. She was locked in Queensland. Anyway, you get the metaphor.

Tegan, Will and I have made *Coronacast* from three different locations throughout the past three years and only been in the studio together three or four times. We would record separately, upload to the cloud and Will would do the rest, including a search-engine-optimised episode summary which we'd edit later in the day or evening.

More than 200 000 questions came in during the first months of the pandemic. They were like a daily, ever-changing barometer of what was on people's minds. Will in particular did a Herculean job of sifting through them and focusing us on what mattered. We hadn't realised we had walked into an information vacuum, which we were filling to some extent in a short, accessible, frequent format available when people woke up. It took weeks for us to realise the audience had become huge and that a careless word from me in jest (like suggesting how bad Perth drivers are) would end up being mentioned in a press conference with a state premier.

One of the toughest moments was when news started to emerge about the blood-clotting complications of the AZ vaccine. The federal government came out strongly saying it wasn't a problem, and implying that the Scandinavians and Germans were panicking and there was no biological reason this could be happening. We knew differently, and the question was whether we should tell it how it was—namely that the sources were highly credible, the science showed there was a biological plausibility, and thankfully it was rare. We made the decision that what counts most in a crisis is trust, and we would be abusing that trust from our audience if we pulled our punches when it counted. Soon after, I got a text from a Coalition

THE SUCCESS OF PODCASTING, CORONA STYLE

MP telling me I was personally responsible for vaccine hesitancy in Australia.

Coronacast reflects the way journalism and reporting responds during a time of crisis. You need to have journalists who are specialists and understand the territory. You can't always rely on outside experts when there's time pressure. You need to be able to read a scientific paper and make your own judgement. It was also high-risk early on because a fact one day would be demolished the next, and we had a firm policy to correct mistakes explicitly in the next podcast. The ABC was in a prime position to mount something as ambitious as *Coronacast* because it had invested in science journalism and broadcasting for over fifty years. I could do what I did not because of anything special about me but by having decades of experience under my belt. Tegan, too, had been in the business long enough to know what she was doing, and Will was battle-hardened and highly skilled. Teams are the recipe for success, but in the end, it's all for nothing without an audience.

What *Coronacast* has proven is the power of the podcasting platform. It has enabled us to regularly, reliably and intimately connect with audiences on a difficult subject. Perhaps for me, the most gratifying audience has been young people who are news- and information-hungry, concerned to do the right thing but not necessarily consumers of traditional news outlets. The most common feedback we get from all our audiences is a thank you for calming them with information. No better compliment.

The Virus: Live, Daily Programming

Jeremy Fernandez, Presenter, *ABC News*, Sydney

'So, MATE, YOU know that coronavirus? They've just announced a case in Melbourne.'

I'll never forget receiving that phone call from my editor on the ABC News Channel, Michael Reid, on 25 January 2020. It's one of those news events about which you remember exactly where you were when you first heard it.

Like most Australians, I largely trusted that the country's scientific and medical experts and public health system would keep us relatively shielded, as they had for countless prior outbreaks of infectious disease—including the ones most of us had never heard of. Of course, epidemiologists had been warning of this exact scenario for decades, but it seemed after years of enduring the hardships and anxiety precipitated by natural disasters, political turmoil, the GFC and other infectious diseases, surely we had earned a break by simply wishing hard enough for better times.

At the same time, I was uneasy about the sense of Aussie exceptionalism in believing our geographic isolation would somehow mitigate the risks of human-to-human coronavirus transmission here. It reminded me of Australia's belated acceptance that the GFC thirteen years earlier was indeed inescapably and devastatingly global.

THE VIRUS: LIVE, DAILY PROGRAMMING

By late January 2020, it was becoming clear this new coronavirus was running faster than even the best experts could in chasing it. 'It's not looking good,' Michael said. 'I think it's time to really ramp up our coverage. Would you be up for hosting a weekly show about it?' Of course I was.

The pitching process for new television shows can be remarkably varied. Sometimes they're detailed proposals spanning months of elevator pitches, treatments, talent scouting, budget reviews and pilots. In this case, we stepped straight out of the elevator and onto the studio floor, resigning ourselves to learning as we went, just like the rest of the world.

There was certainly no pilot. The budget was minimal—our task of producing a new show would be accommodated by 'existing capacity', as they say. There wasn't even time to workshop a catchy name for the program. We simply called it *The Virus*. It would become the ABC's one-stop show for all things COVID-19, sometimes with up to a million views per week via broadcast television, live stream and social media.

The premise of *The Virus* was simple: to have experts answer questions about the outbreak, tackle disinformation, and highlight science-based analysis for a lay audience. In other words, we formulated the program based on what the audience was telling us they needed, then worked backwards from there.

I've spent nearly half my career in rolling news environments. There's sometimes a temptation in newsrooms to get too clever and develop new angles to advance coverage. It can leave the audience short-changed on understanding and potentially alienated and disengaged. One of our main aims with *The Virus*, therefore, was to slow down the news cycle and make space for 'dumb questions', which can prompt the most useful insights.

It was also about striking the right tone—ensuring we didn't worsen people's anxiety by dramatising current events, but also being careful to accurately depict what was going on in the health system, and what it meant for those who rely on it, particularly the vulnerable. In reality, as the show's presenter, I also wasn't equipped to get too clever because I simply didn't know enough. Neither did the experts, especially early in the pandemic.

Unlike the highly produced half-hour nightly news bulletins many of us grew-up with, rolling news allows the audience to witness the news-gathering process live to air. It's both thrilling and treacherous when you have a story developing as quickly as the COVID-19 pandemic, with public health rulings and advice changing several times a day. This was a new disease whose transmissibility and effects were still poorly understood. Even the most expansive research was merely indicative, not definitive. More study was always needed to improve the reliability of results and findings.

We broadcast our first episode on 7 February 2020. Within weeks, the outbreak of COVID-19 was dominating almost entire news programs. The cases of the *Diamond Princess*, *Ruby Princess*, aged-care outbreaks, hotel clusters, lockdowns and face-mask shortages would become bywords for chaos, loss and dysfunction.

Real-time newsgathering and broadcasting also relayed the oscillating public health declarations about surface-to-surface transmission versus airborne transmission, isolation periods, quarantine mandates and vaccine effectiveness. We had two choices: to either withhold confusing communications from the authorities, or broadcast them with a caveat that things could change with a moment's notice.

It compelled people to see the news in a different way—to accept that the facts could become more nuanced, affirmed or outdated within days, or hours. This was clearly fatiguing to many. It also generated distrust in government, systems and even science at the worst possible time. Fear and distrust materialised in the questions submitted to our live-streamed Q&A segments on *The Virus*.

'If a teacher is infected at work, is the school legally responsible?'

'Can people be forced to test for COVID-19, if they refuse?'

'Where are our test kits being supplied from? I'm worried about all the false negatives/positives.'

'Will spritzing tea-tree oil around me kill the COVID?'

'When can I book my next cruise?'

Inconsistently applied rules and advice were also problematic, even if they were unavoidable at times. Masks or no masks? Lockdowns in the west but not the east? How could you possibly short-cut the vaccine approvals process and still guarantee its safety to the same degree? How come 'the best health advice' invoked by premiers differed from state to state? These excellent questions were among the hundreds of thousands people sent us. The answers would depend on which state you were in, what time you were asking the question, who you were asking and how hawkish they were feeling at the time.

An uplifting surprise, however, was that in seeking the advice of general practitioners, epidemiologists, virologists, immunologists, vaccinologists and social scientists, we were inadvertently turning our consultant experts into household names in their own right. I know many people who can now identify their favourite—and most trusted—expert. Their media manner and consistency ended up being critical in helping re-establish the trust that had eroded. You might not have believed the prime minister, but you'd certainly sit up and take notice of the likes of Mary-Louise McLaws.

We continued with our weekly show until well into the third year, only finishing up when all borders were open, all restrictions were lifted, all daily press conferences were stopped and the audience was steadily turning its attention elsewhere. Sustained periods of questions and nebulous answers ultimately proved wearying. It was clear that after nearly three years of crisis reporting, many among our audience had had enough of COVID and were craving the need to return to 'normal' life. We had to acknowledge this alongside the understanding that the pandemic was far from over—it is still a considerable factor in the nation's wellbeing and prosperity.

The media, along with governments, systems and public infrastructure, did, at times, find themselves outrun by the virus itself. In the quest to offer reassurance, however, we saw numerous examples of bravado—from cruise ships and borders, to aged-care homes and hotel quarantine. Therein lies a critical lesson on trust: it shatters at the whiff of pretence.

One of my former bosses had a mantra reminding us always to be honest with the audience, even when we didn't know what was going on. People are sophisticated enough to understand that in live news-gathering, you never really have all the answers. However, the next best thing—a diversity of informed analysis and opinion—goes some way to maintaining credibility.

Many members of our newsrooms were profoundly affected by the events going on around us. We, too, cared for the sick, got locked out of seeing family in other states, missed milestone events, endured lockdowns alone, got sick, and watched loved ones die fearful and sometimes alone. There's no tonic for that. There's no way to make that loss and grief undo itself.

I am proud of our little weekly show, of the questions it answered, the information it presented and the comfort it offered. I suspect that, in the years to come, storytelling about this incomparable time will help soothe psychological wounds that are barely visible but unquestionably present.

The News Media Bargaining Code

Bill Grueskin, Columbia Journalism School, New York

More than a dozen years ago, the US Federal Trade Commission sponsored an ominously titled workshop, 'How Will Journalism Survive the Internet Age?' The gathering included a number of dignitaries, but the marquee name was one familiar around the world: Rupert Murdoch. He used the stage to rail against his digital competitors:

> Our customers are smart enough to know that you don't get something for nothing. That goes for some of our friends online, too. And yet there are those who think they have a right to take our news content and use it for their own purposes without contributing a penny to its production.[1]

It took Murdoch more than a decade before he got his way with some of his online 'friends'—not in the United States, where he had become a citizen, but in his native Australia. While COVID-19 was raging throughout the world, media companies, including Murdoch's News Corp, helped persuade the Australian Parliament to pass a law that is now compelling Facebook and Google to pay substantial sums—sometimes in the tens of millions of dollars—to news organisations whose headlines frequently appear on platforms' pages.

The legislation, known as the News Media Bargaining Code, enabled Australian news organisations to extract more than $200 million within the first year. As a result, the public Australian Broadcasting Corporation placed at least fifty new journalists in under-served parts of the country, while the McPherson Media Group, which publishes such papers as the *Yarrawonga Chronicle* and the *Deniliquin Pastoral Times*, expected tech money to fund up to 30 per cent of editorial salaries. Monica Attard, a journalism professor in Sydney, said at the time she couldn't persuade many students to take internships because it was so easy for them to land full-time jobs, and that change coincided with the gusher of code money: 'I swear to God, I have not seen it like this in twenty years.'

Australia looks like a success story to those who've long yearned to force Big Tech to prop up suffering newsrooms. But it's a murky deal, with critical details guarded like they're nuclear launch codes.

If you want to know how much money the platforms have paid to news organisations, you're out of luck. If you want to learn whether newsrooms are spending that money to bolster journalism, rather than pad executives' salaries, you're out of luck. I've been talking to newsroom managers most of my adult life, and I've never seen a group so reticent to share details of anything related to their business—thanks to iron-clad secrecy agreements insisted upon by the tech companies.

The riches aren't spread equally. SBS, one of Australia's two major public broadcasters, got money from Google but was inexplicably shut out by Facebook. Croakey Health Media, a not-for-profit site that provides valuable information on COVID and Indigenous medical issues, received nothing from either company. In the words of one Sydney media executive, 'It's like a brown paper bag gets stuffed with money, is shoved across the table, and then the platforms can say, "Now just shut the fuck up."'

Still, Australia has managed to force tech companies to do something they've long fought: provide financial support to the news business under government pressure. For years, the platforms have managed to forestall such regulations by donating to noble-sounding initiatives and mounting extensive PR and lobbying efforts. But Australia found a workaround for that, thanks to a wily competition czar named Rod Sims and the heavily concentrated nature of the country's media market, among other factors.

At the heart of the code is the argument Murdoch made at the workshop back in 2009, that digital companies profit when they surface journalists' headlines and news snippets. And yes, it's true that if you search on either platform for 'Ukraine' or 'COVID', you'll see a slew of links and bits from news organisations.

Tech's retort has been twofold. First, journalists need to figure out how to benefit from the visitors sent their way, and it's not Silicon Valley's problem if they can't turn that traffic into meaningful advertising or subscription revenue. And second, as Google notes, a newsroom that wants to withhold its content from search can easily do so.

For years, Australia's media companies have suffered from the same trends plaguing newsrooms around the world: declining ad revenue, shrinking staff, shuttering publications. Into the breach stepped the Australian Competition and Consumer Commission (ACCC), which regulates everything from false advertising to grocery prices. After months of study and reams of submissions from news organisations and citizens, the ACCC determined what journalists already knew: American tech companies were vacuuming up hundreds of millions of ad dollars that once went to news companies. And there was a gaping imbalance of power between the tech and journalism businesses.

To push their argument, media companies were happy to trumpet their own weakness. In mid-2020, News Corp Australia complained that 'digital platforms have become a default conduit for many consumers', and added that the snippets that accompany headlines in search 'are more likely to result in a user remaining within the digital platform, and not reading the publisher's full content'.

The efforts made strange bedfellows, with the progressive *Guardian*, which established a beachhead in Australia in 2013, on largely the same side as Murdoch. 'We had to make sure we were part of this; we could not afford to be excluded,' Lenore Taylor, editor of the *Guardian Australia*, told me. Her colleague, Managing Director Dan Stinton, added that '*The Guardian*, News Corp, Nine, anyone that runs a traditional advertising business, is both dependent on Google and Facebook for traffic and competes with them in the digital advertising market. We're dependent on these platforms to give us more than half our traffic'.

Newsrooms found a powerful ally in Sims, the longest-serving chair of the ACCC. As he said in a recent interview, 'While Facebook and Google need journalism, they don't need any particular media company.' Meanwhile, he noted, 'all the media companies need Facebook and Google. What they've done is intermediate themselves between journalists and people who want to view the content, for their own financial advantage, obviously'. Sims, an economist by training, goes on to say, 'Many market failures you don't have to address. But this one is really important because it affects journalism, and therefore it affects society. Journalism is the classic public good: we all benefit from it.'

The Australian solution was clever. Rather than try to tax the tech companies, or impose a fee based on copyright infringement, regulators decided to let media companies bargain with Google and Facebook—but if Facebook or Google refused to negotiate, they could face stiff penalties. And if a news organisation couldn't work out a deal, it could appeal to the Australian treasurer, who could 'designate' one of the tech companies, setting in motion an unusual process that could end with each company submitting offers, and an arbitrator accepting one of them. So if, say, *The Sydney Morning Herald* thought it deserved $5 million a year while Google thought it should pay $10 000, the arbitrator would have to choose one of those two numbers. No compromise, no splitting the difference.

Tech companies went on the attack. Google threatened to withdraw its search engine from the country altogether, and it surfaced pop-ups with a yellow sign warning, 'The way Aussies use Google is at risk. Your search experience will be hurt by new regulation.' Facebook went further, pulling all news off its platform for Australians. But it bungled the job so badly that it also managed to remove public service information about bushfires and COVID-19, and even support pages for victims of sexual violence. 'It was the worst calculation they could ever have done,' recalls Bruce Ellen, general manager of the weekly *Latrobe Valley Express* and leader of a regional newspaper association. 'It galvanised not just the media but the general public.'

The backlash was immediate, in Australia and beyond. Tech had lost the PR battle even as it did extract some important concessions, particularly in pushing back against sharing information about its algorithms and data. 'We've stood up to the digital giants,' said then Australian treasurer Josh Frydenberg. 'We didn't budge. We want the rules of the digital world to replicate the rules of the physical world.'

Andrew Jaspan, a Melbourne journalist with a long career in Australia and the United Kingdom, had a more acerbic take: The tech companies, he said, made 'a Faustian pact to just get it off the table. If they didn't put the fire out here, it could spread across the world. So they wanted to shut it down and get these people off their backs'.

Tech and media started negotiating even before the legislation was passed. Google agreed to pay Nine Entertainment Co. a reported $30 million or more annually for five years; one source estimates the total value of Nine's deal with the two tech companies at more than $50 million a year. The tech companies also agreed to pay News Corp Australia at least $70 million as part of a larger arrangement that includes advertising and other business, according to people with knowledge of the terms. The UK's *PressGazette* estimated *The Guardian*'s take at around $5 million.

Smaller publishers snagged their own deals. Country Press Australia, a trade group that represents about 160 regional newspapers, got permission from the government to bargain collectively with both platforms. I've reviewed their Google contract, which is loaded with confidentiality requirements, and it showed that the company will pay local newspapers roughly $31 000 to $62 000 per year, depending on their size and how many stories they generate.

Sims estimates the total paid out since the code was passed at more than $200 million, based on what publishers have told him. Neither Facebook nor Google has been 'designated' by the treasurer, so no-one has gone to arbitration. But since there is no public accounting of who's getting what, news organisations can't be sure how much they should ask for or expect. There is no published set of metrics—such as page views or number of reporters—that tech companies use to determine what they'll pay.

Google says its payments are based on scale. The company looks at 'how many news articles' sites are producing, says Richard Gingras, vice-president for news, as well as their 'existing audiences, the size of the market they are serving'.

Such ambiguity leads to 'massive information asymmetry,' says Stinton of *The Guardian*. 'I've done lots of commercial deals in media over the last twenty years, and it's very rare that you come to a position of negotiation with virtually no information as to the basis for determining payment.'

Misha Ketchell is editor of *The Conversation*, a popular non-profit site founded in 2011 that teams up with academics to address topics in the news. He's one of the few newsroom managers willing to talk publicly about how his negotiations went. Both Facebook and Google started with a 'charm offensive,' he says, 'lots of discussion about user values and ways they can help us and how they're experts, blah, blah, blah'. But when it came time to talk numbers, he went 'into the discussion knowing absolutely nothing ... no sense of where the market is, where it's anchored, what previous deals were worth'.

Google eventually offered *The Conversation* enough to fund one to two journalists on a staff of around thirty. 'We were like, is that a lot? Is that a little? I don't know, because the whole thing's entirely opaque. There's no anchoring in the market, there's no history,' says Ketchell. He cut his deal, then heard some similarly sized news organisations did better, so he tried to renegotiate—and got a modest increase.

Tough as that was, it went much better than Facebook negotiations. Those talks also started off on an upbeat note, Ketchell remembers: 'They said, "We love *The Conversation*, we see you're really valuable." And then, at a certain point, they just said, "No, we're not going to offer you anything." No explanation. It's literally just the calculation that "We've paid enough people now, it should be enough".'

Most curious of all, Facebook stiffed SBS, a large public broadcaster that operates TV, radio and digital operations throughout Australia, geared largely to the country's multilingual and multicultural audiences. SBS depends heavily on government funding, as does the ABC, which did pull off a deal with Facebook. So why has SBS gotten nothing? Managing Director James Taylor has no idea. As he told a parliamentary committee last year, 'Facebook has not provided us with clarity as to their rationale for not entering into an arrangement with us ... We're still a little in the dark.'

Facebook did not respond when asked to address individual cases. Gina Murphy, a spokesperson, did state in an email that since Facebook hasn't been designated, 'the law does not apply to Meta'. She also pointed to a three-year, $15 million investment in Australian journalism, separate from the code.

When Google and Facebook do deals, they're careful to ensure they aren't framed as payment for links or clicks. To get around that, they've often positioned these as compensation for participating in the *Facebook News* section, or something called *Google News Showcase*, which is a collection of three-story modules that news site editors assemble, often twice a day.

The showcase is an odd vehicle. Many Australians have never heard of it. Publishers give mixed reviews on the amount of traffic it drives. A Google spokesperson says the showcase isn't so much about page views but 'driving engagement and deepening that relationship with readers'. But for small news organisations, posting multiple stories a day, seven days a week is a big ask. 'That's just an impossible task, unless you're putting absolute rubbish on your website,' says Matt Nicholls, who edits—and writes most of the stories for—the *Cape York Weekly* in Queensland. 'We don't work in that sort of cycle. I've noticed other papers are putting up stories that they would never, ever put in their print publication.'

For companies that did a deal, though, *Google News Showcase* is a minor inconvenience, given the cash flowing in. It 'is far from ideal', says Stinton of *The Guardian*. 'But it was a pragmatic outcome. We were satisfied with the headline number that we got from them. And so we went, "Okay, well, we can do it on these terms."' Taylor, *The Guardian* editor, says tech funds have 'made a huge, huge difference to our newsroom', enabling the site to double its audio offerings and bolster coverage beyond Australia's large metro areas.

Latrobe Valley Express's Ellen said there had to be some mechanism for payment. Several papers 'wanted to approach on the basis that they should give us money for nothing. That was never going to happen. There's got to be commercial negotiation where they get benefit, we get benefit'. In the case of Facebook, that meant an 'innovation fund' for his members, of undisclosed length and amount.

There's no doubt the threat of arbitration, where a newsroom could demand an extraordinarily high number, forced tech companies to negotiate. And they will push back hard if they are forced into designation and arbitration. Facebook is so concerned that, according to several newsroom managers, the company told them their deal will have to be renegotiated if they're designated. A Facebook representative did not respond to a request for comment.

Alternative scenarios for diverting money from tech to news have their own problems. Nieman Lab's Joshua Benton, among others, has advocated a tax on Big Tech's revenue. That would generate billions of dollars. It would also raise the difficult question of how that money would be disbursed, and who would decide. Having a government agency or committee picking winners and losers among news organisations would raise difficult issues around fairness and independence.

And some worry that the new revenue will build a troubling dependency for news organisations on tech dollars. 'What if Google decides it's a bad deal for them?' asks Nicholls. 'If you need Google funding to prop up your journalism, to keep your journalists employed, that's not sustainable.'

Bill Grueskin was invited by the Judith Neilson Institute in Sydney to investigate the News Media Bargaining Code. This essay is an excerpt from his final report, published in 2022 in the Columbia Journalism Review. *He was assisted by researcher Tess Orrick.*

PART VI
A PLACE IN THE COMMUNITY

Digital Transformation: ABC

Gaven Morris, Managing Director, Bastion Transform, Sydney

It turns out nothing inspires viral content more than a virus. On 17 March 2020, *ABC News* published online a story with the humble headline 'Charting the COVID-19 Spread in Australia'. It was a simple data feature with eight charts and some explanatory text. But like the times that followed, the article would redefine our understanding of several fundamentals.

At the time, it was less than a week after the WHO had declared a global pandemic. Scenes of people scrapping over toilet paper in supermarkets faded from newsroom agendas as unfathomable announcements stole the headlines. In a sequence of days, the federal government banned big public gatherings, suspended international travel, and barred non-Australians from entering the nation. Meanwhile, the *Ruby Princess* was steaming towards Sydney, about to disperse hundreds of COVID-positive passengers onto the streets and unleash 'superspreader' into the vernacular. The public was shocked and confused, and desperate for accurate information.

Inside the ABC's Ultimo, Sydney headquarters, a small team of journalists, creators, coders and—respectfully—geeks called the Digital Story Innovations team brainstormed how best to help. They reckoned there was a lack of official detail on COVID cases and their impact on hospitalisations and deaths. With prescience and patience, they manually gathered federal, state and territory data and, as its then editor Stephen Hutcheon puts it, 'smooshed it into a spreadsheet to generate live graphs and charts, which updated automatically as the data in the spreadsheet was changed'.

Within a week of going live, the COVID tracker story had 4.5 million page views. Every day, more people clicked and came back more often to spend more time studying the detail. As more sources became available, more charts were added, the feeds were automated and, like the disease it was tracking, the whole thing grew and spread in unprecedented ways.

By the time the final digest stopped being fed live data in September 2022, *ABC News* readers had spent 134 million engaged minutes with the story across thirty-five million page views. It is a record for any online story published by the ABC, and possibly for any story in contemporary Australian journalism.

Editors and newsroom leaders look back across those initial wild, whirling days of the pandemic and reflect on the redemption of the audience response. People turned to the media in big numbers. Facts mattered. Trusted journalism was restored to its rightful place, informing and empowering citizens in their hour of great need. After years of social media supremacy, the unfashionable mainstream media was back.

But in the haze of this Indian summer of popularity, some important truths were obscured. Efforts like those of the Digital Story Innovations team were not a child of COVID but conceived in days of famine. Journalism's leanest years were just a few seasons before, after multinational platforms channelled away the rivers of gold as the power balance of editorial choice and user behaviour shifted from the publishers and broadcasters to every one of us. Consumers would decide where, when and how they would get their information. A carefully curated summary of yesterday printed on a page was quaint, and being told by the television or radio station what time 'the news' happened was quizzical. For many, the news media became irrelevant and ignorable.

Some news organisations were late to feel the digital climate changing, while others snoozed on the warm sand of yesterday's revenue as, silently, the audience tide went out. Some newsrooms saw the clouds gathering and felt the winds turn. None responded perfectly but, as a different storm approached, those on a transforming path were readier to respond.

At *ABC News*, it had been years of difficult and painful change. During the early 2010s, we could glimpse the dusk of the grand broadcast days. Long accustomed as we were to welcoming more than a million viewers to flagship television news programs, it became clear ratings were sliding steadily. The demographic profile of people watching reached towards the age of retirement, then slipped past it. Lovingly loyal radio audiences set off to explore the inviting frontiers of podcasts, and with the arrival of something called an Amazon Echo, on-demand audio news was on its way.

Some attempts to halt the decline were, in hindsight, predictably futile. At *ABC News*, for a while we pursued a strategy to engage younger or new viewers with the nightly 7 p.m. news, exploring a different story mix, more energetic rundowns, fresher studio presentations and dynamic production techniques. In a bid to be more contemporary, *7.30* lost its '*Report*', and the sentimental themes of *AM*, *The World Today* and *PM* were replaced with more contemporary tunes.

Whether these changes were enticing or misguided, younger audiences were never coming to scheduled broadcast news. By younger, think people aged in their thirties and forties for whom news on a schedule was an oxymoron. We were all online, anytime, and it was hardly surprising habits had shifted. Because for each of the previous three or four generations, the technology and media that would dominate their news and information consumption as adults were not in any home the day they were born. For my grandparents, it was true of the radio. My parents, the TV. The World Wide Web was not the apple of Steve Jobs's eye when I was born. And now, digital content delivered via mobiles was dominant, a little over a decade after anyone had held an iPhone.

～

In the month before the COVID-19 tracker story was launched, the mystically named coronavirus was starting to growl. What was a Wuhan wet market anyway? Nations around the world began to report cases. Still, at the beginning of February, just a dozen had been identified on Australia's shores.

At the time, newsrooms were hoping to catch their breath as the smoke of the devastating Black Summer bushfires across vast parts of the country was just starting to lift. In Australia's east, as Dorothea Mackellar foretold us, the drought was about to turn to flooding rains. Everyone was exhausted, in a way I'd never seen in newsrooms before. In Western Australia, however, the February dragon wasn't done yet. A blaze that came to be known as the Wooroloo bushfire roared to life.

ABC News cadet reporter Evelyn Manfield, with all the journalism talent imaginable but less than a year's experience, was diverted from covering the first scenes of long COVID testing queues, to the hills above Perth. It may have been her first bushfire assignment, but she was armed with a digital native's sharpest weapon: a mobile phone. As part of her cadetship, Evelyn had been trained in MOJO—mobile journalism, essentially the professional use of a phone and customised accessories to produce broadcast-quality coverage. Now she was using it in real time, pumping out photos, social posts, audio and television live crosses. What once required different cameras, a satellite dish, bright lights, a sound recordist and editing machines conceivably could be produced with nimble fingers and a handheld device.

Much of Wooroloo was destroyed in the flames. The fire authorities escorted a small group of journalists into the apocalyptic scene for a very brief look at the smouldering remains. As the television teams set their tripods and mounted their cameras, plugged in their monikered mics, and rehearsed their lines for the evening's pieces to camera, Evelyn flicked on her phone and, with her instincts alight, took us all for a tour live on the ABC News Channel. It was compelling and heartbreaking live TV. As she drifted around the scene, we all saw what she saw for the first time, and sensitively, she narrated the detail of destroyed homes and personal loss.

Little did we comprehend that within weeks, these talents and skills, this type of coverage and this use of technology, would become essential weapons in the pandemic arsenal. As communities locked down and the health and wellbeing of newsroom teams began requiring a very different approach to news-gathering, we found we had unwittingly done essential preparation.

Like the Digital Story Innovations team, MOJO was not a recent epiphany. It had been mapped into the *ABC News* strategy for several years, a plan hatched in those foreboding years when the brew of slashed budgets, departing audiences and rapid technological change boiled on what was often called the 'burning platform'. The craft was no longer what journalists knew it to be. News was now instantly available from anywhere in the world and from the richest variety of sources. News was our most personal moments or interesting insights shared with a vast crowd of strangers. News was raw video as events happened and crafted, narrow narratives whispered personally into our ears. Why rely on a media mogul or an entitled editor to dictate our views? Everyone was empowered, enfranchised and engaged, often without the need for intermediaries.

Then a few things happened.

Clickbait cheated our intelligence for cash. Facebook secretly sold the data of our intimate interactions to the cheapest bidder. Despots and terrorists transmitted their crimes live and unfiltered.

Free speech spread lies and denied democracy. Twitter descended into a nasty nest of bots, bigots and bullshitters. Fake news. Brexit. Bolsonaro. Trump. At the risk of preaching like that Billy Joel song, it turned out that like all revolutions, there were casualties and, increasingly, the truth was dying.

The good news was journalism was still a thing. If the digital-first Lorelei that had seduced newsrooms, luring them towards the rocks, had proved a disaster, then maybe the answer to fighting fake news was quality journalism. In an *ABC News* strategy launched in 2016, we called it an Equal Digital Life. We'd seek to focus on the very best storytelling and content produced for radio and television, and make it equally valuable and equally accessible to contemporary audiences wherever they sought their news—in tune with their habits, on their terms.

If the outstanding reporting produced by, say, the world-class *Four Corners* team could reach the generations of Australians who never watched free-to-air television, we might find a solution. If local ABC newsrooms provided compelling and accurate coverage, not just for traditional viewers at 7 p.m. and for listeners at the top of the hour on AM radio, but across the day on live channels, online and on social media, the public would be better informed, and the news ecosystem better off. If Australia's best audio journalism teams could produce great podcasts and on-demand news, win-win. And if specialist digital skills and new techniques could be developed and deployed using emerging technology to create industry-best story experiences, we might grow, not shrink.

If the lesson from clickbait and fake news was that people valued valuable things, we'd make our digital content the highest quality it could be and loyal to ninety years of ABC excellence.

Could that work? One big problem. Lower budgets meant fewer staff to feed many more outlets. Cuts came, some to cherished broadcast brands like *Lateline* and the 7.45 a.m. radio news. Radio programming was reduced, current affairs seasons shortened. Newsrooms were asked to produce fewer stories fit for different audiences.

Once the government got its fiscal bounty, small strategic investments were placed: the Digital Story Innovations team; an expanded, multiplatform ABC News Investigations team; more specialist rounds; resourcing to produce original broadcast and digital stories in areas like Indigenous, disability, education, environment and technology, business and finance, Asia-Pacific and sport; and audio on-demand resources, increased digital skills in current affairs, MOJO, new technology and expertise, and many, many thousands of hours of digital training across all teams.

Outside of the news division, there were also vital investments in reporting resources and equipment for the ABC's incredible rural and regional teams, and improvements to ABC iView, ABC Listen and, crucially, though invisible to audiences, visionary work to improve the data networks and the digital capability of the ABC's communication infrastructure.

All these things were necessary. But we had no idea how much so until the COVID wave hit.

∼

It's been argued the biggest winner from the ABC's coronavirus journey was Alan Kohler's home library. Alan's an interesting cat, but who knew the breadth and scale of his reading interests until he began broadcasting from home during Melbourne's mammoth lockdown. Each night, Alan would pluck a few tomes off his shelf and lovingly position them on his desk as an adornment to his vital finance and economic insights. From Lou Reed to PG Wodehouse, Alan Greenspan to Tina Fey, each book seemed to carry a topical clue to how Alan was feeling about the world.

It is baffling that Senate Estimates has not interrogated the literary largesse that publishers across the nation must have bestowed upon Alan during this time. A title teetering on the top of Kohler's stack would surely move stock. 'Don't ask, don't tell,' was my approach to this potential public scandal.

Much more notable was that Alan and his wife Deb had turned their hand to producing the segment, shooting it on a mobile and sending it in via an app. A phone, a laptop, a trusty conscript and a library of intrigue made it possible to keep this prime-time staple on air.

Never before had *ABC News* anchored network broadcasts in the living spaces and spare rooms of our most prominent presenters. We got to know Fran Kelly's pooch Buster and Paul Kennedy's penchant for sporting memorabilia. We learned of a locked-down world from within the four confining walls of our foreign correspondents' flats. Even the mighty Leigh Sales beamed into our living rooms from hers. These feats had been logistically inconceivable just weeks before. The speed and skill with which the ABC's technical experts equipped and enabled journalists to work from home was a marvel.

Within the first three weeks of March 2020, the ABC's tireless IT team had acquired more than 300 additional laptops to enable staff to work from home, while eighty were deployed in the field. More than twenty of the ABC's most gifted editors had remote, high-resolution editing capability installed, and 1000 additional virtual private network connections were switched on—by working with the telcos, the capability was quickly lifted to a virtually unlimited capacity.

Obviously, the ABC was not alone in pivoting to working in different ways. All other media, emergency services, health services and public services scaled new mountains as the pandemic's grip took hold. Everyone adapted to 'distributed working'. But not without enormous stress and disruption.

ABC News colleagues in Victoria enduring the world's longest COVID lockdown were incredibly resilient, but like their fellow citizens, at times some struggled or buckled under the strain. The public was angry, and often their ire was directed at media teams out reporting on the pandemic. In Sydney, too, ABC teams were sometimes a target. In the city's south-west, where huge COVID outbreaks and hard borders divided communities, coverage was extraordinarily testing. It meant mobile journalism, smaller teams and reporters working on their own, people working from home and never venturing into skeleton-staff offices, became normal. It wasn't easy, but for the first time, it was broadly embraced.

The *ABC News* director's office shifted to a half-room shack in my suburban backyard. Across countless Zoom and Teams meetings, *ABC News* teams shaped every aspect of their workflows with an incredible spirit to serve the public need for information. The acceleration of newsroom innovation was now at warp speed, and the willingness of people to adapt and respond is something I'll admire forever.

Suddenly, staff asked for MOJO capability so they could report from their neighbourhoods. *Foreign Correspondent* rolled through a season with barely a plane boarded. Studio programs like *Q+A* and *The Drum* kept vital contextual conversations going without people face to face. ABC News Channel and News Radio, operations that are leanly staffed but require immense collaboration to stay on air, found a way to keep providing a critical lifeline to information and those blockbuster live press conferences, even as many staff fell ill or self-isolated and backup was unavailable.

During that time—and hopefully ongoing—the bond of trust between the Australian public and the ABC grew to unprecedented levels. Broadcast audiences continued to ebb and flow around the key moments of the pandemic but remained stronger than they had been in many years. The ABC's digital audiences broke new records. Across 2021, the average weekly audience for ABC news on the web and on the app, as much as can be measured, was 57 per cent above 2019 levels, and even up on the big records set in 2020. Perhaps much more important than the scale of the audience was the appreciation of the service. In a vast landscape of social misinformation, conspiracy theories and political spin, 78 per cent of Australians said they trusted *ABC News*, and it recorded an 88 per cent approval score for the quality of its content.

Before the *ABC News* team set out on its Equal Digital Life journey, the picture was very different. Five years before, the monthly usage of *ABC News* on digital was under a quarter of Australians; now, it was more than half. Then, engagement measures like the time people spent with stories or how often they returned to the service were the worst among any established digital brand; now, they far exceeded all comparable media. Before, too few younger Australians consumed *ABC News*; now, it was one of the biggest touchpoints for people aged under fifty across all ABC content. Once, the audience was very male; now it was majority female.

∼

As the COVID curve began to flatten, a young journalist in the newsroom made a fascinating observation to me. He said: 'There's every chance I've already covered the biggest story of my career.' Whether the planet's climate, China, the global economy or some future scourge proves him wrong remains to be seen, but as the long shadow of the pandemic begins to recede, there are some profound dilemmas for the industry to resolve.

Teams are more productive than ever before, but how can newsrooms be sustainable coming out of the pandemic? Is fostering great teamwork and creative collaboration as valuable as people embracing autonomous and distributed work practices? Digital connections and devices have created opportunities for a much greater diversity of voices, but have we lost the intimacy and intensity of studio interviews? Technology has made news-gathering so much more convenient and accessible, but are the craft skills that produced outstanding content being lost as a result? Has our access to global stories further diminished the value of local perspectives?

There is a risk that what was once news avoidance—modern audiences finding the efforts of journalists much less important in the rhythms of their lives—now becomes news fatigue. Perhaps people, having appreciated the pandemic performance of journalists, will tune out again in a desire for levity after the gravity.

There are also profound truths. All those millions of minutes of engagement with the COVID tracker story, as well as audience appreciation for coronavirus coverage, show facts really matter, journalism is vital, and trust is more valuable than it has ever been.

But the path to relevance for newsrooms is not hoping the next grave event or seismic shift brings audiences home. It takes graft in the leaner times, which may soon enough return. Difficult decisions made with strategic loyalty to audience needs, not newsroom habits and desires, will ensure journalism is ready for the next great wave, whatever and whenever it is.

Multicultural Messaging: SBS

Mandi Wicks, Director of News and Current Affairs, *SBS News*, Sydney

IN JANUARY 2020, the SBS Mandarin team was hard at work reporting on a mystery virus which had surfaced in the Chinese city of Wuhan in Hubei Province. The Chinese Australian community was becoming increasingly concerned about friends and family as images emerged of residents being 'locked down' and in some cases being 'locked in' their homes. Through radio, online and social media, the team reported on the unfolding crisis as the death toll from COVID-19 began to rise. SBS journalists spoke to health experts, shared the stories of those locked down in China, and gave the community in Australia a voice to share their fears for their loved ones.

In February, panic gripped the Italian Australian community as the virus surfaced in the northern region of Lombardy and eleven municipalities were locked down. Both the SBS Mandarin and Italian teams were in overdrive, trying to separate fact from fiction as the crisis escalated, all the while managing their own despair on hearing that loved ones had passed away from this highly infectious virus.

It was only a matter of time before COVID-19 arrived on Australian shores and all our lives were impacted by daily, sometimes hourly health messages and 'stay at home' orders. Australia closed its borders to all residents and non-residents on 19 March 2020. Soon, events were cancelled, restrictions placed on visiting aged-care facilities, 4-square-metre space limits enforced in restaurants (to be replaced by the closure of most venues), restrictions applied to outdoor gatherings including weddings and funerals, and all non-elective surgery suspended. The states and territories started to go it alone, with some closing schools, and parents required to homeschool for the first time.

To the 5.5 million Australians who speak a language other than English at home,[1] SBS is an essential service. The Special Broadcasting Service was established in 1975 to inform migrants in their language of origin about the federal government's new health policy, now known as Medicare. Today, SBS provides Australian news and information in more than sixty languages on radio and online via digital television and social media. When COVID-19 began to impact Australia, SBS realised the enormity of the task ahead. The changes were relentless and often difficult to understand. Each SBS language service was bolstered to increase output, and the phones started ringing with stakeholders and community organisations urgently seeking COVID-19 information in languages other than English to share with their communities.

While each SBS language service was already providing critical updates and health information, it became clear a one-stop shop was needed. On 26 March, only a week after the border closures, the SBS Multilingual Coronavirus portal was launched in sixty-three languages, to curate all COVID-19 content in one easily shareable destination. A link was included on federal government websites and within the official COVID-19 app. Other organisations linked to the portal from their websites and shared the link via emails and social media. There were more than six million unique visitors to SBS language websites in April 2020, and twelve million audio plays and podcast downloads during the first wave in March and April.

The portal provided key information through articles, fact sheets, podcasts, videos and infographics, informing communities about social distancing, mask-wearing, PCR and rapid antigen testing, mental health services, domestic violence services and the vaccination program. It dispelled misinformation and publicised COVID-related scams, which were increasing.

As our lives became increasingly unrecognisable, SBS engaged with different organisations, listening deeply to understand the challenges and determine where we might add value, including bespoke messaging for those with underlying health conditions such as asthma, cancer and dementia. It had never been more important to provide accurate and timely information. Using trusted voices and faces was critical, including doctors and nurses from each community, as well as faith leaders and teachers.

The language services also provided targeted messaging during key events such as Ramadan, Diwali and Lunar New Year to reinforce stay-at-home messaging. This was ever-changing and often included technical terms which didn't easily translate into other languages—words like 'household', which some took to mean 'family' and so continued to gather in large groups.

SBS championed the community heroes supporting the sick, the ageing and those providing food hampers to the homeless and to international students who'd lost their part-time jobs and weren't eligible for the JobKeeper payment program. As restrictions became lockdowns and isolation turned to loneliness, SBS Radio gave audiences access to health experts in their preferred languages via talkback, and provided companionship by encouraging audiences to share moments of joy, acts of kindness, and tips for staying connected with family and friends.

The pandemic brought out the best and the worst in people, with some communities isolated further by racism and discrimination as the virus spread through suburbs, cities and across state borders. When nine public housing towers in Melbourne were locked down in July 2020, with more than 3000 residents confined to their units, SBS Radio printed and distributed flyers via food hampers, providing information in seventeen languages about how residents could stay informed.

SBS's work to serve communities during the pandemic was noted in a federal parliamentary motion on 14 May 2020. Sterling Griff, then an independent South Australian senator, moved that the Senate 'praises the invaluable work of SBS across its radio, television and online platforms keeping culturally and linguistically diverse communities in Australia informed with vital COVID-19–related news and information to help protect themselves and their communities in challenging circumstances'.

SBS also conducted research with community stakeholders in June 2020 on the impacts of COVID-19, finding:

- of those surveyed, 83 per cent were aware of the SBS Multilingual Coronavirus portal, with 96 per cent of those finding it of value
- more than 80 per cent of stakeholders felt SBS had been serving Australian communities 'well' or 'very well' during COVID-19
- stakeholders valued the portal because it was in languages other than English, the information was easily digestible, and they knew the information could be trusted.[2]

During COVID, we were reminded that information must be accessible. Depending on where migrants have come from and their circumstances, they may not read or write in their preferred language, and so audio, video and infographics can be more effective than text articles. Speed of messaging was also key to combatting the misinformation and disinformation that plagued social media during the vaccination rollout. To counter this, SBS provided live interpretations of the daily media conferences in twelve languages.

Fast-forward to 2022, and more than twenty million unique visitors have utilised the SBS Multilingual Coronavirus portal, including eleven million in Australia. The other nine million have listened, read or watched internationally, often in countries with poor health messaging about the pandemic.

Building on the lessons we learnt during COVID-19, SBS launched an additional portal in 2022 called Mind Your Health. This portal provides wellbeing support, especially for the many facing mental health issues. Also in 2022, SBS launched television news services in Arabic and Mandarin—the only weeknight free-to-air news services produced in Arabic and Mandarin by Australia-based journalists, and with a primary focus on Australian news.

And with Australia preparing for a referendum on an Indigenous Voice to Parliament, SBS has translated the Uluru Statement from the Heart into more than eighty languages, including twenty Aboriginal languages from communities in the Northern Territory and Western Australia. These initiatives are focused on breaking down barriers by informing and engaging, in turn assisting to increase social cohesion in Australia.

More than half of all Australians are first- or second-generation migrants. Between the 2016 Census and the next survey in 2021, the number of people speaking a language other than English at home increased by 800 000 to more than 5.5 million. The SBS Settlement Guide, in thirty languages, helps new migrants navigate life in Australia, focusing on everyday topics such as how to call an ambulance, enrol to vote and prepare for a severe storm or flood. COVID-19 has only reinforced how inclusion is critical.

Providing information in languages other than English has been lifesaving during the pandemic. It has increased connection within and between communities, and created a shared understanding of the challenges faced and a greater sense of belonging in Australia for those separated for years from loved ones around the world.

Community Connections: NITV

A Q&A with Tanya Denning-Orman, Director of Indigenous Content, SBS, Sydney

Q [Gavin Fang]: COVID had a significant impact on Indigenous communities. In remote areas this was felt even more. What is your assessment of how the media covered this story and what was it like as an Indigenous broadcaster?
A: The mainstream media responded to COVID with an approach aimed at the broader population. Straight away we could see that First Nations communities were not considered in the reporting. There was a lot of concern from us, from me, because of the media organisation I'm a part of, but also as a First Nations person, about the immediate fear that was being escalated by the media at that time and how that would impact our community. Our community is among the most vulnerable in our society, how we live and our approach to community living is often different, so there was a real concern that the approach of the mainstream media would not be helpful.

I knew it was important that we, as a First Nations media organisation, took a calm approach and worked closely with community health organisations to ensure we were delivering and reporting news in a way that considered our communities and the impact on them.

Q: What were the issues you grappled with to tell this story properly?
A: You've got to consider us as a community of 300-odd nations and clan groups with different information needs across different regional, remote and urban settings. NITV is a very small media player. However, noting that our population is so vulnerable, there was a lot of expectation on our shoulders to make sure we got it right. We didn't want to escalate fear by just repeating what some politicians or health professionals were saying. They were often giving blanket information to the broader community. To be fair, it was unfolding quickly for them as well, but the impact of media misinformation, especially in First Nations communities, was felt heavily.

So, for us, we really needed to try to ensure we worked with health organisations at ground level in [the] community. But as a small outlet, getting that right was hugely challenging.

My team is made up of First Nations people as well, so, at that early phase of COVID, we were dealing with our own personal stresses, including, in some cases, worrying about our own families that we were separated from. We overcame that by working hand in hand with the remote media sector and the First Nations Media Australia organisation. They are right at the community level, so through open communication with them in different communities we could decipher and then deliver correct information as soon as possible.

We also worked with Aboriginal health organisations at a local level to ensure they were getting the information as well. There was a lot on us; we didn't grow as a business, we just had to do things differently.

Q: What lessons did you learn and what lessons should the broader media take on board about reporting on Indigenous issues, especially in an emergency, from the way NITV covered the pandemic?
A: In the media, there are still a lot of assumptions and a mass approach to getting and delivering information. But it's really

important for reporters and newsrooms to consider the audience that receives that information. For me, working with local organisations and local health providers, no matter what the group, First Nations or multicultural group, when there is an unfolding emergency situation, is really important. As a journalist or as a media organisation, you should always be fostering these relationships, not just when a situation is unfolding.

First Nations media organisations are a voice of the community, so we need to reflect them, and we need to look like them. Our communities are not the same as everyday Australians. We have different approaches to family groups, community situations, different languages, our connections are different and what country means to us is very different as well. So it is really important to consider all of that when reporting on an emergency, whether that is a pandemic or a state emergency or any other issue.

My advice to journalists is question harder where you are getting information from, ensure you are holding people accountable to give you correct information, put yourself in the shoes of others so you are actually asking the right questions, make sure you are not creating hysteria and that you are being that trusted voice.

And if there's one thing the pandemic really taught us, it is to keep working hand in hand with communities. Don't take those relationships for granted because you need those relationships to do your job effectively.

Rural and Regional Media

A Q&A with Gabrielle Chan, Rural and Regional Editor, *The Guardian*, Harden

Q [Tracey Kirkland]: Do you think rural and regional journalists have faced unique challenges under COVID compared to the metropolitan media?
A: Yes. The first one, and probably the biggest one, was the shutdown of newspapers during that time. A lot of regional papers suspended or transitioned to digital and never came back, [moving] to an aggregated model where there's a local story to click on and that pulls you into an aggregated news site that offers you more national stories. It was the hollowing out of an already disrupted model.

The other thing that jumps to mind is the daily pressers when premiers came to regional areas. They were hard going for regional journalists. I remember a presser in Newcastle when a local journo wanted to ask about regional statistics but could not get a question in because of the forwardness of the daily press pack—the fact that most of them were confident state journos and the regional journos had less say, less connection to the media staffers. The whole thing exacerbated the lack of information that was happening in regional areas.

We started *The Guardian*'s Rural Network in September 2021 and one of our biggest stories has been the difference between the way regional and metro areas have been treated in terms of pandemic rules. That really hit a nerve with people, I think, and you saw that reflected in the media coverage. We just could not get access.

One of the other challenges for regional journalists was the issues around borders where the journos could not range over state borders because of lockdown rules. So the same old resource–money problems and the practicalities of covering the pandemic within the rule structures were the most fundamental issues.

There were also different pots of money starting to come on board for regional papers during the pandemic: the federal government's PING [Public Interest News Gathering] fund, some funding released through the Walkleys, some ACM [Australian Community Media] papers transitioned to digital or suspended for a while, which all happened at the same time as the arrival of Google and Facebook money. So there was a ripple of businesses opening and closing. That's been a nightmare for a lot of regional journos who are just trying to get some consistency and stability.

Also, a number of reports have exposed the pay levels of regional journos who aren't overly secure anyway. All of that was happening at the same time as lots of social issues in regional areas as a result of the pandemic, and as a result of people moving out of cities, house prices going up, so there was a lot of pressure on regional journos and job losses as well. And I don't think it's stopped yet. I think it will keep going for the next few years.

Q: What, then, will be the ongoing challenges for rural and regional media as the pandemic stretches on?
A: I think resources will continue to be the biggest issue for regional journalism. Who pays for it? Local papers are really important to the social glue of a town, having a common information source so it doesn't run on rumour or conjecture or someone's feelings on Facebook. Papers are fundamental to the way a town sees itself and how it projects out. A good regional journo can lead that conversation up in an uplifting way or down in a Trumpian way. So it matters.

I don't think there's anyone out there saying regional media doesn't matter, but the question is, well, if it matters, who funds it? How do we get a financial model for it? The metros are fine. They have a supply of staff and have a strong business model. In rural and regional media, the business models are unsettled.

After going through the Valley of Death in the first couple of years of the pandemic, I'm broadly optimistic about coming out the other side and seeing really good regional journalists who are being supported, but it remains the biggest challenge in media. Even though it acts as a training ground for young journalists, it's more than that. It is a really, really important job.

Q: What can be learned from the past few years to ensure rural and regional journalists and journalism remain robust and sustainable? What are the opportunities?

A: Citizen journalists have played a pretty important role in the last couple of years. I think we assumed, after the disruption in journalism in the last decade or two, that there would be these trained, out-of-work journalists sitting around waiting for someone to commission them once a month, or something like that. But you can't survive on that. You've got to pay the rent. Yes, there are some good freelance journos out there, but it's a very hard gig to keep rolling that over, chasing the cheques. So I think we could better utilise knowledge on the ground. There is some quite substantial value that people can add, even though they might not be fully trained journalists.

So maybe a model for the future would be to support citizens who want to chase local stories. That requires training and it requires the infrastructure that maybe some metro media organisations can bring, because it does require more liaising and more editing when you are working with someone who hasn't been trained as a journalist. So there could be an aspect of nurturing talent in regions.

Also, let's not be afraid to reinvent the wheel. All of these models are changing and there's lots of different media outlets that are now choosing different ways to do things.

I think one of the warnings is regional media is ripe for takeover. We ignore regional media to our peril. If we get a rich mogul who wants to colonise the media landscape, it would be very easy to do if governments and communities take their eye off the ball as to how important regional media is. It's an exciting landscape in that any model might fly if it gets some funding and backing, but it's also dangerous for the same reason. That's what I would have my eye on, ensuring the regional media landscape stays healthy and diverse.

A Tale of Two Cities: A Divided Sydney

Tu Le, Lawyer and Community Advocate, Marrickville Legal Centre, Sydney

'MAKE SURE YOUR doors and windows are closed tonight for when they spray disinfectant over the neighbourhood,' my mum said to me coolly.

It was the first week of March 2020 and Australia was slowly coming to terms with COVID on our doorstep. My mum was sharing the latest news she had seen circulating in her various group chats. Forwarded messages on WhatsApp, Viber and Facebook Messenger, reminiscent of early 2000s chain emails, are her trusted news source. At the time, no-one I knew had caught COVID yet, but it seemed misinformation and disinformation about the pandemic were already spreading faster than the virus.

By mid-March, I had already postponed my wedding, scheduled for early April. My partner also made the tough decision to permanently close his restaurant in Cabramatta. We could not fathom celebrating our big day with less than the 400 expected guests, and we anticipated the business would not be able to survive a pandemic. I was foolishly hopeful we would be married by the end of 2020. Little did I know, sixteen months and five rescheduled wedding dates later, I would be on the phone with my mum as she tried to instruct me on how to brew a home remedy to protect against COVID. She had seen the recipe on Facebook; it contained a lot of garlic.

While watching the NSW premier's 11 a.m. press conference became the daily norm for some, many people whose first language was not English, like my mum and her friends, weren't relying on traditional media for their coverage of all things COVID. Even the live interpretation by SBS Vietnamese was not enough incentive for her to switch to mainstream media. My mum found the daily presser too exhausting and overwhelming to watch every day. Like a growing number of the population born overseas, she preferred getting her updates from social media.

My work with a local network of multicultural communities in the Fairfield LGA during this time revealed this was a sentiment shared across many community groups. SBS provided COVID information in more than sixty languages, but although it seemed that a lot of resources went into interpreting and translating COVID updates, many questioned their efficacy, particularly as health messages and orders were constantly changing. The mixed messages and translation lag caused a lot of confusion. It seemed as if, by the time the message reached ethnic communities, the information was already changing.

Addressing the language barrier was only a start; it wasn't the only solution. Trust, rather than translation, was the real problem. It is difficult to have confidence in institutions that regularly seek to demonise you.

Everyone felt the sting of the COVID pandemic in their lives, but there is no denying it impacted our lives differently depending on which part of Sydney you lived in. Images of seemingly crowded eastern suburbs beaches splashed all over the media offended many western Sydney residents who could not even enjoy outdoor exercise as basketball rings were removed from local parks. COVID exposed these deep-rooted inequalities.

The inconsistent treatment of residents across the city left those living in western and south-western Sydney LGAs, and subjected to harsh lockdown rules, feeling frustrated yet mostly unsurprised. The longstanding stigma associated with being a 'westie' has often been reinforced by the negative narratives about the region with racist and classist undertones. The sense of postcode prejudice was further exacerbated during the pandemic.

Rather than building trust and engaging meaningfully with the diverse communities in western Sydney, extra police officers were sent in to patrol the area. Every day when I left the house for my one hour of exercise, I would see the police on the streets. The occasional soldier I encountered on my daily walks looked wildly out of place in the suburbs.

The media coverage and government response to the COVID outbreak deepened the wedge between the 'haves' and the 'have nots' across Sydney. Limited representation in politics and mainstream media revealed just how out of touch these pillars of democracy truly are with a significant percentage of the population. It showed the lack of connection and empathy with local communities in western Sydney who felt misunderstood and unfairly targeted.

The majority of people were not deliberately trying to break the rules, but it seemed like our decision-makers just could not understand and appropriately address the underlying circumstances leading to COVID clusters sprouting in the suburbs. In reality, the largely working-class population in the west did not have the luxury of working from home. Many employees in insecure, low-wage jobs were deemed essential workers and had no option but to risk their health and that of their families on a daily basis to maintain their livelihoods and keep the economy afloat. A lot of families also live in multigenerational households, which increased the risk and rate of transmission.

Instead of supporting the already vulnerable communities in the 'LGAs of concern', we were punished with curfews and had to wait hours in line for mandatory testing every three days. Yet when I think back on the news coverage at the time, it was incidents like the funeral at Rookwood Cemetery, where the gathered mourners were stopped by police, and the arrest of a maskless man at Bass Hill Plaza, that made headlines. The spotlight on the few people doing the wrong thing meant that residents in western and south-western Sydney were generally typecast as law-breakers who either did not understand the rules or simply ignored them.

Despite the challenges faced during lockdown, community groups and civil society organisations rallied to help each other and fill the void left by an inadequate government response. Local organisations packed and distributed food hampers and supplies. They checked in on families and delivered extra electronic devices to schoolchildren who shared a single computer in their household. A focus on these positive stories would have lessened the hurt permeating these communities, and local spokespeople would not have had to constantly defend their communities to rebut the negative portrayal of western Sydney

The media's treatment of people hailing from the western side of that pseudoscientific, socioeconomic indicator known as the 'Red Rooster line', most of whom are from ethnically diverse communities, most likely reflects the lack of diversity within mass media outlets. The 2020 report *Who Gets to Tell Australian Stories?* by Media Diversity Australia found that 75 per cent of presenters, commentators and reporters have an Anglo-Celtic background, while only 6 per cent have an Indigenous or non-European background.[1] It is therefore unsurprising that news coverage during the lockdowns continued to misrepresent those in the 'ethnic west', who already faced pre-pandemic marginalisation. It might also explain why people continue to abandon traditional media, as they lost trust in these outlets to represent their perspectives and voices accurately and authentically in news content.

While we may be encouraged by the noticeable increase in diverse faces reporting news across some channels, like the ABC and SBS, there is still a long way to go until newsrooms are truly reflective of our culturally and linguistically diverse population. Addressing the lack of representation in the media will change the way our stories are framed, and can lead to greater inclusion and belonging, no matter which side of the metaphorical line you live on.

Generation COVID: Storytelling for Gen Z

Sarah Curnow, Senior Reporter, and Ben Knight, Senior Reporter, *ABC News*, Melbourne

On sunday, 15 March 2020, the ABC directed all employees who could work away from the office to stay home for the next seven days. Within a fortnight, only skeleton staff were left onsite. By the end of the following week, most of the country had been shut down. Every aspect of Australians' lives—domestic, social, study, work—was up-ended, and no-one had any idea when, or if, it would change back.

It might be hard to recall now, but by late April most of us were in shell shock, none more so than teenagers. Kids who had been exploring their freedom, finding their first financial independence, going out with friends, staying out a bit later, even starting to do stuff their parents might not approve of, were suddenly locked back in their homes with no end in sight. Their lives became more screen-based than ever. All their schooling, their social networks and their recreation was conducted through laptops and phones.

That gave us an idea. If we could get a wide-enough representative group of gen Zers to film their lives and record their thoughts over an extended period, we could build a first draft of history. Was COVID scarring a generation of kids at a crucial time in their lives? ABC Investigations boss Jo Puccini asked us to find out. First-person storytelling wasn't new to us, but this was an experiment in asking members of the community to film themselves and their own personal reflections in big-enough numbers to enable us to paint a diverse and collective picture. We called it 'Generation COVID'.[1]

First, we needed to find them. We looked at Australian Bureau of Statistics and other data to work out what range of backgrounds and attributes to include in our group. None of it surprised us. We needed to find students, apprentices, workers and out-of-workers. We needed migrants and children of migrants; the Indigenous and non-Indigenous; kids who lived with their families and those who didn't; people without wealth behind them and others from economically secure backgrounds; people who'd experienced anxiety or depression, drug use or family dissolution, and people who hadn't; people whose gender or sexual orientation was from across the continuum.

We rang youth groups, local councils and dozens of organisations across the country to find young people who might want to be involved. We did call-outs on various social platforms. Triple J's *Hack* program was an incredibly valuable conduit thanks to its credibility with the cohort we were reaching out to. It turned out there were dozens and dozens of young people who wanted to be involved. They brought with them the range of experiences and backgrounds that our research told us was a true picture of Australians aged 16–25 in 2020.

Each participant had to film their own video diary entries each week for us. They could do it more often if they liked—that was up to them. Many did; some filmed in spurts, with long stretches when they went silent. Regardless, we stayed in touch. We gave them some pointers, and steered them to talk about whatever was most important to them, and tell us what they were feeling. But we were totally in their hands as to what they delivered. What started coming in was incredible—sometimes thoughtful, sometimes angry or fearful, occasionally funny.

GENERATION COVID: STORYTELLING FOR GEN Z

It was a fascinating and poignant experience getting to know some of these young people through their diary entries, watching their moods go up and down, swinging from hope to despair and back again. The overriding theme was uncertainty. And often the reality of that uncertainty was awful.

'The anxiety I felt was through the roof, and I never really felt it before to this extent. I also felt this childlike feeling of wanting everything to go back to the way it was, which I knew wasn't an option.' Bailey Hohn, 21, Brisbane

'I was just so sad and tired all the time. I was getting headaches every day, almost sort of like I couldn't shake these feelings of hopelessness and worthlessness. I went from working like 30-hour weeks, and spending every spare moment I had out with friends, to doing absolutely nothing and just being cooped up in the house. It took a global pandemic for me to realise I'm the most boring person ever, and desperately, desperately need to find a hobby.' Erin Brown, 20, Wyong

They were endlessly trying to adapt to their new reality.

'I feel like COVID-19 kind of gave me time to myself—time to work on my reading, my gaming, my projects and everything—so that I kind of had those three keeping me sane, keeping me intact, not thinking about what's happening out there, but just focusing on what I have right now right here and with me.' Robin Njobo, 22, Perth

But perhaps what was most surprising was the constant search for the silver lining.

'I would like to think that this has made everyone reflect on how much time they spend at work, how much time they spend travelling to and from work. I know that speaking to people in the community while I've gone for a walk ... they've realised how little time they spend with their children. I would like to think that we come out of this kind of more appreciative people and less stressed for unnecessary reasons. Like if you are stuck in traffic, if you miss the green light [it] doesn't really matter.' Jacqui Fahey, 24, Sydney

While we were working on this project, we found out that Susan Rossell and her team at Swinburne University were researching the same issue, but on a far bigger scale. Their early results were shocking. Depression scores for 18–25-year-olds were almost four times higher than usual for that age group. The anxiety and stress scores were nearly as bad.

To economists, the worry was disrupting that critical window between late school and a first adult job, the one that leads to every job you have until retirement. Young people who don't successfully make that transition feel the impact throughout their working lives. And this group was well aware of it.

'The pandemic has raised questions about whether I can find work at all, let alone graduate ... I just got an email today saying that I didn't get the job for one of [my applications]. So I'm probably assuming I didn't get the other one either. So, you know what? The rat race to finding a job continues on.' Alain Nguyen, 22, Melbourne

'I started my résumé which is really important that I get out soon, because I've got just under three weeks to find a new salon to take me on as an apprentice. Otherwise my apprenticeship will be put on hold ... I feel like I'm already going a little bit insane because I have no job and I can't work. I feel like if I can't even do the course work, I'm just gonna feel even more stuck.' Syrenite Hewson, 18, Warrnambool

And we noticed something else about COVID which threatened to affect some of our contributors for many years. In taking away their agency, it both stunted their developing maturity and simultaneously forced them to grow up fast. For instance, COVID was the first event in many of their lives that made them engage politically. Some were angrier at our elected representatives than they were at the virus itself.

'The federal government kind of went through and said how great Centrelink would be to support people who have been displaced and affected by coronavirus. And a lot of people didn't see any of it. We didn't see any of it.' Bailey Hohn, 21, Brisbane

What emerged from this project was the overarching importance of mental health—being aware of it and taking care of it.

'I think the whole experience has kind of solidified for me the idea that although we do have the power to steer ourselves as individuals in the direction that we choose, we can never have complete control over everything. And that's okay. I'm actually grateful that I experienced this at the beginning of my 20s because I think that's set me up for a better future. I think it's made my generation a bit more resilient and a bit more understanding of the world.' Emma Haddy, 22, Adelaide

The stories had huge engagement (over 800 000 views). But of most importance to us was our primary target audience: gen Z. More than any other, that cohort has lost trust and interest in mainstream media in recent years. To reach them, we needed to deliver something that was patently as much *for* them as it was by them and about them.

Our digital team—Clare Blumer and Jack Fisher—researched extensively to craft something that in structure, content and design would appeal to gen Z, right down to the colour palette, pace, and the relationship between text, sound and image. The end result looked and felt different to anything else published on the ABC website. It delivered our reporting in a way that showed an awareness of how media content and consumption has been defined by gen Z. In other words, it signalled respect for our subjects.

That approach is a critical component of the suite of skills journalists need to develop if we are to re-establish trust with the public. In an era when audiences are increasingly media-savvy, we need to show a reciprocal understanding and appreciation of them.

PART VII
GOING GLOBAL

Tom Hanks, Trump's America and COVID Journalism

Damien Cave, Australian Bureau Chief, *The New York Times*, Sydney

O N 12 MARCH 2020, two people in my orbit caught COVID, in two very different countries, leading to stories in *The New York Times* that revealed far more than I realised at the time. I use the term 'orbit' very loosely here—the first person was Tom Hanks. I don't know Tom (obviously) but as *The Times*'s bureau chief in Sydney, it fell to me to write a story about when he and his wife, Rita Wilson, caught COVID while filming a movie in Australia.

Looking back, I played it relatively light. 'Tom Hanks had a cold, or so he thought,' I wrote, 'slight fever, body aches, chills, the usual.' I went on to note that while those symptoms would not have been enough to guarantee coronavirus testing in the United States, where testing was scarce, in Australia, testing was accessible, common and free. That contrast—an organised, if overzealous Australia and an ad-hoc, divided America—would frame many of the COVID stories I wrote over the next two years. Almost immediately in 2020, it was clear to me the pandemic would be a test of societal values and government competence in country after country. The United States, where I grew up, was slow off the mark and would struggle to catch up.

What I failed to recognise, at least early on, was that America's failures would also affect my own colleagues and the way COVID journalism evolved in the United States. On 24 March, I discovered the first hint of what was to come when Jessica Lustig, the managing editor of *The New York Times Magazine*, and a creative and efficient force in the newsroom, wrote a harrowing account of seeing her husband fall ill with COVID in New York. She described twelve days of hell. Her husband, 'a tall, robust 56-year-old who regularly goes—who regularly went—on five-hour bike rides from our Brooklyn neighborhood to Jamaica Bay in Queens and back,' she wrote, 'has been lying on his back, staring at the ceiling, or curled on his side, wearing the same pajama bottoms for days because it is too hard to change out of them, too hard to stay that long on his feet, too cold outside the sheets and blankets he huddles beneath.'

She had become his isolation nurse, his caretaker, delivering food and medicine to his bedroom door while also trying to deal with an overwhelmed medical system. And she was far from the only one to be pulled into the story we were all trying to cover.

Other friends and colleagues from *The Times* and other American outlets went down with the illness too. At least one beloved former *Times* editor, Alan Finder, died from COVID, in late March. Facebook later pointed me to a friend whom I used to brainstorm with about digital transformation—a young father—who ended up in a hospital bed. Others endured one case, then another, or a bout of long COVID that kept them from returning to five-day work weeks.

Slowly, I began to see the gap widen between my experience and that of my American colleagues. In the United States, COVID was not just something journalists covered; it was not just a topic that led, as it did in Australia, to tough (sometimes ridiculous) questions at news conferences and the elevation of public health experts who favoured the most frightening outbreak projections. It was something that journalists lived, up close and personal. It was traumatic. It was deadly. It was life-affirming. It was confusing.

American journalism was shaped by its surroundings, a mess of what-me-worry individualism, trauma, sadness, imperfect data, local variation, alarm and competition. When the media in America responded to the urgent dynamics of COVID, our scribbling tribe (including those who we don't see as members) did so in much the same way America seems to respond to so many things these days: with intense, extreme division.

On one side were those who favoured 'doing their own research', often by creating or relying on YouTube videos or experts of dubious distinction. A former *Times* colleague, Alex Berenson, became famous for claiming COVID posed no serious risk. Some of my own Trump-voting relatives insisted I watch the lengthy diatribes of a delusional doctor spreading fear about vaccines. I also recall arguing with a very left-leaning friend in San Francisco who—relying on teacher-driven online discussions centred around fear—insisted that children were better served by staying out of school for an entire school year rather than enduring the minimal risk of COVID in classrooms.

But even as these extreme elements created their own do-it-yourself media echo chambers, serious journalism counterpunched and rose to the occasion. The desperate need for clarity and credibility in the United States eventually produced a series of very strong examples of how to cover an evolving, uncertain global health disaster. Several journalists—Ed Yong at *The Atlantic*, for example, and Zeynep Tufecki, a sociologist who now writes for *The Times*'s 'Opinion' section—broke through the emotional, irrational fog of polarisation and built large audiences for clear-headed, logical, explanatory journalism that went above and beyond what public health coverage used to be in American journalism.

At *The Times*, too, my colleagues found new ways to approach the challenge. In January 2020, our graphics team published a tracking page that presented coronavirus data from China. Over time, that grew into a global tracking page that pulled together cases, deaths and vaccine rates from across the world, showing trend lines of growth or reversals of fortune. At its peak, seventy-seven staff members worked on the project, including twenty-nine reporters, eleven data managers, and nine people doing design and software development. Several other outlets, including *The Economist* and *The Guardian*, produced their own COVID trackers—an example of global data journalism that will likely inspire similar efforts on other issues.

All of these innovations deserve recognition for beginning to capture the paradox of the pandemic. COVID was in many ways a unifier—the virus travelled across the world bringing the same symptoms to rich and poor, regardless of location and language spoken. And yet, the impacts of COVID varied because the responses varied. The virus has acted, from the start, like a magnifying glass, letting journalists zero in on the essence of a country—how people relate to government, to science, to risk, to fear, and ultimately, to each other.

Did our coverage ultimately match that moment? I'm still not sure any of us in the media, in Australia or America, have done as much of that deep thinking and reporting as we could have or should have. In that early COVID story I wrote about Tom Hanks, I described COVID as 'an international stress test for public health performance', but now, I think of it as a test of national cohesion and human interaction.

Have Australian journalists truly and deeply explored what held the country together, and what led to a cruel degree of shut-the-door-keep-everyone-out overreach? Have media companies examined when it makes sense to send a political journalist to cover a health crisis, and when to send a reporter with more of a background in science or sociology?

Looking north, too, have journalists in America done enough to step back and look at how their experience of the virus shaped the way they covered it? Or the way their social circles or culture—or the many cultures of America—shaped the country's reaction to the threat?

Perhaps the question is even broader. Have journalists in any country done enough to climb out of their own pot of boiling water to see COVID and their country's response with proper perspective?

I suspect not.

'Not much more to it than a one-day-at-a-time approach, no?' Tom Hanks wrote in a Twitter post about his COVID diagnosis on 12 March 2020. Exactly, Tom. And with COVID journalism, maybe that's been the problem all along.

Chasing Truth and Facing Jail

Drew Ambrose, International Correspondent and Investigative Journalist, Al Jazeera, Kuala Lumpur

I CLAMBERED EXHAUSTED INTO our van. The local media pack rapidly snapped photos of my six Al Jazeera colleagues and I as we left police headquarters in Malaysia's capital, Kuala Lumpur. For the first time in my career, I had become part of the story instead of reporting on it.

Over several tense hours, each of us had been interrogated as part of a criminal investigation launched by the authorities after our documentary revealed the country's shocking treatment of migrant workers during the COVID-19 lockdown. While bustling cities across Asia became ghost towns during the pandemic due to government-imposed movement-control orders, Malaysia's approach was controversial because the authorities erected barbed wire and barricades around neighbourhoods home largely to migrants.

This foreign workforce of seven million people, consisting of legal and illegal labourers from poorer countries like Bangladesh, Nepal and Indonesia, do Malaysia's dirtiest, most dangerous, low-paid jobs. The Malaysian Government promised no action would be taken against them if they presented for testing, even if undocumented, but this guarantee was not upheld. Instead, the authorities raided these vulnerable communities, arresting more than 2000 migrants with or without visas. They were chained together, loaded into trucks and taken to overcrowded, unhygienic detention centres where many contracted COVID-19.

For almost a decade, I had worked as a roving international correspondent for Al Jazeera's award-winning program *101 East*, based in the network's office in Malaysia. Our team has a proven track record in investigating human rights issues, corruption and government misconduct across Asia. We recognised highlighting the mistreatment of Malaysia's migrants during the lockdown was in the public interest.

Cameraman Craig Hansen and I filmed raids the authorities didn't want the public to see for our documentary *Locked up in Malaysia's Lockdown*. While our press passes enabled us to travel freely throughout a city in tight lockdown, these raids were often conducted a long way from public view, behind barricades. We used our knowledge of the streets to find places where we could film arrests. The *101 East* team also cultivated sources living in the fortified neighbourhoods who provided us with phone footage of the raids that we could verify.

Our story featured previously unheard testimony of migrants detained in the controversial incursions, who accused the authorities of misconduct. I also interviewed abandoned foreign workers in slums who depended on charities for their survival. Despite intense pressure from the authorities during the police interviews, we refused to disclose the identities of the anonymous whistleblowers featured in our documentary.

A number of government leaders rejected or ignored repeated requests for interviews, and international media were barred from attending government press conferences. This reporting environment was a dramatic contrast to when I'd covered the avian influenza epidemic in Indonesia fifteen years earlier. Back then, journalists could freely interview government officials and film bird-culling operations.

Despite the barriers, we presented the Malaysian Government viewpoint by featuring comments from the defence minister, recorded in a press conference with local state media. While Malaysian officials sought to avoid scrutiny, I interviewed local frontliners who were concerned the country's punitive approach was driving migrant workers into hiding, deterring them from seeking testing and treatment out of fear of deportation. The documentary also featured Malaysian employers who questioned the cleanliness of foreign workers and their presence in the country. This balanced story showed all societal perspectives on a controversial pandemic response.

Locked up in Malaysia's Lockdown garnered two million views online and sparked a torrent of government criticism. The authorities accused us of sedition, defamation and violation of the country's *Communications and Multimedia Act*, offences which carry jail terms. Al Jazeera's Malaysian bureau and two local satellite companies that broadcast the news channel were raided by the police. Two computers were seized from our premises. Along with other Al Jazeera staff, I was doxxed, and subjected to death threats and other sustained forms of vicious trolling on social media platforms after the program was broadcast. Mysterious callers contacted my former colleagues, asking where I lived, and I was forced to go into hiding.

The most chilling response was the extensive manhunt for the Bangladeshi whistleblower who spoke out in our documentary about the mistreatment of migrant workers. Malaysia is a signatory to a number of international human rights declarations which protect freedom of speech. Rayhan Kabir should have been able to express his opinion but instead was treated like a fugitive and paraded in handcuffs on national media. After having his work permit revoked, and being held for days in a detention centre, Rayhan was deported back to Bangladesh and blacklisted from returning.

Despite no evidence of criminal misconduct, the government also refused to renew the work visas of myself and another Australian producer, forcing us to leave Malaysia.

During this whole saga, Malaysian Government representatives refused repeated requests to be interviewed live on *Al Jazeera News* to state their position. Nor did they produce a shred of evidence to refute the facts reported in the documentary. A number of international and local human rights groups defended the veracity of the program based on their own work throughout Malaysia.

Al Jazeera is not the only news organisation to have been the target of the Malaysian Government's crackdown on media freedom. Local reporters continually suffer harassment, are subject to police investigations, and in some cases are charged with offences that carry jail terms. In the first year of the pandemic, when our own reporting came under attack, Malaysia suffered the worst drop of any country on the World Press Freedom Index.

Scrutiny of the pandemic emergency in Asia has been a major blind spot for all media organisations. According to one study in *Australian Journalism Review*, COVID-19's impact on South-East Asia only accounted for 5 per cent of international pandemic coverage by Australian media outlets.[1] Closed borders, few foreign correspondents and the growing death toll in Western nations contributed to poor reporting of what was happening in Asia.

Neglecting the region during this critical time has meant that the actions of authorities have not been given the necessary examination to ensure human rights are being upheld. It has shown how, in many countries across Asia, weak legislation and legal loopholes have allowed some governments—even those in so-called democracies—to exploit this health emergency to crack down on critics and curtail independent reporting. Amid this climate, it has never been more important for foreign correspondents to ensure they are fulfilling their watchdog role and standing in solidarity with their local counterparts, who often bear the brunt of government restrictions on media freedom.

The ostracising, cruelty and discrimination migrant workers in Malaysia were subjected to during the lockdown is a disturbing example of a government increasing its powers and control during this critical time in the world's history. We journalists never expected that we would be the ones making headlines. But in a reporting environment where most local media is government-owned or politically affiliated, this type of independent investigative journalism, which exposed the government's actions to public scrutiny, was not welcomed.

Investigating the truth is often difficult. I found that out the hard way while reporting on this extraordinary disregard for human rights which, in the end, stripped me of my own in Malaysia.

Dome of Despair

James Oaten, North Asia Correspondent, *ABC News*, Tokyo

It's impossible to sleep in the mornings. My mind is just too active. I'm living in Delhi and it seems everywhere you look there is grief, despair and anguish. But as a journalist living here, I use adrenaline to push aside the creeping sadness. There's news to write.

Every morning I check my phone first thing to scan news articles, Twitter, and check any messages I may have received.

'Feeling very sick,' one message read. 'It must be the virus. Field reporting is too dangerous. Those who have an option of leaving the city/country should do that immediately. Then at least you are assured of treatment.'

I WROTE THESE WORDS back in May 2021, for what was meant to be an online story. At the time, I was working as the ABC's South Asia correspondent, watching New Delhi's healthcare system collapse under the weight of the most vicious COVID wave experienced during the pandemic.

Footage of mass cremations being held anywhere from car parks to the banks of the Ganges River was being beamed across the world. Television crews captured the sick gasping for air as they slumped outside hospitals that were unable to help, relatives wailing in agony as their loved ones succumbed to the virus. The message from the journalist was correct: it had become too dangerous for me to venture outside.

A few weeks prior, I had visited an intensive-care ward in the city of Nagpur, in central India, which was experiencing an explosion of COVID cases and where the notion of 'herd immunity' was still kicking about. Experts pondered whether India was past the worst because serological surveys showed far more people had been infected than official data suggested. It was assumed a level of immunity would slow the spread of the virus where outbreaks had previously occurred. Nagpur, it was initially believed, was experiencing an outbreak because it had avoided the worst of the year before. But what I saw was just a preview of the catastrophe that was to soon sweep across the country.

Every intensive-care ward in the city was full and all ventilation units were occupied. In a public hospital, COVID patients were being forced to share beds. Outside, long queues of people waited for news about their loved ones inside. I watched a man and a woman sobbing uncontrollably.

'They cry, they beg,' one volunteer outside explained to me, 'but there are no beds available for them.'

My producer, Som Patidar, and I ventured inside a private hospital intensive-care ward. A doctor took me from room to room, pointing out every person who would not survive infection, despite receiving the best care available. I saw a family come in to say goodbye to an elderly man—he was dead just a few hours later.

But it wasn't just the elderly. A woman a few years younger than me was also marked for death. She had given birth only ten days earlier. The virus was literally taking lives before my eyes, and there I was standing in the same room as it, hoping it was not also infecting me.

Som and I had taken every possible precaution. The hospital provided the necessary safety gear, and its nurses ensured our behaviour was COVID-appropriate. On the outside, we regularly changed face masks, wore face shields and sanitised our hands. We had a third hotel room that was designated for storing items that were potentially contaminated, such as camera gear and previously worn clothes, which were placed in rubbish bags.

When we returned to Delhi, I was to isolate for five days and undertake a COVID test on the final day. I took the precautions seriously as I did not want to infect my partner, who was pregnant at the time. I wanted to get the test over with, given what I had just witnessed, but the medical advice at the time was COVID tests were most accurate five or six days after exposure, and anything before that was unlikely to be reliable. So I waited in isolation, stuck with thoughts of those who died in Nagpur before me, wondering if I too had caught the virus.

Fortunately, my fifth-day test was negative. But Som wasn't so lucky; he tested positive. Our driver called me soon after to say he was feeling ill, and his wife was also sick. I was a close contact, so back into isolation I went.

It was clear what was happening in Nagpur was now happening in Delhi. Social media filled up with posts from people pleading for advice about where to find a spare hospital bed. People turned to the black market to find oxygen tanks. The cruel reality was the difference between life and death might have been the contacts one had in their phone.

Som, who fortunately was asymptomatic, called his contacts to identify the best way to secure an oxygen tank, just in case, and by doing so found the necessary healthcare treatment for my driver's wife, whose blood-oxygen levels were dropping into worrying territory.

At this stage, it was becoming clear that a new form of the virus was wreaking havoc. At the time, it was called the 'double mutant' variant. We now know it as Delta. Doctors told me the virus had become far more hostile. Teenagers were ending up in intensive care and pregnant women were now considered vulnerable. Whole families were being infected, despite efforts to isolate. The government urged households to keep windows and doors open to maximise air ventilation, but it was far too late. The notion of herd immunity was smashed with terrifying speed and brutality. Delhi became a dome of despair.

'It's impossibly bad,' one hospital superintendent told me. 'It's way beyond even what the media is able to capture. Not because they don't want to. Even doctors don't realise how bad it is.'

The risk of infecting my pregnant partner with this new, mysterious version of the virus was too high, so I, like many others, stayed home and reported remotely. I did interviews over Zoom or my phone. Footage was provided from a mix of sources, and live crosses were done on my rooftop or directly in front of my house. Those brave journalists and camera operators still venturing outside did the heavy lifting.

When the Australian Government finally organised evacuation flights, my partner and I secured a seat on the first plane, as her pregnancy made her a priority. We were placed into pre-flight quarantine, and I filed what I thought would be my last report from Delhi. It was about a pregnant woman infected with COVID who recorded a video message urging others to take the virus seriously. Nine days later, both she and her unborn baby were dead.

Then, just hours before my escape to safety, I received news that shocked and gutted me. My mandatory pre-flight COVID test was positive. A flood of emotions hit my body. I feared the symptoms to come. But I was far more scared by the realisation that I had likely infected my pregnant partner.

It was not long before messages started to arrive from other passengers who had also tested positive. While we shared our distress, I also started to realise something was wrong.

ABC News broke the story that half the flight had been kicked off due to either testing positive or being a close contact. I assumed the detail was leaked to the media to demonstrate the hard border was necessary. But everyone messaging me had the same test result as me:

'low' viral load. Sadness turned to anger. And then my journalism instincts kicked in.

Once again, I forced my emotions to the side and I went down the rabbit hole of gathering test results from fellow passengers, and investigating the company that did our tests as well as Indian testing regulations. I discovered the company Qantas had hired to conduct the pre-flight tests had, in fact, outsourced them to another company that had lost its testing licence due to inaccurate testing. I, like many others on the flight, was indeed negative, as subsequent testing proved. It was bittersweet.

Qantas said it was unaware of the outsourcing but refused to apologise or conduct our tests again. The ABC, wasting no time, secured me another flight out of India, on a different airline.

Journalists never like to become the story.

Journalists also don't like to leave the story.

I arrived back in Australia carrying a dense ball of emotions, something which took months to process. The fact I was in Perth, a city which had not suffered long lockdowns or catastrophic COVID waves, made my new home and the people in it feel alien.

Australia did eventually start to suffer its own Delta outbreak. Lockdowns spread and the border was greatly tightened. Thankfully, COVID never became as destructive here as what I had witnessed in India.

In the end, I knew I had made the right call. My partner and I made it to safety and I was there to welcome my son into the world.

Hong Kong's Citizen Journalist

Aaron Busch, the brains behind @tripperhead, Hong Kong

There's a certain level of irony in becoming one of Hong Kong's leading social media journalists, as I never wanted to be a journalist. I studied journalism at Curtin University in Perth, but it was only a means to an end. After working as a newspaper journalist in rural Western Australia for eight months, I finally took a job in commercial radio and never thought of being a journalist again. That was 1999.

The COVID-19 pandemic was the perfect storm for me, an ex-journalist with a love of numbers and plenty of time on my hands as a stay-at-home dad. My wife's job took us around Australia, and then from 2007, around Asia, living in Jakarta, Da Nang and Bangkok, before finally arriving in Hong Kong in 2014.

Our first visit to Australia in eight years was at Christmas 2019. Rumours of a new virus had already started circulating on social media before New Year's Eve. I can't really say why, but very early on I had an inkling this was going to be something very big. By the first week of 2020, in the small WA town we were visiting, I went to the local chemist and bought all their face masks before we returned to Hong Kong.

From the outset, I tracked the numbers—first out of China, then Hong Kong from the day it recorded its first case on 23 January 2020. I had all the data, but what to do with it? I decided to start putting the daily numbers on my Twitter account, @tripperhead. At the time I had roughly 300 followers, none from Hong Kong, and at a guess, a majority were bots. The first daily numbers went up on 29 March 2020 and I've tweeted them every day since.

Hong Kong is 90 per cent Cantonese speaking, and the media landscape reflects that. As someone who is not a Cantonese speaker, I found it annoying that I couldn't receive news about the pandemic fast. So, armed with Google Translate (and now Bing Translate and DeepL), I began reading the local news online and translating it for an English-speaking audience. The ability to put out news in English that wasn't readily available to those on English-language twitter helped grow my follower count.

By the end of 2020, I had 1000 followers; at the time, I expected that would be as many as I could ever get. A follower suggested I set up a 'tip' system so people could chip in, given I was doing this every day. While I've never made a living wage from this work, donations from followers on Twitter allowed me to replace my broken laptop in 2021, and in 2022 fly my parents from Australia to Singapore to see them for the first time in three years.

With heavy restrictions on travel and 21-day hotel quarantine on arrival in Hong Kong, much of 2021 was pretty quiet, pandemic-news wise. By the end of the year, I was surprised to find I had 9000 followers.

Then 2022 arrived, along with Hong Kong's fifth wave. Within three months, Hong Kong recorded one of the highest mortality rates from COVID in the world.[1] The elderly were dying in car parks; hospitals were overloaded, with dead bodies stacked in wards with patients. That's when there was an exponential growth in @tripperhead followers.

At the peak of the fifth wave, I would spend fourteen hours a day reporting. And when not tweeting out the latest news, I was answering hundreds of questions via replies and direct messages: 'What are the current rules to enter Hong Kong?', 'When do I need a PCR test?', 'What are the current rules if you test positive overseas?' etc. I made a decision from the outset that I would answer everyone's questions.

It was time-consuming, but what I didn't realise at the time was it built a network around the @tripperhead brand whereby people knew they could come to me for answers. It continues to this day.

I also developed a 'dot point' system for my tweets, explaining the main points outlined in press conferences or new articles. It was such a successful social media ploy that Bloomberg started teaching the system to new journalists.

Random followers began reaching out to help. One high-school kid wrote me a script to generate the nightly Compulsory Testing Notices; another follower wrote a script for Google Sheets to generate the daily case numbers tweet. When I finally took a holiday in August 2022, another follower watched the daily press conferences for me and sent me the numbers to tweet. I call all of them friends in real life now.

For the first two years of the pandemic I remained anonymous, using only my first name and a cryptic user icon (it was a photo I'd taken in Seoul many years beforehand). People thought I was Chinese due to me tweeting so many Chinese-language articles. Some even thought I was Korean due to the Twitter icon. I refused more media interviews than I'd care to count. It wasn't until early 2022, when a journalist friend moved from the *South China Morning Post* to Bloomberg, that I was finally 'outed'. He was asked if this 'tripperhead' would be interested in an exclusive interview. After much cajoling I finally relented and the rest is history. I went on to record interviews with *BBC World News*, ABC Radio Perth and local Chinese newspaper *Ming Pao*.

This also afforded me the luxury of meeting scores of journalists, both local and foreign correspondents. With their help, I could have my questions posed to the powers-that-be of Hong Kong. It also saw me granted membership of the Foreign Correspondent's Club of Hong Kong—its first ever social media journalist.

However, being a social media journalist is a precarious job at the best of times. In Hong Kong, the 'blue tick' journalists receive protection via their various media outlets. After the protests of 2019–20, a clear delineation on social media arose between those who are pro-protest and those who are pro-government. Navigating that line has tended to be the toughest part of the job. Anything deemed straying from the median means instant social media attacks. Plus, the government in Beijing implemented its National Security Law in Hong Kong in 2020, meaning there are 'red lines' everywhere. So far, it seems I've managed to avoid them.

Even now, while the rest of the world appears to mostly have moved on, the Hong Kong Government's rhetoric is 'The pandemic isn't over'. To that end, I still report every day. As Hong Kong slowly opens up, I've pivoted to reporting on other news aside from COVID-19. But of course the primary focus remains restrictions on travel into Hong Kong, the constant PCR testing of inbound travellers and locals, and the ever-changing social-distancing measures imposed by the government.

The sheer beauty of social media journalism is its immediacy. The second a news story breaks, it's up on social media. There are no cumbersome editors to deal with—you are the editor, you are the video producer, you are the print producer. Its immediacy can also be its downside. Social media is fleeting, especially on Twitter. If people aren't online at the time the tweet goes out, chances are they'll miss it. That's social media journalism.

China and the Virus of Tyranny

Stan Grant, International Affairs Analyst and Presenter, *ABC News*, Sydney

IT IS 2019. There is a virus lurking in China. The Chinese Communist Party (CCP) is warning that if it is not contained, it could infect the entire country. It could turn the country upside down. Tear at the social fabric. The CCP's dream of harmony cannot withstand this. So they tell their people: This must be wiped out. Memories are too fresh in China of what happens when things spiral out of control.

China is a nation that barely hangs together. Throughout time, empires have risen and fallen. Bloodshed beyond imagining—on a scale almost unseen in human history—marks each turn in China's fate. The hundred years between the mid-nineteenth century and the Communist Revolution in 1949 were brutal. The Opium Wars with Britain, the fall of the Qing, the Taiping Rebellion, the Boxer Rebellion, the civil war between nationalists and communists, the Japanese occupation—tens of millions were slaughtered.

The CCP knows it should fear its own. It knows what happens when people rise up. The party seeks stability, but stability can only come with force and threats. Nothing can be tolerated that strays too far from the reach of the party.

Now, a virus is loose. In 2019, the world is not watching. Not really. Some warn of what is happening, what is to come. But who listens? It is too far away. We are trading with China and we grow rich as China grows rich.

So, the Communist Party goes to work in secret. It is rounding up people infected with the virus. It is locking them away in secret facilities. Prisons. Isolating them. Choking off the virus at its source. Nothing short of elimination will do.

This virus has a name. Uighur. Many, if not most, in the West cannot spell it. Nor can they pronounce it. Uighurs. Muslims. A people in the outer western regions of this vast country. People who have been yearning to be free. Who speak their own language. Practise their culture. Pray to their god.

They are a virus. At least, that's what the CCP calls them.

The Communist Party transmits 'health warnings'. As reported by Sigal Samuel in *The Atlantic*,[1] and translated by Radio Free Asia, it aims them at Uighurs via WeChat, a popular social media platform in China:

> Members of the public who have been chosen for re-education have been infected by an ideological illness. They have been infected with religious extremism and violent terrorist ideology, and therefore they must seek treatment from a hospital as an inpatient ... The religious extremist ideology is a type of poisonous medicine, which confuses the mind of the people ... If we do not eradicate religious extremism at its roots, the violent terrorist incidents will grow and spread all over like an incurable malignant tumour.[2]

In 2018, Human Rights Watch released a report titled *Eradicating Ideological Viruses*. The warnings are there. Even if the world is slow to wake to them. The report says:

> Perhaps the most innovative—and disturbing—of the repressive measures in Xinjiang is the government's use of high-tech mass

surveillance systems. Xinjiang authorities conduct compulsory mass collection of biometric data, such as voice samples and DNA, and use artificial intelligence and big data to identify, profile and track everyone in Xinjiang. The authorities have envisioned these systems as a series of 'filters', picking out people with certain behaviour or characteristics that they believe indicate a threat to the Communist Party's rule in Xinjiang. These systems have also enabled authorities to implement fine-grained control, subjecting people to differentiated restrictions depending on their perceived levels of 'trustworthiness'.[3]

Note the language. Biometric data. Voice sampling. DNA. This is ideological and it is biological. People are treated as viruses that transmit illness. If not stopped, they will threaten us all, is the message.

Human Rights Watch says in the name of stability and security, authorities will 'strike at' those deemed terrorists and extremists, to rid the country of the 'problematic ideas' of Turkic Muslims. Not just Muslims, but anyone not expressing the majority ethnic Han identity. As Human Rights Watch says: 'Authorities insist that such beliefs and affinities must be "corrected" or "eradicated".'

∼

This is not new. What the CCP is doing is what other tyrannical regimes have done. They seek to create what's been called a 'harmony of souls'. They want nothing less than to produce the perfect, subdued, sublimated human. Compliant. Passive.

In the words of Joseph Stalin: 'The production of souls is more important than the production of tanks.' Historian Timothy Snyder says the Nazi and Soviet regimes turned people into numbers. And tyrants everywhere have used the language of germ warfare. They define their enemies as diseases or infections and they seek to inoculate their own societies.

Authoritarian regimes seek to sterilise and 'purify' society. Listen to them.

Stalin's henchman Vyacheslav Molotov spoke of purging or assassinating people who 'had to be isolated' or, he said, they 'would spread all kinds of complaints, and society would have been infected'.

The architect of Hitler's holocaust, Heinrich Himmler, in sending millions to the gas chambers, said he was exterminating 'a bacterium because we do not want in the end to be infected by a bacterium and die of it'. He said: 'I will not see so much as a small area of sepsis appear here or gain a hold. Wherever it may form, we will cauterise it.'

And then there is Adolf Hitler, who compared himself to the famed German microbiologist Robert Koch who found the bacillus of tuberculosis. Hitler said, 'I discovered the Jews as the bacillus and ferment of all social decomposition. And I have proved one thing: that a state can live without Jews.' To Hitler, Jewish people were 'no longer human beings'. He described the Holocaust as a 'surgical task', 'otherwise Europe will perish through the Jewish disease'.

It is no mistake these regimes use the language of virus, disease and contamination. Just as a virus is to be eradicated, so too people are to be removed, eliminated or exterminated. These attitudes do not belong to a time past. There are leaders today who exploit the same fears, who focus on difference and create division using the same language of disease.

Remember what Donald Trump said of Mexican immigrants? That they are responsible for 'tremendous infectious diseases pouring across the border'.

And in China, the Communist Party has locked up a million Uighur Muslims in 're-education camps', where human rights groups say they are brainwashed with Communist Party ideology. A virus to be eradicated.

The virus of tyranny has haunted our world. Albert Camus warned us of this in his novel *The Plague*: the story of a rat-borne disease that overruns an entire city. His was a bleak vision of death and fear, of a city sealed off and a people locked down, then shot when they tried to escape. Written in 1947, just two years after World War II, when the West was still celebrating the victory of freedom, Camus's plague is an allegory of authoritarianism.

Camus wanted to tell us of the courage that swells within us, that when the plague was at its worst, brave people fought against it. But he cautioned us, too, that the plague can return. It is 'a bacillus that never dies or disappears for good', but bides its time 'slumbering in furniture and linen'. It waits patiently 'in bedrooms, cellars; trunks, handkerchiefs, old papers', until one day it will rouse again.

~

In coronavirus, tyranny may have found the perfect host: a fearful population and all-powerful government. French philosopher Michel Foucault long ago made the link between the plagues of the seventeenth century and authoritarian control. Behind state-imposed discipline, he wrote, 'can be read the haunting memory of contagions': not just the memory of a virus but of rebellion, crime, all forms of social disorder, where people 'appear and disappear, live and die'. It is the state that brings order to the fear: 'everyone locked up in his cage, everyone at his window, answering to his name and showing himself when asked'. In the response to the plague, Foucault saw the forerunner of the modern prison: the panopticon; the all-seeing eye.[4]

The plague-stricken village, wrote Foucault, is 'traversed throughout with hierarchy, surveillance, observation, writing; the town immobilised by the functioning of an extensive power that bears in a distinct way over all individual bodies—this is the utopia of the perfectly governed city'.

The coronavirus shutdowns remind us freedom is the province of the state. The crisis has centralised government control. Around the world, governments have used physical and biological surveillance to control the pandemic. To eradicate the virus.

We have all become, to varying degrees, a little bit like China.

∼

Coronavirus emerges out of China in the dying months of 2019. I remember reporting on it. A strange illness is being detected in the city of Wuhan. Dozens of people are being treated for pneumonia-like symptoms. In January 2020, there is the first reported death. Then quickly, deaths in Europe, the United States, South Korea, Japan, Thailand.

We are still so blasé. It feels so far away. We have seen this before, haven't we? SARS, swine flu, Ebola. They come and they go. Life goes on. We go to the beach. We get on planes. We have parties. And if we have a cough or feel a bit under the weather, we most likely still go to work.

We don't realise what is happening. I am on ABC's *Q+A* program in February 2020. Footage is shown of lockdown in Wuhan. People are barricaded in their apartments while police forcibly remove and restrain. The audience is appalled.

It couldn't happen here, could it? An epidemiologist on the panel says, actually, yes. We have laws to allow for just these extreme emergency measures. Surely though, we agree, it isn't likely.

On the same program is China's deputy ambassador to Australia, Wang Xin. Minister Wang, as he is known, is an old acquaintance. A sparring partner. When I was based in China for CNN, he was my minder. He was appointed by the Ministry of Foreign Affairs to watch everything that I did.

In China I was arrested and detained, taken to Chinese police cells for doing stories the authorities did not approve of. I was, on several occasions, physically attacked and beaten. My family was under constant surveillance. Now the man responsible was sitting next to me in an ABC studio.

In the audience, a Uighur man asks a question. He was separated from his wife and child. He had come to Australia ahead of them, hoping to settle and secure visas so they could follow. He didn't know where they were. He had family in the Chinese 're-education' camps. He was clearly worried.

Minster Wang defends the China COVID lockdown. And he defends the lockdown—soon to be called the genocide—of the Uighurs.

In this moment were twinned the two crises—the two 'viruses'—threatening our world. COVID-19 threatened our health. Soon, we would indeed follow China's lead and introduce lockdowns. And the virus of tyranny was spreading.

∼

In 2020, as COVID crossed borders, so, too, did tyranny. Liberal democracy was in retreat. Freedom House, which measures the health of democracy, now counted fifteen straight years of democratic decline. From the post–Cold War boom, freedom was now being crushed.

Within democracies, too, people were falling under the sway of autocrats and demagogues. This had been a slow burn. Growing inequality, war-fuelled refugee crises and a blowback against globalisation had eroded trust. The poor and left behind felt abandoned.

The devil dances in empty pockets. Anti-immigration attitudes grew. Racial division became even more stark. Far-right parties made a comeback in Europe as barbed wire went back up on borders. People wanted their countries back and they were primed for populists. Türkiye's Recep Tayyip Erdoğan, Hungary's Viktor Orbán, India's Narendra Modi, Rodrigo Duterte in the Philippines, Brazil's Jair

Bolsonaro—all would come to power. Each spouted easy solutions to complex problems. Each divided to conquer.

Into the picture came a political circus act. A Manhattan real estate billionaire and reality television star. Donald Trump styled himself as the anti-politician. He promised to 'drain the swamp' and 'make America great again'. Eight years of the first Black president of the United States, Barack Obama, ended in 2016 with the election of a man who exploited racism.

To populists, COVID-19 initially was a boon. They seized on it to strengthen their grip on their countries. This was the state of the world in 2020, when the virus took hold. This was a perfect storm. A virus that robbed us of our freedom just as democracy was imploding and freedom was in retreat. And China was proudly boasting that its authoritarianism was ascendant.

If the twentieth century was a triumph of democracy, the twenty-first century, to China's Xi Jinping, would crown the China dream.

∼

Plagues have historically been a harbinger of political repression and violence. The Spanish flu after World War I contributed to the rise of the extreme right in Germany. The Black Death in the fourteenth century unleashed violence against Jews.

Sydney University Professor of Jurisprudence Wojciech Sadurski, in his book *A Pandemic of Populists*, says COVID has been a 'powerful accelerator of many of the pre-existing trends, both negative and positive, in business, culture and politics'.[5] Populist leaders declared states of emergency and, as Sadurski writes, pushed them 'well beyond the limits of the necessary'. Viktor Orbán set aside parliament. He was a one-man government. People critical of him could be arrested. In the Philippines, as in India, police were given powers to detain anyone 'spreading misinformation' or inciting mistrust.

Sadurski points out that, in most cases, these authoritarian leaders used militaristic language. Fighting COVID was a war. The people were conscripted.

Xi Jinping is not a populist leader. He doesn't seek legitimacy at the ballot box. He is an authoritarian. And he believes his system is better. To Xi, the battle against coronavirus is also a war: a 'people's war'.

It has been a war without end. Xi cannot allow the virus to win. Long after lockdowns have passed elsewhere, Xi continues to keep a stranglehold on COVID flares. It has weakened the economy. It is straining nerves. People are angry. There have been protests. Some are even calling for Xi to go.

But Xi has strengthened his grip. By altering the constitution, scrapping two-term presidential limits, he is now leader for life. Under cover of fighting COVID, he has used enhanced surveillance and tracking technology to peer into every part of people's lives. The COVID crackdown coincided with crushing democracy in Hong Kong. He has arrested dissidents. Silenced rivals. He is threatening war on Taiwan.

And Uighurs remain a target. Still a 'virus' to be eliminated.

∽

We are at a hinge point of history. Thirty years after the end of the Cold War, there is talk of Cold War 2.0. The United States is staring down a new rival: China. We are witnessing a return of great power rivalry. It is a supercharged great power rivalry. China is more powerful today than the Soviet Union was then, and the United States is unquestionably diminished. America is politically fractured, it is deeply divided along racial and class lines; it has an epidemic of gun violence and it has been devastated by coronavirus.

Donald Trump thought he was bigger than COVID. He was slow to act, he was dismissive and his populism was eventually revealed as reckless. Yes, he fast-tracked vaccine research and production.

But he was a master of mixed messaging and so much damage was done. At the time of writing, in the United States there have been more than 100 million cases and one million deaths. The only country to reach that number. Trump lost office.

By contrast, Xi Jinping is entrenched in power. The country where COVID first emerged is the world's biggest engine of economic growth. It is on track to usurp the United States as the single biggest economy in the world. It is extending its influence and economic reach via the Belt and Road Initiative, the biggest investment and infrastructure program the world has ever seen.

Xi is building an army to match his economic might. And he is leading the way on artificial intelligence research. The numbers tell the story. In the twenty years between 1997 and 2017, China's global share of research papers increased from just over 4 per cent to nearly 28 per cent. And what is it focusing on? Speech and image recognition. The Chinese Communist Party can track anyone, anywhere, anytime.

Technology was meant to liberate us. Some saw the death knell for authoritarian regimes. How can you control the internet? But China has. Cyberspace has become a tool of tyranny. China has taken the digital age and put it in service of genocide.

There are lessons here for journalists. Our job is not to simply report events, it is to connect them. To join the dots. To reveal the big forces at play in our world. We missed this opportunity.

We cannot understand the COVID pandemic and its impact without understanding the currents shaping our world. COVID emerged out of China at a time when Xi Jinping had his eyes on global supremacy. He had shown how far he would be prepared to go to 'harmonise' the nation. He had trialled his lockdown measures on what he callously called the 'virus' of the Uighurs. Around the world, democracy was in retreat and authoritarianism on the march. And now a virus was spreading that would attack the liberal democratic West where it believed it was strongest: its freedom.

Media can so easily be overwhelmed by events. One of the most common failings—particularly of television—is to report what we see, not what it means. Images can drive coverage. And images of people in white suits locking down entire cities obscured what was even more important. COVID was a twenty-first century virus; a virus of a globalised world, of high-speed travel and borderless trade. It was also a virus of an increasingly authoritarian world.

The COVID-19 pandemic was a stress test. It revealed and accelerated fault lines already there. Populists were stripped bare. Their slogans, easy answers and arrogance meant they were slow to act. Millions died who might otherwise have lived. In strong democracies where there is trust in science and authority, countries emerged stronger. Yet they, too, walked a fine line between surrendering liberty and saving lives.

In China, Xi Jinping believes the People's War is a victory for the Communist Party. The Party—the all-seeing eye—can control everything. It sits at the heart of everything. Xi believes he is the fulfilment of prophecy. The man who follows the great leaders, Mao Zedong and Deng Xiaoping. The one who delivers on China's greatness.

Xi walks a tightrope, too. He has strained the nation to breaking point. The relentless, cruel lockdowns have slowed the economy and crushed the spirit of Chinese people. And they are angry and rising. China, like the rest of the world, is also reaching a tipping point.

The virus of tyranny sleeps within democracy, too. It has always been in our bloodstream. China has edged us, the democracies, closer to what political scientist Vladimir Tismaneanu has called 'the age of total administration and inescapable alienation'.

The COVID pandemic has passed, at least as a political crisis. Our minds are turned now to war in Ukraine and economic strife. But journalists must remember that, as in contagions past, COVID will shape us. It leaves behind the trace of tyranny. And that is the true virus. The virus that will not die.

Acknowledgements

To create this book, we approached journalists from across all of Australia's major news organisations and platforms to share their personal reflections with us and were overwhelmed with the positive response. This book is a tribute to the honesty, integrity and hard work of people on the front lines of COVID news, pulled together in just a few weeks.

Ironically, but not surprisingly, at least two of us had serious bouts of COVID as we wrote our essays. One contributor birthed her first child during the process. (Welcome to the world, Boston!) Several contributors were heavily involved in coverage of the Victorian election. Some are writing books of their own. Thank you to all of the contributors, for making this book a priority and for sharing your valuable stories.

The very few who politely bowed out were either still deeply affected by the pandemic experience and finding it still too raw to write about, or needed time away from thinking about work, or too busy working on their own projects. To all of you, our fondest good wishes.

To the crew at Monash University Press, thank you for your partnership in this. It has been an absolute privilege and pleasure to

ACKNOWLEDGEMENTS

work alongside such a professional, passionate and fun team: Julia Carlomagno, Paul Smitz, Sarah Cannon and Rachel McDiarmid. Your support has been unflinching since the first time we spoke about *Pandemedia* near the end of 2022. It has been a wild ride but we'd do it again in a heartbeat.

A very special shout-out to the two powerhouses who led us to the brilliant team at Monash: Lisa Millar and Louise Adler. Thank you both for your generous spirits, your incredibly insightful advice, for championing writers and for encouraging our vision for this book.

A huge thanks to Phil Campbell for your creative ingenuity on the cover design. We knew it was perfect the first time we saw it! Thanks to our fabulous cartoonist Warren Brown for your sharp and insightful creations. And thanks to the team at *The Betoota Advocate* for allowing us to reproduce some of your clever Instagram posts, which kept us laughing even as the pandemic was at its worst.

Many people shared contacts and suggested writers and topics, as we cold-called some of Australia's most decorated and experienced journalists and asked them to write for us. For that, we thank Peter Doherty, Katie McRobert, Alice Mulheron, Lisa Millar, Leigh Sales, Paul Lamond, Mark Mallabone, Michelle Ainsworth, Sam Clark, Ticky Fullerton, Jennifer Hewitt and Gaven Morris.

Thank you to our early readers: Katie McRobert, Sumi Skellam, Tim Ayliffe, Flip Prior, Lyndal Parker, Alice Mulheron and Stuart Watt. Your insightful feedback and genuine encouragement were invaluable.

From Tracey

A special thanks to those cherished friends who supported me during this project, which ended up being more of a sprint than I could have imagined, especially Mimi Kwa, Katie McRobert, Andrew Scott, Sumi Skellam, Jo Rolland, Leanne Jeffs, Francine Dawson, Lyndal Parker, Julie-Anne Jones and Tom Vujevic.

ACKNOWLEDGEMENTS

A shout-out to many of our amazing ABC colleagues, who work so diligently beside us, and who helped to shape the original idea, especially Ynja Bjornsson, Lee Brooks, Simon West, Andrew Robertson, Peter Gotting, Paul Lamond, Tim Ayliffe, Sarah Naughton, Lauren Higgins, Reed Robinson, Alice Mulheron and Mawunyo Gbogbo.

Thanks especially to my dear friend and co-editor Gavin Fang, who brought his A-game to this book even though he was up to his eyeballs in work and baseball training. Thank you for sharing your big brain and creative energy.

Finally, thanks to my beautiful family for their endless support. To my amazing mum Carolyn, for her tireless enthusiasm and utmost belief in me. It has made all the difference. To my children Sean and Laura, for creating a home of laughter and joy, and teaching me how to laugh at myself. Also, for sharing your mobile hotspots as I worked during our holiday. And to my husband Ian, who has had to endure thirty-five years of listening to me talk about writing a book. Your patience and confidence in me is, and always has been, more than I could wish for.

From Gavin

A big thanks to all of the colleagues I've worked with in the media for the past two decades. This book is in part inspired by your hard work and dedication to the craft we all love.

Thanks to my friend and co-editor Tracey Kirkland, for letting me follow in your slipstream on this project. Without your passion, talent and drive, this book would not exist.

To my parents, Chang Sha and Barbara, who are still bemused as to why I became a journalist, thanks for being my biggest fans.

And finally, thanks to my family for letting me be distracted by more work. My buddies Sam and Gabriel for being the best sons a dad could ask for. And my wife Bronwyn, for always supporting me in everything I do and never once questioning whether I can do it.

The Betoota Advocate: Light Relief in Dark Times

Man Heading Overseas Next Week Taking Virus More Seriously Than He Ever Did During Lockdown

"Day For It" Says Coronavirus Staring At A Packed Beach

Nation That Used To Watch Their Premier's Daily Conferences Now Shrugging At 33,000 Cases A Day

Grown Adult Honestly Thinks World Leaders Created COVID-19 To Ruin Their Economies On Purpose

Contributor Bios

Aaron Busch is the citizen journalist behind Hong Kong's @tripperhead Twitter COVID news blog. He's been tracking case numbers every day in Hong Kong since 23 January 2020, the date of the first COVID case recorded in the city. Aaron grew up in regional Western Australia. After thirty-three years, he and his family packed up and left Australia for Asia, living in Indonesia, Vietnam and Thailand before settling in Hong Kong in 2014. Aaron studied journalism at Curtin University.

Alan Kohler is the finance presenter on *ABC News* and a columnist for *The New Daily*. He is also the founder and editor in chief of *Eureka Report*, which offers daily commentary on wealth management and markets. Alan has been a journalist for fifty-two years, including periods as editor of the *Financial Review*, editor of *The Age* and economics correspondent for the ABC's *7.30 Report*.

Andrew Lund started as a reporter at Channel 7 Queensland in 2002 and moved to Melbourne in 2006, before joining Channel 9 in 2010. As Nine's Victorian state political reporter for more than ten years, he covered three premiers, while also regularly filling in in as the network's London-based Europe correspondent. Andrew attended the bulk of Victoria's daily COVID-19 press conferences and was front and centre of Nine News Melbourne's nightly coverage of the pandemic. In August 2021, he joined Melbourne Airport as Head of Communications and Engagement, where he maintains a keen interest in both journalism and politics.

Anita Savage is the News Director at Sydney radio station Hope 103.2fm. A highly respected international journalist, she was employed by Hope Media in 2019 to establish a news service aiming to provide a credible, balanced voice in Sydney's news media. She can be heard reading the news each morning. Her experience includes news reading and reporting for ABC, 2UE, Sky News and the NINE Television Network. Anita also has been a US foreign correspondent, the Washington, DC correspondent for a US television network affiliate, and Bloomberg Television's first international anchor in New York.

Anne Connolly is a seven-time Walkley Award winner. In 2022 she won her second Gold Walkley for her investigation into Public Guardian and Trustee agencies. Anne has twenty-five years' experience specialising in investigative journalism for ABC Radio and TV. In 2018, her *Four Corners* 'Who Cares?' series uncovering neglect, abuse and understaffing in Australian nursing homes led to a royal commission into the aged care sector.

Ben Knight is a senior reporter with *ABC News* and led the in-depth investigations unit in Melbourne, documenting the impact and experience of living through the city's extended lockdowns through projects such as 'Generation COVID' and 'The COVID Diaries'. He was part of the team that quickly developed new methods of news-gathering and reporting for television as the newsroom adjusted to COVID restrictions. He has previously reported for *Four Corners* and as a correspondent in the ABC's Washington and Middle East bureaus.

Bill Grueskin is a professor and former academic dean at Columbia Journalism School in New York. In early 2022, he served as the first international journalist in residence at the Judith Neilson Institute in

Sydney. While in Australia, he spent nearly two months researching the News Media Bargaining Code. He has held senior print and online editing roles, including deputy managing editor of *The Wall Street Journal*, city editor of *The Miami Herald* and an executive editor at Bloomberg.

Casey Briggs is a data journalist and presenter with *ABC News*. After studying mathematics and statistics at the University of Adelaide, he decided to swap academia for journalism and joined the ABC in 2016. He spent much of the past three years charting how COVID-19 spread across the world. Previously, he covered politics, cyclones and crocodiles for the ABC in several states. Casey was named the SA Press Club Young Journalist of the Year in 2019.

Claire Kimball is the founder and Managing Editor of Squiz Media, which was created in her kitchen in 2016–17. Squiz Media now employs fifteen people across *The Squiz*, *Squiz Kids* and commercial/growth functions. Before that, Claire was an adviser/press secretary to National and Liberal ministers during the Howard government years, and to Tony Abbott during the remarkable 2010 election year. Claire was Woolworths Group's head of retail/corporate communications and director of corporate affairs between 2011 and 2016.

Damien Cave has worked for *The New York Times* since 2004, reporting from more than twenty countries. He was a finalist for the Pulitzer Prize in international reporting in 2008 with a team in Baghdad, when covering the Iraq War. He came to Australia in 2017 to open *The Times*'s first bureau in the country since World War II. He lives in Sydney with his wife and two children, and is the author of *Into the Rip* (Simon & Schuster), a memoir about risk, community, and his family's unexpected effort to become more Australian (and a little less American) before and during the pandemic.

CONTRIBUTOR BIOS

David Speers is the host of *Insiders* on ABC TV, where each week he tackles the big issues in politics and national affairs, interviewing a senior politician and a panel of leading journalists and commentators. David also writes weekly analysis for ABC Online and appears each week across radio and TV programs. David is a former Press Gallery president, having spent twenty years working from Parliament House in Canberra. He has won multiple awards for his journalism, including Walkleys and a Logie. He is the author of *On Mutiny* (MUP), a short book on the downfall of Malcolm Turnbull as prime minister.

Drew Ambrose is an international correspondent and investigative reporter for Al Jazeera English. Since 2011, he has produced more than 100 documentaries from forty countries in the news channel's programs unit and has been a digital lead on numerous groundbreaking online journalism projects. His reporting has won thirty-five global media prizes including three Walkleys, the Wincott Award, the Venice TV Award, six New York Festival Gold Medals, three Overseas Press Club of America citations and the coveted 'International Journalist of the Year' category of the One World Media Awards. Before joining Al Jazeera English, he worked across a range of news and current affairs programs for Australia's two public broadcasters, the ABC and SBS.

Emily Arnold worked as a news reporter and producer at *7NEWS* from 2016 until 2022, across several newsrooms including Bundaberg, Mackay, Maroochydore and Brisbane. Emily now works as a Senior Media and Communications Specialist at Urban Utilities, one of the largest water utilities in Australia. Emily has a Bachelor of Journalism from the University of Queensland and is also studying a Master of Business, majoring in Management, at the Queensland University of Technology.

CONTRIBUTOR BIOS

Dr Erin Smith is Dart Centre Asia Pacific's CEO. Dr Smith is a long-time advocate for supporting the mental health and wellbeing of those impacted by trauma. Her research, writing and expert opinion can be found published widely in academic journals, magazines, textbooks and news media, including *The Conversation*. Her commentary on the traumatic impact of the 2019–20 Australian bushfires, the twentieth anniversary of the 9/11 terrorist attacks, and the COVID-19 pandemic reached a global audience of over 600 million. In 2022 she was nominated for a Volunteering Victoria Leadership Award for her contributions to mental health advocacy within the community.

Gabrielle Chan is Rural and Regional Editor for *The Guardian*, based in Harden, New South Wales. She has been a journalist for more than thirty years, including a political journalist and politics live blogger at *Guardian Australia* from 2013 until late 2022. Prior to that, she worked at *The Australian*, ABC Radio, *The Daily Telegraph*, in local newspapers and politics. Gabrielle has written and edited history books, biographies and even a recipe book. Her latest is *Why You Should Give a F*ck about Farming* (Penguin Random House). The daughter of a Singaporean migrant, Gabrielle moved from the Canberra Press Gallery to marry a sheep and wheat farmer in 1996.

Gaven Morris is the Managing Director of Bastion Transform, a digital transformation and content strategy consultancy. He is also Industry Professor at Western Sydney University. From 2015 to 2021, Gaven was the director of news, analysis and investigations at the ABC. During a decade in international news, he was a senior member of the team that built and launched Al Jazeera English and on the team that expanded CNN.com to become one of the first global online news services. With thirty years' experience in the Australian and international media, he spent many years covering global conflicts and terrorism attacks, natural disasters and political upheaval, and many years in the Australian parliamentary Press Gallery.

Gavin Fang is the ABC's Deputy News Director and Head of the National and International reporting teams. He is also the ABC's News Diversity lead. Gavin has twenty-five years' experience in print and broadcast journalism, with most of the past decade spent in a senior leadership role. He's a former Indonesia correspondent and video journalist for the ABC's *Australia Network*. During the pandemic, Gavin led the daily national editorial meeting at *ABC News*.

Grant Sherlock is the Managing Editor for ABC News Digital, which includes the *ABC News* website and app. After beginning his career as a newspaper journalist, he shifted his focus to digital fifteen years ago and has since worked for the BBC and ABC, helping those organisations to adjust to changing audience behaviours and developing new ways of delivering news content on digital platforms.

James Oaten is the ABC's North Asia correspondent, covering Japan, South Korea and North Korea. He was previously the ABC's South Asia correspondent based in New Delhi. During this time, he covered the COVID-19 pandemic extensively, including India's catastrophic Delta surge in 2021, and the Taliban takeover of Afghanistan. James has previously worked as a broadcast and digital journalist in ABC newsrooms in Melbourne and Darwin, as well as for the flagship current affairs programs *7.30* and *AM*.

Jeremy Fernandez is a journalist, producer and presenter specialising in live events and multiplatform news coverage with the ABC. He has anchored and reported in the field for some of the network's most complex broadcasts over two decades, including coverage of the death of Queen Elizabeth II, the Black Summer bushfires, the COVID-19 outbreak in Australia, Melbourne's Commonwealth Games and the

Australian of the Year Awards, and New Year's Eve live on Sydney Harbour. Jeremy regularly appears on ABC television and streaming services, including the News Channel, and NSW 7 p.m. news.

Jess Malcolm is a political reporter in *The Australian*'s Canberra bureau. She won Student Journalist of the Year at the 2021 Quill Awards after making her start in regional journalism. She holds a Bachelor of Arts majoring in Politics and Sociology, and a Master of Journalism from the University of Melbourne.

Josh Zimmerman is the State Political Editor at *The West Australian* newspaper. He began covering WA politics in mid-2019, and for the past two and a half years, much of his focus has been on WA's response to COVID and the health, economic and political impacts of the virus on the state. Prior to *The West*, Zimmerman spent two and a half years at *The Sunday Times*, and has also worked in community newspapers in Bunbury and the Perth council of Melville. He won the 2022 WA Media Award for best print news coverage for a series of reports focusing on the deterioration of St John WA ambulance services in the face of the pandemic.

Lee Hunter is the General Manager of TikTok Australia and New Zealand. He's a former head of marketing strategy and innovation at Google and a former global head of brand at YouTube. Lee has a degree in Psychology and a masters in Marketing. He is a regular commentator on digital technology and future digital trends.

Lisa Millar is a Walkley Award–winning journalist who has worked across audio, digital and TV for the ABC for thirty years. She is the co-host of *News Breakfast* based in Melbourne, a guest presenter on *Back Roads* and the narrator of hit series *Muster Dogs*. She was one of the ABC's longest-serving foreign correspondents, serving as bureau chief in Washington, DC and London between 2001 and 2018.

She has written about those experiences in her bestselling memoir *Daring to Fly* (Hachette).

Dr Kimina Lyall is Dart Centre Asia Pacific's Deputy CEO. She spent almost fifteen years as a journalist, including a period as South-East Asia correspondent for *The Australian*. Her experiences during that posting led to a Walkley Award nomination, along with the publication of her first book, *Out of the Blue: Facing the Tsunami* (HarperCollins). Kimina has reported on and experienced disasters firsthand. She works in private practice as a psychologist as well as for DCAP.

Mandi Wicks is the Director of SBS News and Current Affairs and has nearly thirty-five years' experience in the media industry. Mandi oversees *SBS World News*, *SBS News* in Arabic and Mandarin, SBS News Digital, *Insight*, *Dateline* and SBS WorldWatch, a television channel broadcasting news in more than thirty languages. Prior to joining News and Current Affairs, Mandi was the director of SBS Audio and Language Content for almost ten years, with a team of more than 200 journalists producing news and information in more than sixty languages.

Mark Kenny is a Professor at the Australian National University's Australian Studies Institute. He is a former chief political correspondent for *The Sydney Morning Herald* and *The Age*, and is a weekly columnist for *The Canberra Times*. Presenter of the *Democracy Sausage* podcast, he was a director of the National Press Club for more than a decade and has regularly appeared on national and international broadcasts including CNN, BBC World, Al Jazeera, as well as the ABC's *Insiders*, *The Drum* and News Channel.

Max Futcher is a news presenter for Seven News in Queensland. He has worked as a journalist for more than twenty-five years, reporting on major stories across Australia and around the world. During the early period of COVID, Max presented daily news bulletins and breaking news items as Queensland went into lockdown and the borders were closed. Throughout this time, he regularly interviewed stakeholders such as the state's police commissioner and chief health officer. Like most everyone else, he also supervised his daughters through homeschooling, without doing any lasting damage.

Michelle Grattan is one of Australia's most respected political journalists. She has been a member of the Canberra parliamentary Press Gallery for more than forty years, during which time she has covered all the most significant stories in Australian politics. She was formerly editor of *The Canberra Times* and political editor of *The Age* and has been with the *Australian Financial Review* and *The Sydney Morning Herald*. Michelle currently has a dual role, with an academic position at the University of Canberra and as Associate Editor (Politics) and Chief Political Correspondent at *The Conversation*. She is the author, co-author and editor of several books, and was made an Officer of the Order of Australia (AO) in 2004 for her long and distinguished service to Australian journalism.

Dr Norman Swan co-hosts the ABC's COVID podcast *Coronacast*, as well as Radio National's *Health Report*. He is also a reporter and commentator on ABC's *7.30*, *Midday*, *News Breakfast* and *Four Corners*, and a guest host on *RN Breakfast*. He is a past winner of the Gold Walkley and has won other Walkleys, including one with his *Coronacast* colleagues in 2020. He created *Invisible Enemies* on pandemics and civilisation for Channel 4 UK and SBS, which was subsequently broadcast in twenty-seven countries. Norman has been awarded the Medal of the Australian Academy of Science, an honorary MD from the University of Sydney, and in October 2022 a Fellowship of the Australian Academy of Health and Medical Sciences.

CONTRIBUTOR BIOS

Patrick Durkin has been the Melbourne Bureau Chief of the *Australian Financial Review* for more than eight years and Deputy Editor of the *AFR*'s *BOSS* magazine and leadership content for more than a decade. He has won multiple awards during his sixteen-plus years as a journalist writing on business, politics and economics, including the National Press Club's joint Financial Journalist of the Year and Citi Journalism Award for Excellence. Patrick was previously a litigation and insolvency lawyer at a top-tier law firm and an in-house lawyer at a Big Four bank. He is an Asia Pacific Journalism Fellow and a member of the Dromana Life Saving Club.

Peter Law is Media Manager at Mineral Resources Ltd. During the pandemic, he was the state political editor for *The West Australian*, where he reported on—among other issues—the state's hard border and the policies of the McGowan government. He has held roles as chief of staff for *The West Australian* and head of news at *The Sunday Times*.

Rachel Baxendale started as a cadet in *The Australian*'s Melbourne bureau in 2012 and has since covered federal and state politics for the paper in Canberra and Melbourne. She has been *The Australian*'s Victorian Political Reporter since 2018.

Raina MacIntyre is Professor of Global Biosecurity, NHMRC Principal Research Fellow and Head of the Biosecurity Program at the Kirby Institute, UNSW. She leads a research program in the control and prevention of infectious diseases. Her area of vaccine expertise is vaccination of older adults and immunosuppressed people, and she has done several clinical trials of vaccines in adults and immunosuppressed populations such as transplant patients. Raina has over 450 peer-reviewed publications. She is the author of *Dark Winter* (NewSouth), an insider's guide to pandemics and biosecurity.

CONTRIBUTOR BIOS

Rick Morton is an award-winning journalist, Senior Reporter for *The Saturday Paper*, and the author of three non-fiction books: *My Year of Living Vulnerably* (HarperCollins), *One Hundred Years of Dirt* (MUP) and the extended essay *On Money* (Hachette). Rick is the winner of the 2013 Kennedy Award for Young Journalist of the Year and the 2017 Kennedy Award for Outstanding Columnist.

Sarah Curnow started as a journalist at the ABC in 1999. Since then, she has worked on *Four Corners*, *7.30*, *Media Watch* and a number of other programs across news, documentary and television. Sarah has been with the ABC's investigative team since it was founded in 2018. Sarah has also worked in the law and the public service. From March until December 2020, based in Melbourne, she researched, produced and reported exclusively on COVID.

Stan Grant is a proud Wiradjuri man and one of Australia's most respected and awarded journalists, with more than thirty years' experience in radio and television news and current affairs. He is currently the ABC's International Affairs Analyst and presenter of *Q+A*. Before joining the ABC, Stan served for a decade as a senior international correspondent for CNN in Asia and the Middle East, broadcasting to an audience of millions around the world. He is an award-winning and bestselling author of several books and has contributed articles to many major Australian newspapers, magazines and journals.

Tanya Denning-Orman, a proud Birri and Guugu Yimidhirr woman from central and north Queensland, has led National Indigenous Television since it joined SBS in 2012, and became SBS's first Director of Indigenous Content in 2020. Tanya manages NITV as a channel dedicated to Indigenous voices, overseeing its diverse and innovative multiplatform content. She also plays an instrumental role in the development and delivery of First Nations storytelling across the SBS network. With more than twenty years' experience working in media, Tanya has previously held positions as a journalist and producer for the ABC and SBS, and a number of different roles at NITV since its inception in 2007.

Tory Maguire is the Executive Editor of Nine Publishing's metro mastheads *The Sydney Morning Herald*, *The Age*, *Brisbane Times* and *WA Today*. Prior to July 2021, she was national editor of the same mastheads, responsible for all their federal politics, business, world and environment coverage. Before joining Fairfax Media in 2018, Tory was editor in chief of the Australian edition of *The Huffington Post* and worked at News Corp in a range of roles over fifteen years.

Tracey Kirkland is a career news journalist, working in broadcast and print for more than thirty years. During COVID, she held two key editorial roles at the ABC, first as the national newsgathering editor, then in her current role as the Continuous News Editor for ABC News Channel. Since joining the ABC in 1999, Tracey has been a reporter, presenter and producer for most of the ABCs major news programs, including *7PM*, *Midday*, *News Breakfast*, *The Business*, *Stateline*, *News-24* and local radio.

Tu Le is a community education lawyer at the Marrickville Legal Centre who made headlines in 2021 after speaking out about the lack of diversity and representation in Australian politics. Tu was a spokesperson and advocate for western Sydney when it was locked down under COVID. She won the 40 Under 40 most influential Asian Australians award in 2022. The co-founder of YCollab, a social enterprise based in south-west Sydney, and the Vietnamese Australian Forum, Tu also sits on the board of Addison Road Community Organisation, a charity focusing on social justice, arts and culture, and community sustainability.

Notes

The Storyteller's Story
1. D Nolan, C Hanna, K McGuinness and K McCallum, *Covering COVID-19: How Australian Media Reported the Coronavirus Pandemic in 2020*, News and Media Research Centre, University of Canberra, 2021. This report used data obtained by media monitoring company Streem.
2. Ibid., p. 7.
3. Ibid., p. 20.
4. Edelman, *Trust Barometer 2022 Australia*, https://www.edelman.com.au/trust-barometer-2022-australia (viewed January 2023).
5. Ibid.
6. Reuters Institute, *Digital News Report 2022*, https://reutersinstitute.politics.ox.ac.uk/digital-news-report/2022 (viewed January 2023).
7. Ibid.
8. Ibid.

An Honest Conversation
1. S Park, C Fisher, J Young Lee and K McGuinness, *COVID-19: Australian News and Misinformation*, News and Media Research Centre, University of Canberra, 7 July 2020, https://www.canberra.edu.au/research/faculty-research-centres/nmrc/research/covid-19-australian-news-and-misinformation (viewed January 2023).
2. Edelman, *Trust Barometer 2022 Australia*, https://www.edelman.com.au/trust-barometer-2022-australia (viewed January 2023).
3. Andrea Carson and Denis Muller, *Undercover Reporting, Deception, and Betrayal in Journalism*, Routledge, London, 2023.

The Economic Pandemic
1. The Treasury, Australian Government, *Insights from the First Six Months of JobKeeper*, 11 October 2021, https://treasury.gov.au/publication/p2021-211978 (viewed January 2023).
2. Robert Gottliebsen, 'Stores Cash in on Home Spending Splurge', *The Australian*, 15 May 2020.

NOTES

Fit to Print

1 *The Age*, 'Victoria Can't Go on Like This', 1 September 2021, https://www.theage.com.au/national/victoria/victoria-can-t-go-on-like-this-20210901-p58nql.html (viewed January 2023).
2 Gay Alcorn, 'Loved, Hated, Read: The Editorial with the Extraordinary Response', *The Age*, 4 September 2021, https://www.theage.com.au/national/victoria/loved-hated-read-the-editorial-with-the-extraordinary-response-20210903-p58opw.html (viewed January 2023).

Power Switch

1 Jack Neary, 'What a Multi-Year Analysis of Traffic Sources, Device Type, and Loyalty Tells Us about the Year ahead', Chartbeat, 2021, https://blog.chartbeat.com/2022/04/11/what-multi-year-analysis-traffic-loyalty-device-tells-about-2022 (viewed January 2023).
2 Google Search, 'How Results Are Automatically Generated', 2023, https://www.google.com/intl/en_au/search/howsearchworks/how-search-works/ranking-results/ (viewed January 2023).
3 Stephanie Dalzell, 'Gatherings Restricted to Two People to Slow Spread of Coronavirus', *ABC News*, 29 March 2020, https://www.abc.net.au/news/2020-03-29/public-gatherings-limited-to-two-people-coronavirus-covid-19/12101162 (viewed January 2023).
4 *ABC News*, 'Scott Morrison Has Announced the Two-Person Rule on Gatherings in the Fight against Coronavirus, But What Does It Actually Mean?', 29 March 2020, https://www.abc.net.au/news/2020-03-29/scott-morrison-coronavirus-covid19-two-person-rule-explained/12101212 (viewed January 2023).
5 Neryssa Azlan and Widia Jalal, 'You Asked Us 100 000 Coronavirus Questions. We Read Them All and They Helped Shape the *ABC News* Coverage of COVID-19', *ABC News*, 20 September 2020, https://www.abc.net.au/news/redirects/backstory/2020-09-20/how-abc-news-answered-coronavirus-covid19-questions/12624260 (viewed January 2023).
6 Simon Elvery, 'What Is within 5km of Your Victorian Home?', *ABC News*, 4 August 2020, https://www.abc.net.au/news/2020-08-04/how-to-measure-whats-within-5km-radius-of-your-home-coronavirus/12517868 (viewed January 2023).

Nightly News

1 PwC Australia, *Australian Entertainment & Media Outlook 2020–2024*, 2020, https://www.pwc.com.au/entertainment-and-media/2020/2020_australian_entertainment_media_outlook_report.pdf (viewed January 2023).

A Question of Balance

1 Ipsos, *Ipsos Global Advisor: Trust in the Media*, 2019, https://www.ipsos.com/sites/default/files/ct/news/documents/2019-06/global-advisor-trust-in-media-2019.pdf (viewed January 2023).

2 Media Entertainment & Arts Alliance, 'Opening Statement to Senate Inquiry into Media Diversity in Australia', 12 March 2021, https://www.meaa.org/mediaroom/opening-statement-to-senate-inquiry-into-media-diversity-in-australia/ (viewed January 2023).
3 Alex Schultz and Jay Parikh, 'Keeping Our Services Stable and Reliable During the COVID-19 Outbreak', Meta, 24 March 2020, https://about.fb.com/news/2020/03/keeping-our-apps-stable-during-COVID-19 (viewed January 2023).
4 Timothy Graham et al., '#IStandWithDan Versus #DictatorDan: The Polarised Dynamics of Twitter Discussions about Victoria's COVID-19 Restrictions', *Media International Australia*, vol. 179, no. 1, 2021, pp. 127–48, https://eprints.qut.edu.au/207260/1/1329878x20981780.pdf (viewed January 2023).
5 Ibid.
6 Mildred F Perreault and Gregory P Perreault, 'Journalists on COVID-19 Journalism: Communication Ecology of Pandemic Reporting', *American Behavioral Scientist*, vol. 65, no. 11, 5 February 2021, https://journals.sagepub.com/doi/full/10.1177/00027642211992813 (viewed January 2023).

Public Backlash
1 Annabel Crabb, 'Facebook or YouTube? What Does Your Favourite Social Media Site Say about You?', *ABC News*, 28 June 2021, https://www.abc.net.au/news/2021-06-28/annabel-crabb-australia-talks-social-media/100241888 (viewed January 2023).

The Role of the Expert
1 Great Barrington Declaration, 4 October 2020, https://gbdeclaration.org/ (viewed January 2023).
2 For one of several studies showing the same thing, see Yan Xie et al., 'Long-Term Cardiovascular Outcomes of COVID-19', *Nature*, no. 28, 2022, pp. 583–90, https://www.nature.com/articles/s41591-022-01689-3 (viewed January 2023).

Febrile Nation
1 Richard Willingham and Dan Harrison, 'Victorian Hotel Quarantine Inquiry Report Unable to Determine Who Made Private Security Decision', *ABC News*, 21 December 2020, https://www.abc.net.au/news/2020-12-21/final-victorian-hotel-quarantine-inquiry-report-released/13002882 (viewed January 2023).
2 Donna Lu, '"I Love You!" Australian Epidemiologists Grapple with Newfound COVID Fame', *The Guardian*, 4 July 2021, https://www.theguardian.com/world/2021/jul/04/i-love-you-australian-epidemiologists-grapple-with-newfound-covid-fame (viewed January 2023).

3 Ibid.
4 Mark Evans and Gerry Stoker, *Saving Democracy*, Bloomsbury Academic, London, 2022, p. 136.
5 Governance Institute of Australia, *Ethics Index 2022: What Would You Do?*, 2022, https://web.governanceinstitute.com.au/media/887237/ethics-index-2022.pdf (viewed January 2023).

The Power of Purpose
1 David Lipson, 'A Year of Living and Reporting in the US through COVID, Civil Unrest and a Drama-Packed Election Campaign', *ABC News*, 31 October 2020, https://www.abc.net.au/news/redirects/backstory/2020-10-31/abc-us-correspondent-david-lipson-election-covid19-civil-unrest/12825520 (viewed January 2023).
2 Georgia Hitch, 'AstraZeneca Coronavirus Vaccine Approved for Use in Australia by TGA', *ABC News*, 16 February 2021, https://www.abc.net.au/news/2021-02-16/coronavirus-astrazeneca-vaccine-approved-for-use-in-australia/13115784 (viewed January 2023).
3 *ABC News*, 'October Vaccine Hopes All But over after AstraZeneca Blood Clot Concerns Prompt Roll-out Shake-up', 8 April 2021, https://www.abc.net.au/news/2021-04-08/australia-new-coronavirus-vaccine-rollout-plan-what-we-know/100057354 (viewed January 2023).
4 Australian Government, Department of Health and Aged Care, 'Vaxzevria (AstraZeneca) Vaccine and Thrombosis with Thrombocytopenia (TTS)', https://www.health.gov.au/our-work/covid-19-vaccines/advice-for-providers/clinical-guidance/tts (viewed January 2023).
5 Stephanie Zillman, 'Queensland's Chief Health Minister Rejects Prime Minister's Comments on AstraZeneca's COVID-19 Vaccine for Under-40s', *ABC News*, 30 June 2021, https://www.abc.net.au/news/2021-06-30/qld-cho-rejects-morrisons-astrazeneca-comments-covid-vaccine/100256022 (viewed January 2023).
6 Ibid.
7 News and Media Research Centre, *Digital News Report: Australia 2022*, University of Canberra, 2022, https://www.canberra.edu.au/research/faculty-research-centres/nmrc/digital-news-report-australia-2022 (viewed January 2023).

From Moral Injury to Trauma Resilience
1 Ricki Morrel, 'Reporting and Resilience: How Journalists Are Managing Their Mental Health', *NiemanReports*, https://niemanreports.org/articles/reporting-and-resilience-how-journalists-are-managing-their-mental-health/ (viewed January 2023).
2 S Jukes, K Fowler-Watt and G Rees, 'Reporting the COVID-19 Pandemic: Trauma on Our Own Doorstep', *Digital Journalism*, vol. 10, no. 6, 2022.

3 World Health Organization, 'COVID Pandemic Triggers 25% Increase in Prevalence of Anxiety and Depression Worldwide', 2 March 2022, https://www.who.int/news/item/02-03-2022-covid-19-pandemic-triggers-25-increase-in-prevalence-of-anxiety-and-depression-worldwide (viewed January 2023).
4 G Tyson and J Wild, 'Post-Traumatic Stress Disorder Symptoms among Journalists Repeatedly Covering COVID-19 News', *International Journal of Environmental Research and Public Health*, vol. 18, no. 21, 26 October 2021, p. 8536.
5 A Feinstein, J Owen and N Blair, 'A Hazardous Profession: War, Journalists, and Psychopathology', *American Journal of Psychiatry*, vol. 159, no. 9, 2002, pp. 1570–5.
6 E Newman, R Simpson and D Handschuh, 'Trauma Exposure and Post Traumatic Stress Disorder among Photojournalists', *Visual Communication Quarterly*, vol. 58, no. 1, 2003, pp. 4–13.
7 C McMahon, 'Journalists and Trauma: The Parallel Worlds of Posttraumatic Growth and Posttraumatic Stress—Preliminary Findings', *DEP*, vol. 29, no. 2.2, 2005, p. 2.
8 Daniel P Aldrich, 'How Social Ties Make Us Resilient to Trauma', *The Conversation*, 24 May 2017, https://theconversation.com/how-social-ties-make-us-resilient-to-trauma-78223 (viewed January 2023).

The Great Resignation
1 Crystal Wu, 'Survey Reveals One in Five Australians Quit Their Job Last Year, One in Four Consider Leaving with COVID-19 Shifting Expectations', *Sky News*, 18 February 2022, https://www.skynews.com.au/australia-news/survey-reveals-one-in-five-australians-quit-their-job-last-year-one-in-four-consider-leaving-with-covid19-shifting-expectations/news-story/638ae6bfe5ae11fa860309d8aba93eb5 (viewed January 2023).

The Use of Data for Storytelling
1 Inga Ting et al., 'Charting the COVID-19 Spread in Australia', *ABC News*, 5 September 2022, https://www.abc.net.au/news/2020-03-17/coronavirus-cases-data-reveals-how-covid-19-spreads-in-australia/12060704 (viewed January 2023).
2 CovidBaseAU, https://covidbaseau.com/ (viewed January 2023).
3 COVID Live, http://www.covidlive.com.au (viewed January 2023).

The Rise and Rise of TikTok
1 Jack Shepherd, '20 Essential TikTok Statistics You Need to Know in 2023', Social Shepherd, 3 January 2023, https://thesocialshepherd.com/blog/tiktok-statistics (viewed January 2023).

The News Media Bargaining Code

1. Rupert Murdoch, 'From Town Crier to Bloggers: How Will Journalism Survive the Internet Age?', Centre for Journalism at the University of Kent, 3 December 2009, http://centreforjournalism.org/blogs/rupert-murdoch-town-crier-bloggers-how-will-journalism-survive-internet-age-full-text (viewed January 2023).

Multicultural Messaging: SBS

1. Australian Bureau of Statistics, 'Census', 2021, https://www.abs.gov.au/census (viewed January 2023).
2. SBS Community Brand Tracker. Base n = 111.

A Tale of Two Cities: A Divided Sydney

1. Media Diversity Australia, *Who Gets to Tell Australian Stories? Putting the Spotlight on Cultural and Linguistic Diversity in Television News and Current Affairs*, 2020, https://www.mediadiversityaustralia.org/wp-content/uploads/2020/08/Who-Gets-To-Tell-Australian-Stories_LAUNCH-VERSION.pdf (viewed January 2023).

Generation COVID: Storytelling for Gen Z

1. Sarah Curnow and Ben Knight, 'Generation COVID', ABC Investigations and ABC Victoria, *ABC News*, 6 July 2020, https://www.abc.net.au/news/2020-07-06/generation-covid-faces-an-uncertain-future/12388308 (viewed January 2023); and Sarah Curnow and Ben Knight, 'Coronavirus Pandemic May "Scar" Generation COVID for the Rest of Their Lives', *ABC News*, 7 July 2020, https://www.abc.net.au/news/2020-07-07/coronavirus-young-adults-facing-difficult-economic-future/12426886 (viewed January 2023).

Chasing Truth and Facing Jail

1. R Tapsell, 'The Australian Media's Foreign News Coverage of COVID-19 and Its Declining Reportage of the Asia Pacific Region', *Australian Journalism Review*, vol. 43, no. 2, 2021, pp. 193–209.

Hong Kong's Citizen Journalist

1. Our World in Data, 'Hong Kong: Coronavirus Pandemic Country Profile', February 2023, https://ourworldindata.org/coronavirus/country/hong-kong (viewed February 2023).

China and the Virus of Tyranny

1. Sigal Samuel, 'China Is Treating Islam Like a Mental Illness', *The Atlantic*, 28 August 2018, https://www.theatlantic.com/international/archive/2018/08/china-pathologizing-uighur-muslims-mental-illness/568525/ (viewed February 2023).

NOTES

2 Radio Free Asia, 'Xinjiang Political "Re-Education Camps" Treat Uyghurs "Infected By Religious Extremism": CCP Youth League', 8 August 2018, https://www.rfa.org/english/news/uyghur/infected-08082018173807.html (viewed January 2023).
3 Human Rights Watch, *'Eradicating Ideological Viruses': China's Campaign of Repression against Xinjiang's Muslims*, 9 September 2018, https://www.hrw.org/report/2018/09/09/eradicating-ideological-viruses/chinas-campaign-repression-against-xinjiangs (viewed January 2023).
4 Michel Foucault, 'Panopticism', in *Discipline & Punish: The Birth of the Prison*, translated by A Sheridan, Vintage Books, New York, 1995.
5 Wojciech Sadurski, *A Pandemic of Populists*, Cambridge University Press, Cambridge, 2022.